THE
WHAT
TO EAT
WHEN
COOKBOOK

THE WHAT TO EAT WHEN COOKBOOK

135+ Deliciously Timed Recipes

Michael F. Roizen, M.D.,
Michael Crupain, M.D., M.P.H.,
and Jim Perko, Sr., CEC, AAC
with Ted Spiker

NATIONAL
GEOGRAPHIC

WASHINGTON, D.C.

CONTENTS

PART 1

THE
WHEN
WAY

EAT ONLY WHEN
THE SUN IS UP;
EAT MORE EARLY,
LESS LATER

99

CHAPTER ONE

WHAT TO EAT WHEN: THE CHEAT SHEET

A Quick Look at the Main Ingredients of the When Way

Nutritional information can sometimes be confusing and conflicting (just say the word "carb" if you want to start a fork-to-fork fight among food aficionados). But we have a hunch that whatever your nutritional knowledge, you probably know the basics of fiber: Although it can come in many forms (beans, veggies, powder), the bottom line is that it's very good for you and it's easy to digest.

Well, consider this cheat sheet your literary fiber. It's really good for you *and* easy to digest.

In our first book, *What to Eat When,* we explained why timing is so important when it comes to your diet—in other words, *when* you eat is just as vital as *what* you eat. Before you start cooking these delicious and easy recipes that follow, you need to know about *What to Eat When* (what we call the When Way). Thinking more about the timing of your meals will set the stage for what's to follow: a heaping helping of dishes that are as great for your tongue as they are for the rest of your body.

THE TWO MAJOR PRINCIPLES OF THE WHEN WAY

The When Way is beautifully simple: Eat only when the sun is up and eat more earlier in the day. Adapting this lifestyle will greatly change how your body interacts with food. That's because biology shows us that our body has a food clock, just as it has a sleep clock (or circadian rhythm); we're better equipped to eat, digest, absorb, and fuel our systems during certain parts of our daily cycle. Here's how it works:

- **Eat only when the sun is up:** This tenet provides your body a specified window for eating—approximately 12 hours, depending on the time of year. More importantly, it allows for a resting period (or "fasting"). In today's modern era, when many Americans eat all day up until they go to bed, our nutritional systems are less efficient, creating more health problems and not allowing our bodies to use that fuel properly. Give your eating window a start and finish time that's dictated by the sun (or when the sun should be out, such as 7 a.m. to 7 p.m.) and break the habit of bingeing on snacks and *The Office* for the sixth time. The longer the window of fasting, the better. Start with 12 hours of fasting, but if you can get to 14 or 16, even better.

- **Eat more earlier in the day:** One of our biggest mistakes is that we often eat most of our calories toward the end of the day, with a heavy dinner and late-night snacking. The When Way is about flipping that ratio: You should eat most of your calories early in the day via some combo of breakfast and lunch. That doesn't mean you have to have a heavy breakfast if you're not a breakfast person, but you should consume 80 percent of your daily calories before 3 p.m.

WHY TIMING MATTERS

Next time you're at a cocktail party and a well-meaning gentleman strolls up to you holding a pyramid of Swedish meatballs, tell him you're not hungry because of chrononutrition. Sure, the word still hasn't appeared as a puzzle on *Wheel of Fortune*, but you can probably figure out the derivation—*chrono* (time) and *nutrition* (food). The science tells us that clocks and plates have more in common than just their circular shapes; they're intricately linked to how our bodies work.

Your biological clock—your body's automated system for conserving energy—influences behavior from sunset to sunset. It does so by sending messages throughout your body via hormones. The signals tell us when to sleep and when to eat. This cycle is your circadian rhythm. These natural cues are relatively consistent from day to day, so that you can follow your biological rhythm effectively and efficiently.

Scientists looking at these patterns found that animals have food clocks that are tied to their circadian rhythm: an instinct that ensures we get the right amount of food throughout the day so that we have plenty of energy for survival. The easiest way to think about it: The job of the circadian rhythm is to get the body ready to do the right thing at the right time. Multiple studies show that it's better for your body to consume calories earlier in the day, rather than later. One study in particular examined participants and weight loss over a 20-week period; those who ate lunch earlier lost 25 percent more weight than those who ate later.

Your body prefers to use carbohydrates as a fuel source during the day and burn fat at night. One reason for this may be that it's most sensitive to insulin in the morning. In practice, this means that your body is better able to shuttle the sugar (or glucose) circulating in your blood into cells as energy. At night, you're more insulin resistant, which means what you eat after sunset is less likely to be used as fuel and more likely to be stored as fat. Over time, that increases your chance of developing serious health issues like obesity, heart disease, diabetes, arthritis, cancer, memory dysfunction, and more.

But here's the rub: Although research shows that our bodies respond better when we eat earlier, our biology nudges us to *want* to eat later. Evolutionarily, that makes sense: Prehistoric man ate after a hunt to store fat to compensate during times of famine. Now that we have easy access to food, the desire for survival directly competes with what's best for our long-term health. The When Way helps *convince* your desires and cravings to shift, so you can live healthier, longer, and with more energy. It will also make your body younger. Yes, you read that right: Turns out, your food choices change your genetic expression—which of about 1,500 of the 22,500 genes you have are "on," or expressed. There is considerable evidence that eating the When Way shifts your genetic expression to one that makes your physiological age younger. (This is called your RealAge, Dr. R's groundbreaking science that showed diet and lifestyle factors determined your true age, not a calendar date.)

New research is suggesting that the principles of the When Way also have implications for aging, longevity, and fending off disease. In 2015, a study with the University of Southern California Longevity Institute demonstrated that fasting could increase stem cells' ability to reproduce. This could have big implications for increasing life span, because stem cells are responsible for repair of injured or aging organs. In addition, some studies suggest that time-restricted eating over 18 months reduced biological markers of aging and limited age-related cancer development. Such changes show evidence in your biomarkers in as little as four days. And today, researchers are exploring new ways to measure a person's circadian rhythm for better health—for example, determining customized timing plans for medication delivery. Although much of this research is in early stages, the conclusions so far support our mantras of eating early and eating only when the sun is out—with benefits that extend far beyond weight management.

STOP STEREOTYPING FOODS

Oatmeal is for breakfast, beans are for dinner, and never shall the two mix. We say: Bull scrapple! With the When Way, there's no such thing as breakfast food, lunch food, snack food, or dinner food; you can have our recommended foods whenever you want them. In practice, that means you can have fish or chicken as your first meal of the day and a frittata as your last. And that's what we do all the time: Dr. R eats salmon burgers most mornings. Dr. C cooks up a *bellissimo* dinner every night but doesn't touch it until the next day for breakfast or lunch (our best When Way tip: Cook the night before to make eating early in the day easier). And Chef Jim "dares to pair," always trying new When Way food combinations to complement his morning coffee.

Consider this new way of eating "meal agnostic." When you're following our rule of more early, less later, you want to eat *what* you like best *when* you can afford to take in the calories. So if you like

chicken, beans, and sweet potatoes, make that your early or midday meal; a couple of egg whites, veggies, and berries may be the perfect light fare to end the day. Just this slight adjustment is one of the most crucial things you can do to eat according to your biological rhythm. It also opens up your kitchen to a world of new possibilities. Here's how:

- **Follow the three P's: Plan, prep, plate.** We don't want to simplify today's health crisis, but we can certainly say that poor food choices are some of the biggest contributing factors. And this is understandable: So many of us are stressed out, busier than hive-building bees, or just dog tired. So what do we reach for? Whatever is easiest—a drive-through window, delivery service, or frozen meal. Although those options might feature healthy choices, nothing will *ever* compare to food you prepare yourself. When *you* cook, you will always know exactly what ingredients go into the dish—and into your body. You don't even have to commit to eating healthy; you just have to commit to *planning* to eat healthy. That's our challenge to you: Find 15 minutes to sketch out what you plan to eat for the week (use our recipes and grocery lists, please). When you do that, you can create shopping lists and have everything on hand when you're ready to cook.
- **Experiment with timing.** Some people don't like eating too early and would rather have a heavier midday meal. That's OK. Or you may like three medium-size meals all before late afternoon and then finish the day with a light salad or a couple of egg whites. That's okay, too. Try cooking a day's worth of meals the night before *or* prep a week's worth of meals on a Sunday night. Two hours of cooking one night can save a big burden of 30 minutes of

cooking per meal. This helps not only with preparation, but also with shifting your mindset. As you experiment with timing by eating what you already have on hand, eating "dinner" foods earlier will start to feel more natural. Always follow the When Way principles: Eat more early rather than late, and eat only when the sun is up.

- **Drum up support.** It helps to have friends (or family) who are also practicing the When Way. Offer one another support and ideas. Host a "dinner for breakfast" with your When Way pals to make eating pasta first thing in the day feel a bit more normal. Share recipes you love (hopefully ours!).

- **Find your own rhythm and routine.** Some diet plans only work when you're told exactly what to eat and when to eat it. That ensures calories and nutrient control. Although that can be effective for short spurts, it's nearly impossible to maintain for the long haul. That's why it's crucial you find variations of the When Way that work for *you:* What recipes are your favorites and the easiest to make for your lifestyle? What recipes help you feel satisfied and energized? When do you like to have your biggest meal of the day? And what will your routine be for shopping, cooking, and eating?

YOUR MIND MATTERS

Look, we could talk until we're blueberry in the face about macronutrients and scientific studies and the equations about how much food you should have per day. But it doesn't mean squash if you can't wrap your head around a new way of thinking—that dinner should not be your royal feast and 11:30 p.m. does not signify cookie time. Those folks who have adapted the When Way have done it not just by following a few guidelines and cooking up some recipes. They've been successful because they've changed not just what and when they eat, but also the way they think about and prepare food. You can steer your stomach to doing the right thing by creating new habits.

Yes, this is a cookbook. And yes, we have more than 135 tongue-titillating recipes that we hope you try. Our guess is that you're going to find at least a handful that become your absolute favorites. Stick with them. Make them often. Get into the habit of new eating patterns. This ensures consistency. This takes the guesswork out of meal prep. This automation keeps you on the right track.

Keep in mind that recipes are meant to be guides focused in technique—once you've mastered the skills, mix and match what you learn and experiment with flavors and new ingredients. By all means, you should experiment whenever you want. We're just trying to avoid you having to reinvent your meals every day. When your body operates on autopilot with good foods and optimal timing, you increase your chances of reaching and keeping your health goals.

THE BEST WHEN WAY FOODS

If the When Way was all about timing, we would happily tell you to go ahead and have that large pepperoni pizza for breakfast. But *when* and *what* have to work together like two salsa dancers (*mmm,* salsa!). Coordinating the *when* and *what* will give you the best results. A small study in the journal *Cell Metabolism* looked at what happens when people ate a diet of largely ultraprocessed foods. As it turned out, that type of diet led people to eat too quickly, consume more calories overall, and gain weight. Whole foods—fruits, vegetables, lean proteins like salmon and ocean trout, whole grain carbs, and foods with healthy fat like walnuts, avocados, and dark chocolate—are keys to making the what and when dance elegantly together. This is how we think about the best When Way foods chart.

NEED-TO-KNOW NUTRITION: *Your Go-To Glossary*		
IN YOUR FOOD	**WHAT IT IS**	**WHAT IT DOES**
Protein	1 of the 3 macronutrients (a type of food required in large amounts of our diet)	Protein is made up of amino acids that are the building blocks of your cells. It is found in all foods—animals and vegetables.
Carbohydrates	1 of the 3 macronutrients	Carbohydrates come in two forms: simple carbs (such as sugars) or complex carbs (such as whole grain fiber). Complex carbs are healthier because they take longer to digest, and consequently raise your blood sugar level more slowly and to a lower peak.
Fat	1 of the 3 macronutrients	This macro contains a little more than double the energy of carbs. There are a few different forms of fat: Saturated fat is typically derived from animal products, and unsaturated fats, which come in a variety of forms, are usually derived from plants. Unsaturated fats with an odd number such as omega-3 (found in avocados, fish, and walnuts, among other foods) or omega-9 (found in extra-virgin olive oil) are the healthy kind. (Trans fats are manufactured fats currently being phased out of production.)
Vitamins, minerals	Micronutrients (essential nutrients found in small amounts)	Vitamins and minerals help the body perform a variety of essential functions, including speeding up key processes like production of energy, building bones, facilitating nerve transmissions, and repairing cellular damage. They're found in fruits, vegetables, and other foods.
Phytonutrients, antioxidants	Other elements found in food	Phytonutrients and antioxidants have disease-fighting and disease-protecting effects on the body. They're found in fruits, vegetables, and many other foods, and boost immunity and protect energy-processing capabilities.
Glucose	Blood sugar	Glucose is the sugar from digested food that is transported to organs, tissues, and systems as fuel and energy. When the body has too much glucose, it is turned into triglycerides and is stored as fat.
Insulin	Hormone	This hormone, secreted by the pancreas, acts as a delivery service for glucose. When there's not enough insulin to take glucose into cells (from lack of production of insulin or from insulin resistance), that glucose stays in the bloodstream and is often stored as fat. Insulin levels are low in type 1 diabetes and high in type 2 diabetes. Insulin growth factors are secreted with insulin and age us. That's one of the reasons (in addition to causing fat storage and cancer growth) that we think simple sugars cause us to age faster than complex carbohydrates. And it's why you should keep insulin low by eating the When Way.

We've made it easy by breaking foods into three categories:

- **YES! foods** are choices that, at the right time of day, you can eat in unlimited quantities.

- **LIMITED foods** are ones you want to eat sparingly, such as red meat (less than four ounces a week) and pork (less than six ounces a week). Be sure to avoid egg yolks, cheese, or other red or processed meats in the same week.

- **NO! foods** should be avoided at all times, except on special occasions.

WHAT YOU'LL GET FROM THE WHEN WAY

Goals are like opinions and celebrity crushes: Everybody's got one. The great thing about the When Way is that it isn't focused on one health goal over another. Instead, it will help you reach a variety of positive healthy outcomes. In the big picture, the meals in this book can help you lose weight (if you want to), live longer healthily (who doesn't want that?!), and gain the vitality and energy of someone five to 10 years younger. At a glance, recipes and ingredients of the When Way have been linked to:

- Weight loss
- Improved cardiovascular health
- Increased energy
- Better brain function
- Lower stress levels
- Less fatigue, more energy
- Less desire to eat in the evening
- Increased longevity
- Better sleep
- Improved muscle function
- Lower risk and pain from arthritis
- Lower risk of cancer

WTFASTING?

The number one question we received after we published *What to Eat When* was: What's the deal with fasting? You may have heard the term "intermittent fasting" as a trendy approach to dieting, and you may have been scared off. We don't blame you; "fasting" conjures up images of starvation.

The solution is simple: Think of it as a way your body can use periods without eating as a time-out—a chance for your biological players to recharge and renew. Sometimes—as with the When Way—that means about 12 to 16 hours of fasting. Just by following the When Way of eating with the sun, you're essentially putting yourself into a mini-fasting state every night—and most of that fast period takes place while you're sleeping.

This stretch of fasting, appears to have some benefits to the body in terms of weight loss, energy, and longevity. Some other benefits include reducing blood markers of aging, increasing chemicals that protect the brain, and increasing the ability to generate more stem cells.

By restricting the window in which you eat, that cycling gives your body, cells, and system, a chance to repair and recharge. This is what helps protect against heart disease and other chronic diseases. In the brain, fasting may give the body a chance to increase a chemical called BDNF (brain-derived neurotrophic factor), which helps build brain cells and stimulate other processes that help clear plaque and gunk from the brain (linked to brain inflammation and subsequent problems like Alzheimer's disease).

Keep in mind we're not suggesting that you go extra-long periods without eating. The main idea is to eliminate late-night snacks or meals to reap huge benefits for your body. That is one of the advantages of these short periods of fasting, and it is one you will notice when you shift your time frame.

YES! FOODS			
Plant- and Sea-Based Protein and Poultry	**Whole Grains**	**Healthy Fats**	**Resistant Starch & Vegetables**
Legumes (beans and peas) Tofu Tempeh Fish and seafood (salmon and ocean trout are best) Chicken and turkey Egg whites Nondairy milks (like almond, hemp, or oat) that do not have any added sugars	Bulgur (cracked wheat) 100% whole wheat flour Whole oats/oatmeal Whole grain corn/ cornmeal Popcorn (unsalted and without butter) Whole rye Whole grain barley Whole farro Wild rice Buckwheat Buckwheat flour Triticale Millet Quinoa	Extra-virgin olive oil (unlimited for salad dressing or sautéing, not frying) Nuts and seeds (1 ounce a day; walnuts may be best, but whatever you choose always opt for raw or dry roasted, which means no oil is used, and no salt added) Avocado (½ a day)	Sweet or white potatoes (cooked and cooled, but not fried!) Green bananas Black beans and legumes Intact whole cooked grains, and cooled whole grain pastas

Fruit: Enjoy unlimited quantities of your favorite fruit (at the right time of day).

Non-Starchy Vegetables			
Artichokes Asparagus Beans (green, wax, Italian) Beets Brussels sprouts Broccoli Cabbage (green, bok choy, Chinese) Carrots	Cauliflower Celery Cucumber Eggplant Greens (collard, kale, mustard, turnip) Hearts of palm Jicama Kohlrabi Leeks	Okra Onions Peppers Radishes Rhubarb Ramps Rutabaga Salad greens (chicory, endive, escarole, lettuce, romaine, spinach,	arugula, radicchio, watercress) Sprouts Squash (summer, crookneck, spaghetti, zucchini) Sugar snap peas Swiss chard Tomatoes Turnips

LIMITED FOODS	NO! FOODS
Animal protein: Red meat (less than 4 ounces a week) and pork (less than 6 ounces a week)—avoid egg yolks, cheese, or other red or processed meats that week	Added sugar (especially in drinks and desserts)
Egg yolks (at most once a week and without cheese or red meat that week)	Added syrups
Dairy (limit most, but plain, no-sugar-added, strained yogurt like Greek or Icelandic yogurts are OK)	White flour
Cheese (less than 4 ounces a week)	Processed foods
Starchy vegetables (fried plantains, hot white potatoes)	Fried foods
Rice	Coconut and palm oil
Alcohol (limit to 1 drink for women and 2 for men a day; men and women tend to metabolize alcohol differently, because of different levels of alcohol dehydrogenase in their stomach linings), including alcohol without added sugar. Avoid all alcohol with added sugars or combined with sugary mixes.	

FOUR WAYS TO HAVE A SUCCESSFUL WHEN WAY KITCHEN

Strategize: Shop for the week and meal prep several meals at once.

Create an Emergency Response System: Store When Way foods you can grab in a pinch like veggies and hummus or a handful of nuts.

Eat Mindfully: Eat slowly and think about the taste of your food; don't rush.

Play: Find new favorites by experimenting with creative combos of veggies and spices.

HOW TO FILL YOUR TANK

No doubt about it: Some people like to count calories. Others measure their food and count the grams of each micronutrient they eat. And still others tear through their meals without a thought about what or how much they eat.

One of the best parts about the When Way is that it doesn't take a lot of calculating to eat right. It all comes down to this simple breakdown:

EAT 80 PERCENT OF YOUR FOOD BEFORE ABOUT 3 P.M.
EAT THE REMAINING 20 PERCENT OF YOUR FOOD BEFORE ABOUT 7 P.M.

Granted, that may not be easy at first, and you may want to measure out your meals to try to hit the right number. But in a few weeks, the proportions will become second nature—just remember that your last meal is the lightest of the day.

WHAT HAPPENS WHEN LIFE GETS IN THE WAY?
The number one obstacle to eating consistently healthy isn't a single venti Frappuccino. It's the fact that everyday life—schedules, choices, stresses and illnesses, or pressures from friends—can often derail even the best of intentions. So many things can drive us to eat too quickly or too haphazardly. And as so many yo-yoers know, once you fall out of the routine, it can be pretty hard to jump back in.

We've designed the When Way so that you can be flexible with your eating. Being well prepared will go a long way to thwarting temptation and other challenges. But we also know that our bodies need and crave certain things at certain times. In *What to Eat When,* we outlined 30 common life scenarios and dissected the nutrients and foods that would best help you manage them. We looked at everything from being hangry to being depressed, from preventing heart disease to improving memory, from being on a first date to going on a job interview.

Your body's ecosystem changes as much as your environments do. That is, hormones, chemicals, and other systems are often affected by the outside world. But good foods are good foods; you can always find ways to maximize their nutrients. Just keep these factors in mind:

Boost brainpower and mood with foods rich in omega-3 fatty acids, like salmon and walnuts.

Find energy by drinking water (dehydration is a key factor in low energy levels) and eating healthy fats (avocados and nuts) and protein (lean white meat or ocean trout), which provide more sustained energy than fast-acting carbs.

Prevent diseases with fruits, veggies, and black coffee or tea. Their various nutrients and ele-ments have been shown to assist in fighting off many conditions. They're also key in reducing inflammation, a major factor in chronic disease.

Battle chronic pain with extra-virgin olive oil, known for its anti-inflammatory effects.

GET STARTED THE WHEN WAY
The good news is that eating the When Way is actually pretty easy, and your body and appetite will adjust quickly. Here are tips to get started:

1. Record what and when you eat for four or five days so that you can observe patterns and see where you may need to shift.

2. Gradually shift your eating patterns toward the 80/20 rule: Eat 80 percent of food before 3 p.m., the remaining 20 percent before 7 p.m. This may take a few weeks of adjusting your schedule—starting with a 10 percent shift from your normal proportions, and gradually increasing the percentage and shifting the time. If you have a setback, just pick up where you left off.

3. Scan the recipes starting on page 32; pick the two or three that appeal most to you. Designate a time to prepare and shop for the meals, so that you have enough food for about five or six days.

4. Make a large salad bowl full of your favorite veggies. Divide it up into portion sizes that can serve as a meal, a snack, or late-night emergency when you don't have time to prep. When you are ready to eat, drizzle with balsamic vinegar and extra-virgin olive oil, and top with walnuts.

5. Look for foods in your pantry and fridge that fall on our NO list (see page 16). Swap them for When Way–approved foods.

CHAPTER TWO

THE KITCHEN SINK

Tools, Tips & Techniques to Make Cooking Fast & Fun

n a perfect world, the intersection between health and food work like an extra-virgin olive well-oiled machine. Food should work for, not against, your body (but all those processed foods and added sugar cause biological collisions). Trust us, we know what you're up against.

Cooking can feel daunting. It can feel like a time suck. It can feel like you spend all this time prepping and cleaning for just a few short minutes of tongue-pleasing payoffs.

Part of the challenge—if you're not passionate about cooking by nature—is to (1) learn to embrace the joy that comes from preparing new and love-you-back flavors and meals, and (2) turn cooking from a chore into something you adore. How do we do that?

The solution is simpler than you think: being as efficient as possible so you can enjoy the process more. This is one part preparation, one part cooking techniques, and one part experience; the more you learn and the more you try, the better you'll get—not just at efficiency, but also at achieving deliciousness.

In this chapter, we'll help you stock up with ingredients, tools, and techniques designed to make the cooking experience one you'll love.

INGREDIENTS
KEEP STOCKED AT ALL TIMES

Stock your kitchen with the following ingredients so you can whip up a When Way recipe—or dish of your own—at a moment's notice.

SPICES

❏ Allspice ❏ Cloves ❏ Black pepper
❏ Caraway ❏ Cayenne ❏ Chili powder
❏ Cinnamon ❏ Coriander ❏ Cumin
❏ Fennel seeds ❏ Garam masala
❏ Ginger ❏ Kosher salt ❏ La Baleine sea salt
(in the blue can, Dr. C takes it everywhere)
❏ Mustard powder ❏ Nutmeg ❏ Oregano
❏ Paprika ❏ Red pepper flakes
❏ Smoked paprika ❏ Thyme ❏ Turmeric
❏ Urfa chili ❏ Za'atar

OILS & VINEGARS

❏ Balsamic vinegar (white balsamic)
❏ Distilled white vinegar
❏ Extra-virgin olive oil, first cold pressed

PRODUCE

❏ Avocado ❏ Broccoli ❏ Cauliflower
❏ Fresh Basil ❏ Fresh fruit and vegetables of choice
❏ Fresh garlic ❏ Fresh mint (or other preferred herbs, like cilantro or parsley) ❏ Fresh rosemary
❏ Leafy greens (like spinach, arugula, and kale)
❏ Lemons and lemon juice ❏ Lime and lime juice
❏ Organic raisins ❏ Prunes ❏ Sweet potatoes
❏ Turkish apricots ❏ Onions

MEAT

❏ Chicken ❏ Salmon

NUTS, SEEDS & GRAINS

❏ 100% whole grains ❏ Almonds
❏ Almond butter ❏ Black sesame seeds
❏ Cashews ❏ Chia seeds
❏ Farro or whole wheat semolina pasta
❏ Flaxseed ❏ Millet ❏ Oatmeal
❏ Quinoa ❏ Walnuts

DAIRY

❏ Alternative unsweetened and unflavored milks
such as almond, hemp, and soy
❏ Buttermilk ❏ Egg whites ❏ Greek yogurt

CANNED & PACKAGED GOODS

❏ Black beans (dried) ❏ Canned crushed tomatoes
❏ Lentils ❏ Other beans and legumes
(like heirloom beans from Rancho Gordo)
❏ Tomato paste

OTHER

❏ Baking powder ❏ Baking soda ❏ Cornstarch
❏ Dark, bittersweet chocolate (70 percent cocoa)
❏ Low-sodium tamari ❏ Tahini
❏ Unsweetened cocoa powder

TOOLS

THE TOOLS EVERY KITCHEN NEEDS

Having all the ingredients you need on hand cuts down on preparation time, as does a well-outfitted kitchen. Make sure you have the following gear at the ready:

❏ 8-inch and/or 12-inch chef's knife
❏ 10-inch and 12-inch sauté pan ❏ Bread knife
❏ Can opener ❏ Cast-iron skillet
❏ Cooling racks ❏ Corkscrew
❏ Dry measuring cups

❏ Dutch oven ❏ Food processor
❏ Heavy-duty aluminum baking sheets
(Get heavy-duty aluminum that won't warp from online restaurant supply stores. Always cover with parchment paper when using.)
❏ Immersion blender ❏ Kitchen scale
❏ Liquid measuring cup ❏ Loaf pan
❏ Locking tongs ❏ Measuring spoons
❏ Microplane grater
❏ Mixing bowls of various sizes
❏ Muffin tin ❏ Multiple high-quality polyethylene cutting boards ❏ Nonstick skillet
❏ Parchment paper ❏ Rolling pin ❏ Saucepan
❏ Vitamix or high-speed blender

SNEAKY SUBSTITUTIONS

How to make something sweet without sugar:
Use naturally occurring sugars coupled with fiber—like prunes, figs, blueberries, or raisins. The Raisin Reduction on page 69 is a great sugar substitute that adds bulk, flavor, and nutrients.

How to make something moist without fat:
Swap butter, unhealthy oils, and lards with fruits and veggies to moisten grains, salads, and prepared meals. High-moisture foods like grapes, mushrooms, green beans, peppers, tomatoes, zucchini, jicama, turnips, dark leafy greens, onions, and celery work well.

How to make something savory without salt:
Use herbs, acids, and spices with heat to make dishes with complex flavors. Vinegars are a great choice for acids, as are wines. Hot or medium-hot chili peppers can reduce the desire for added sodium. Balsamic vinegar goes great on greens, especially genuine balsamic vinegars with no additives. But if you have a less expensive one, put it in a pan on the stove, reduce it down by a third to concentrate naturally occurring sugars, and it will help to mimic the flavor profiles of four-leaf and higher-end balsamic vinegars.

EASY INGREDIENT CONVERSIONS

The following gives approximate ingredient yields and conversions of a few common foods found throughout this book.

INGREDIENT	AMOUNT	APPROXIMATE YIELD BY VOLUME
Arugula	1 pound	8 cups
Asparagus	1 pound	2 cups
Bananas	1 pound	3 bananas
Beets	1 pound	2½ cups
Bell peppers	1 pound	2½ cups
Blueberries (fresh)	1 pound	2 cups
Broccoli	1 pound	2½ cups
Butternut squash	1 pound	2½ cups
Canned beans	15-ounce can	1½ cups
Carrots (fresh)	1 pound	2½ cups
Cauliflower	1 pound	1½ cups
Celery	1 pound	4 cups
Cilantro (fresh)	1 ounce	5 tablespoons
Crimini mushrooms	1 pound	5 cups, sliced
Cucumbers	1 pound	2 cups
Dark chocolate (70 percent cocoa)	1 pound	3 cups
Eggplant (fresh)	1 pound	5 cups
Farro	1 pound	2½ cups, raw
Garlic (fresh)	1 ounce	2 tablespoons
Grapes (seedless)	1 pound	3½ cups
Green beans	1 pound	3 cups
Jicama	1 pound	3½ cups
Leeks	1 pound	2½ cups
Lemons	1 lemon	3 tablespoons juice
Onion	1 pound	2½ cups
Raisins	15-ounce box	2½ cups
Red skin potatoes	1 pound	5 cups
Shiitake mushrooms (fresh)	1 pound	4 cups
Spinach (fresh)	1 pound	6 cups
Sweet potatoes	1 pound	2½ cups
Walnuts (pieces)	1 pound	4 cups

BETTER THAN BUTTER

Who doesn't love butter or a cheese spread on bread or a creamy salad dressing? These ingredients add luxurious mouthfeel and flavor. But they're also loaded with saturated fat: the worst kind. We've got a really cheap gourmet hack that cuts the fat and adds tons of flavors—what we like to call vegetable crema or cream.

What's a vegetable cream? Basically, it's pureed vegetables. Dr. C got the idea perusing the olive oil section of his local grocery store. Stuffed among the golden and green liquids was a very small but very expensive jar labeled *crema di carciofi* ("artichoke cream" in English). Dr. C loves artichokes because they are delicious and loaded with inulin, a prebiotic fiber that feeds good gut bacteria. A quick look at the ingredient list revealed there wasn't much to this interesting treat: just artichokes, lemon juice, garlic, and a little olive oil.

So, Dr. C decided he could probably make this himself (see the recipe on page 47). The taste was absolutely amazing, and he had a huge jar of the stuff for just a few bucks. Artichokes aren't the only cream you can make. We also have recipes for carrot crema, corn crema, and Cauliflower Cream (pages 46–47). And once you've mastered the technique, you can try to make your own versions with any vegetable you like.

The cremas are great smeared on a piece of whole grain bread by themselves, or topped with some smoked salmon. You can also stir them into a hot soup, instead of crème fraîche, to add some extra body, or add some to your salad dressing to create a creamy dressing. Top healthy tacos with them like sour creams, too.

KEEP IT CLEAN:
Why Kitchen Sanitation Is Crucial

If eating is the best part of cooking, cleaning is the worst. But when it comes to being neat in the kitchen, it's not just about saving time; it's also about your health. There are more than nine million cases of foodborne illness in the United States every year, and many of them are believed to be the result of the way food is handled in the home.

After spending years in the operating room, kitchen sanitation is a no-brainer for Dr. C and Dr. R. Follow their best practices to keep your own kitchen safe and clean. In particular, pay attention to how you handle raw meat like chicken:

Be prepared: Have all the plates, knifes, scissors, cutting boards, and paper towels you need ready before you even take chicken (or raw meat) out of the fridge.

Keep bacteria contained: Open the chicken in an empty sink, not on the counter. Make sure you don't have clean dishes in the dish rack next to the sink, which could become contaminated. Don't rinse the chicken, which can cause splashing and cross-contamination, but do drain the juices and wipe up anything that might contaminate other foods or dishes with a damp paper towel. Dr. C likes to prep his chicken in a clean sink with a knife or scissors, so he doesn't even have to worry about dirtying a cutting board.

Notice what you touch: If you touch something after handling raw meat, make sure you clean it up later (more on that in a minute).

Clean your sink: Wipe up any juice in the sink with a paper towel and then run water gently to rinse it out. Wash your hands with soap and water and then wash the sink handle and soap dispenser where you touched it. Also wash any dishes that touched the raw meat or may have been splashed by its juices.

Transfer your chicken: When your hands are clean, you can transfer the chicken to wherever it needs to go, like the refrigerator. Remember to wash your hands again if you touch the raw chicken.

Clean your counters and sink: Use a wet, soapy paper towel to wipe down your counters, then do the same to your sink. Rinse and dry.

Wash your hands: Soap and water get rid of the majority of bacteria and viruses, but if you think your kitchen is particularly contaminated (especially after chicken), use a kitchen cleaner that contains bleach. (Don't use antibacterial wipes, which can actually spread contamination around your kitchen. Use a kitchen spray or Dr. R's favorite—just a towel with diluted bleach.)

This isn't just about chicken and raw meats, however. Most people don't wash their garlic, onions, or shallots first. They just put them on the cutting board and begin peeling, thereby cross-contaminating their cutting board. Those onions probably were handled a great deal by people at the store before you got them. Cover your cutting board with paper towels and peel the onion, garlic, and shallots on the paper towels. Not only will this significantly prevent cross-contamination, but it will make cleaning up the peels easier, too. Then wash your hands and the knife before cutting the onion and shallot or chopping the garlic.

You can't sanitize vegetables that you are going to eat raw, but you do need to clean them. For green leafy vegetables, like lettuces, kale, and herbs, we recommend using a salad spinner. Put the vegetables in the spinner (most have to be cut to fit in the spinner to make things easier), and fill it with enough water to cover and swish the veggies around. Drain the water and repeat, usually three times. You may need to do this in batches—this method won't work if the water bath is too crowded.

When you're done, take a look at the water. Are dirt or sand in the bottom? If so, dump out the water and do it again and again and again. Worried about wasting water? Use the dirty water in your plants. Repeat the steps until you don't see any grime at the bottom of your spinner. Then spin the veggies dry.

Always wash cutting boards well with warm, soapy water and rinse well. Store cutting boards upright (and not on top of one another) to air-dry.

TECHNIQUES

When it comes to cooking, there are two kinds of people: "Mad scientists" love creating new concoctions, no matter how many dishes get dirty or how long it takes, but meal prep for "bottom-liners" is pressing 2:00 on the microwave. Both styles are okay—we all have different barometers for how we approach cooking, from one end (a necessary chore) to the other (a love-every-minute passion).

Whatever your views on cooking, one thing is universally true: The number one way to use food to control your health is to control your kitchen. If you master healthy, whole ingredients and smart cooking techniques, you'll also master your health. Just as you have to make time to exercise and do yoga, you have to make time to cook!

This chapter will reveal all the techniques you need to learn to prepare your foods efficiently and effectively, maximizing both health and flavor.

PREPARATION

It feels fitting to start with *mise en place*—the art of preparing to cook. Mise en place is a French term that means "everything in its place" and is a common practice in almost every restaurant kitchen. In your own kitchen, this means having all the required equipment—pans, measuring cups, spoons, whisks, and so on—to prepare a recipe easily accessible. It also means prepping ingredients—chopping garlic, herbs, and vegetables, for instance—and having them ready in small bowls, along with spices. Staple ingredients like whole wheat flour, pepper, and extra-virgin olive oil should also be within arm's

reach. Mise en place allows you to concentrate on the task at hand, rather than being distracted by hunting down a tool or ingredient in the kitchen. This allows you to mindfully focus on critical elements like time and degree of doneness when preparing and cooking.

A serious and constant companion of mise en place is another culinary code of conduct termed "clean as you go." As you prepare your mise en place, clean finished dishes and tools along the way to avoid a pile of dirty utensils and bowls at the end of meal prep. This isn't just a time-saver; it's also a critical step to prevent any cross-contamination of ingredients.

Another mise en place tip: Even when cutting the same ingredient—for example, mushrooms—keep adding them to a bowl so you don't have a mound crowding your cutting board. Cutting on a clean, uncluttered board makes the process safer and more fun.

In the 21st century, mise en place has changed—and in many ways, for the better. Today, we have videos and demos of cooking techniques at our fingertips and an amazing array of new culinary gadgets that speed the process. Immersion blenders, spiralizers, electric pressure cookers, and professional-grade cutlery are easily available and affordable at many stores. So keep in mind that you can multitask when preparing your mise en place: Get water boiling while you're peeling and chopping garlic; roast vegetables in the oven while you're cleaning, spin-drying, and cooking chard.

A common problem is that many home cooks don't allocate enough time for mise en place—and cleaning as you go—or underestimate the time it takes to do it. But with a little practice honing knife and cooking skills, you'll get faster and more efficient, build confidence, and end up with great-tasting and satisfying healthy meals.

CUTTING

The kitchen knife is your most important tool in the kitchen. You don't need a set of 20, either—a chef's knife can accomplish almost everything you need to do while cooking. Because this will become your most used kitchen tool, we recommend you buy the best 8- or 12-inch chef's knife (non-serrated) you can afford.

We also recommend having at least four cutting boards (two smaller and two larger) in your arsenal. Food safety is a primary concern, so distinguish cutting boards for produce, grains, gluten-free grains, and for fish or poultry. A high-quality polyethylene board with a slightly rough surface to keep food from slipping is best. Wood boards are more sanitary in theory, but we find people wash the polyethylene boards in their dishwasher more often for maximum sanitation. Speaking of, wash your boards every time you change what you are about to cut—along with your hands.

Follow these tips to make slicing and dicing fast, efficient, and safe:

- Place a damp paper towel or dish towel under your cutting board to keep it from slipping as you work.
- Keep the pointed edge of your knife (the tip) on the cutting board. As you cut, this becomes a lever system.
- Always cut ingredients moving away from you (the same goes for peeling vegetables).

- To hold ingredients as you cut, slightly indent your fingers under the first knuckle so you can grab the food with a clean nail. Let your first knuckles, not your whole fingers or fingertips, be the guide.
- The golden rule to keep in mind is that the smaller and more uniformly you cut, the greater the seasoning surface and taste. The trick is to cut the vegetables into relatively uniformly small pieces so they all cook at the same rate.

MAKING VEGGIES GREAT AGAIN

Maybe the word "vegetables" conjures up nightmares of Meemaw trying to force sprouts down your throat. Or maybe you just yawn at the prospect of what some people consider to be crunchy mouthfuls of no-taste plants. Perhaps you even equate vegetables with a colonoscopy—good for you, yes, but once every ten years is plenty.

We all know the restaurant way to make veggies delicious: Drape them in butter, cheese, or some other calorie-dense sauce that, for all intents and purposes, robs them of their nutritional powers. Zucchini isn't zucchini when it's fried. Broccoli isn't broccoli when it's costumed in melted cheddar. Potatoes aren't potatoes when they come in a bag and can be ordered in small, medium, and backpack.

And that's the real problem: The average American doesn't eat a wide variety of vegetables, and the ones we consume most often aren't exactly model citizens. Three varieties cover about 60 percent of all vegetables the average American eats: Potatoes are mostly consumed as fries and chips. Tomatoes come in the form of processed ketchup and sauce. And lettuce is often smothered with a creamy dressing.

The real power of the vegetable—of which you can have unlimited quantities, with a few notable exceptions on page 16—is that preparation can make a huge difference in the way they taste. And isn't that really the end goal here? If you like the way good-for-you foods taste, you'll likely eat more of them. If you hate broccoli, there's a good chance it's because broccoli is often overly steamed, boiled, or cooked, rather than prepared in a way that maximizes its flavor, texture, and even color. So really take a look at the different ways to prepare your favorite vegetables.

ON THE STOVE
BLANCHING

To blanch simply means to cook quickly in water. Here's how to do it:

- **Put a pot of water on the stove to boil.** Set the stove to high and cover to boil water in about eight minutes or less.
- **Parboil, then cool.** When the water boils, add salt, then gently submerge the vegetables in the water (the water will stop boiling). Cook until the water just about returns to a boil, then pour the contents into a strainer in the sink. Shake out any excess water—you can even gently press on the vegetables to drain more water. The dryer veggies are, the better. Put them into the refrigerator immediately to cool—we believe in stopping the process with cool air, not cool water, which can add moisture to the vegetables and ruin their texture. Cool air makes veggies taste crisper and look brighter.

STEAMING

Steaming is often used for foods that cook quickly (like broccoli) or foods that might fall apart on the grill or in the pan (like delicate fish fillets); the ingredients are cooked by hot steam that rises from boiling water, teas, or broths seasoned with aromatics below. Steaming is a particularly healthful and low-calorie way to cook, as no extra aging fats are used. It's also a great alternative to boiling, which can void vegetables and other foods of their water-soluble vitamins. Delicate fish can be wrapped in leafy greens or even in parchment paper (see recipe pages 234–5) to prevent moisture loss by capturing juices and any added herbs, spices, and aromatics for intense flavors. Try not to oversteam vegetables; when the colors turn bright, they're usually ready.

BROWNING

Browning not only adds color and flavor to your meal, but the cooking process also leads to the accumulation of little bits that stick to the pan. In culinary lingo, these bits are known as fond and are the secret to developing richer soups and sauces made from nothing more than water.

So how do you get started? First and foremost, it's going to be easier to brown your ingredients if you have the right pan. Choose something heavy that holds heat—cast iron works best. We love French-enameled cast iron because it is beautiful to look at *and* beautiful to work with. The enamel layer makes them easier to care for than regular cast iron, and the lighter-colored surface makes it easier to see if you're burning anything. They are typically very expensive but can last a lifetime. Dr. C bought his first one in medical school and has used it regularly for the last 18 years. Chef Jim has had the same pots and pans for more than 30 years.

Here are the best practices for browning:

- **Preheat the pan.** Use medium to medium-high heat. Add the oil only once the pan is hot. Let the oil heat up a bit, then add your ingredients.
- **Don't overcrowd the pan.** If the pan is too full, the moisture from what you are cooking will steam the other ingredients instead of evaporating into the air. This can interfere with browning.
- **Leave it alone.** This is probably the hardest technique for people to master: the art of letting food be. For good color on ingredients, you have to let them sit and cook; unless the heat is too high, they probably won't burn. If you're not sure, try to pick up some clues from the sounds and smells coming from the pan. We know sizzling is hot, so whatever is in the pan needs to be watched carefully, but a gentle soft sizzle is fine with lower heat for slower cooking at longer lengths of time. Smells are the aromatherapy of the kitchen: When you begin to smell the onions cooking, the sugars are beginning to caramelize, and the sweetness permeates the room. Also look at the edges of ingredients to see how they are browning. If you must check, pick up a representative sample without disturbing everything else in the pan.
- **Deglaze the pan.** To take advantage of those tasty little bits stuck to the pan, remove the browned ingredients from the pan, add a liquid like wine or water, and scrape up all the stuck-on pieces with a wooden spoon. Stir over medium-high heat to dissolve them into your liquid and form a sauce or the base of a soup.

SOUPING UP YOUR SOUPS

Making flavorful and healthy soups is easy and can be a big time-saver when you're eating the When Way. Soups make for great on-the-go breakfasts or lunches because they transport easily and stay hot in a thermos.

The trick to a good soup: Develop a flavorful broth. To do so, be sure to cook your vegetables, especially the onions, well in the pan. Onions contain sulfur, and if onions are combined raw with a liquid, that sulfur leaches out into the broth. If those same onions are cooked at least to the point of being translucent, then the sulfur dissipates. If cooked longer, then the sugars caramelize and the onions will sweeten the soup. If you're going to add spices like cumin to soup, toast them at the bottom of the pan after the vegetables are cooked (but be careful—spices can go from toasted to burned and bitter in a heartbeat). If you're using tomato paste, add it before other liquids so that it can caramelize a bit and bring out the tomato's naturally occurring umami flavors. (Many children and people like ketchup because tomatoes contain umami that's more pronounced when cooked.) All that dark brown stuff that sticks to the pan bottom will be dissolved by the water or broth used and will add both color and flavor. Herbs, especially fresh, are generally added in the final stages of cooking. When it's time to eat the soup, adding a little bit of fresh lemon or lime or chili flakes will help amp up the flavor without adding salt.

IN THE OVEN
BAKING

Baking—cooking food in dry heat without direct exposure to a flame—is basically cooking in the oven. But what's the difference between baking and roasting? Roasting can be done in the oven or on a stovetop with exposure to flame; it's also typically done at a slightly higher heat than baking. Baking typically refers to cooking a liquid or dough into something more solid, like a custard or bread. Of course, if you bake your bread in a wood-burning oven, is it really roasted? It doesn't matter. What *does* matter is technique. Here are the best baking practices:

- **Get an oven thermometer.** Oven temperatures vary across the board, and the actual temperature in your oven may be different from what you see on the dial or display. Get

an oven thermometer to check it, and adjust temperatures accordingly to ensure you are baking dishes at the temperature the recipe calls for.

- **Use aluminum sheet pans.** Most cookie sheets—no matter how cheap or expensive—are lousy. Almost all warp pretty quickly under the oven's heat, usually on first use. This leads to food rolling around or tilting, which can mean uneven cooking. The best sheet pans are made of aluminum and are typically $10; they also come with PFOA-free, nonstick coatings that require less oil and make for easier cleaning. (Two good sources for high-quality sheet pans are *jbprince.com* and *restaurantsupply.com*.) Look for 18-gauge half-size sheet pans (the kind that fits in a regular oven). It's good to have a few on hand for times when you're doing a lot of baking. Quarter-size sheet pans can also come in handy for toasting nuts or breadcrumbs, or for baking in smaller batches.

- **Always use a piece of parchment paper on top of the sheet pan.** This keeps the pan cleaner and doesn't interfere with heat transfer.

- **Use the center of the oven.** Adjust your oven racks so they are in the center for even cooking. But there is an exception, depending on your heat source: When roasting, it's sometimes advantageous to cook items on a higher rack, because the heat bouncing off the top of the oven will brown what you are cooking.

- **Rotate and switch.** Evenness is key in baking, and temperatures in an oven can vary, so it's a good idea to rotate the dish about halfway through the process. So, if you are baking something for 60 minutes, turn the sheet pan 180 degrees after 30 minutes. (Of course, opening the oven door causes heat to escape, so do this as quickly as possible.) Also, if you have more than one sheet pan in the oven, plan to swap the racks they are on halfway through the baking process. Convection ovens have a fan that blows heat around for more even cooking; if you have one, you'll still need to rotate your pans. Plus, you'll need to pay close attention—items baked using a fan-forced oven tend to cook more quickly.

- **Follow directions.** Baking is as much a science as an art. Following steps precisely is the key to success.

FLAVORS AND TEXTURES

BLENDING

No, this isn't about plopping a bunch of ingredients into a blender. Blending is about making ingredients work together, or as the dictionary defines it, to make flavors work together "to produce a harmonious effect" and "to combine into an integrated whole." However, making the taste of a dish sing while reducing sugar, sodium, and fat from your diet can be challenging. Take, for example, the textbook version of vinaigrette: three parts oil to one part acid. How do you make those same great flavors with a one-to-one ratio or with no oil at all? Both the ingredient selection and the blending mechanics become really important when trying to prepare healthier meals that taste great to *you*.

Back to our vinaigrette: Chef Jim makes a healthier version that tastes equally great by adding the acid to the oil while whisking. He also mashes in cooked legumes to create viscosity and denseness along with great flavors. It works great, adds a ton of healthy protein and fiber to the dressing, and holds together long enough to toss in a salad or over a vegetable.

Another example would be how much water to blend with raisins for a reduction to use in place of added sugars (see recipe page 69). If you want a thinner reduction for a light sauce, blend in two parts water to one part raisins. But you may want a thicker reduction in a vinaigrette that adheres to the salad ingredients.

Timing of blending is important. Tossing a lemon juice vinaigrette with broccoli too soon will turn the broccoli yellow after 20 minutes; mashing avocado too early without an acid will cause the fruit to brown; and adding fresh herbs and spices should come at specific times (later for herbs, earlier for spices).

DONENESS

Judging doneness is important, as it dictates not only food safety (no one wants to consume raw chicken!), but also the texture, mouthfeel, and taste of what you eat (for example, cutting a fibrous fresh mango against the grain can make it easier to chew). Or consider this: Three different people can make the same recipe and get three different outcomes. A four-ounce piece of salmon that is small but thick will not cook the same as a piece that is thin and wide; both are the same weight, but by virtue of their shape, they will render differently. Likewise, a toaster oven will cook nuts differently than a standard gas oven. The cut of the nut—whole, halved, pieces—is also a factor, as is the type of sheet pan material (stainless versus aluminum, coated versus ceramic).

Given these varying factors, how do you know when it's time to flip and turn? Here are four keys:

- **Cut consistently.** It's important to practice cutting ingredients into similar-size pieces. Consistency in size equates to consistency in cooking. Even if you're making a cold salad, cutting ingredients in smaller pieces makes the texture pleasing and gets more ingredients into every bite. (This is the concept in the Tempeh Salad Véronique, page 202.)

- **Practice.** The more you cook, the better you'll get at determining when salmon is considered done or broccoli is just al dente. It takes some time, but you will master it as you keep at it.
- **Go ahead and taste it.** The best way to determine if grains, pasta, or vegetables are cooked properly is to taste them for tenderness. If you want to test the doneness of a roasted chicken breast and you do not have a food thermometer, you can pierce the thick part of the breast with a skewer. If pink juices come out, it's not done. If clear juices come out, it's done. If no juices come out, it's overdone.
- **Use your eyes.** Fresh fish is translucent when raw and becomes more opaque as it cooks. You can lift and gently bend a piece of salmon until it just begins to break and expose the inside; then consider the color and opaqueness to see if it's done to your liking. For vegetables, look for bright colors when blanching as they diminish when overdone. For roasting vegetables, avoid burning and blackening, as potential carcinogens are associated with *anything* blackened or burned. Chicken should not be pink or glossy when cut into; instead, it should look densely white with no gloss and have clear juices. To be safe, use a meat thermometer to judge doneness for chicken.

NOW LET'S COOK!

There's no question that cooking is in part clinical: You use X amount of one ingredient, Y amount of another, combine them, and come up with something delicious. There are formulas and measurements—teaspoons, tablespoons, and cups—machines and utensils.

But we can't ignore the fact that cooking is as personal as it is tactical. We're sure it's meaningful to you, too. Maybe you grew up eating Grandma's favorite recipes and honor her legacy by making them today. Or perhaps you've established your own traditions to warm your family's hearts and fill their bellies. In any case, we believe the joy of cooking is made of three main ingredients:

1. the social—and frankly, spiritual—aspect of breaking (whole grain) bread with friends and family;
2. the joy of preparing and serving foods that feed and fuel your body with healthy ingredients; and
3. the creativity of using what you know to make something different and all your own.

As you try the When Way recipes that follow—whether you're an experienced cook or a newbie—you will continue to be part clinician and part artist. Experiment and find what works best for you and your family.

Always keep in mind one of the golden rules of the When Way: Don't stereotype food. All our recipes can be eaten at any time of day—with our 80/20 system in mind: Eat 80 percent of your foods before 3 p.m., the remaining 20 percent before 7 p.m. There is no traditional breakfast or dinner recipe in this book. Try our Whole Beet Linguine (page 81) in the morning and our Egg-White Frittata (page 245) at night. Make our When Way Vegetable Platter (page 66) for a healthy—and easy!—family dinner; keep our Whole Grain & Dark Chocolate WTEW Bars (page 253) on hand for mornings on the go. Whenever you choose to eat these delicious snacks and meals, make sure you're eating when the sun is out (or should be out), and that you're eating more in the morning, less later on.

We hope that as you try each new recipe, you see food for what it is—nature's best medicine with the power to heal and make your body (and mind) work as optimally as it can.

Diced

Chiffonade

Small dice

Minced

Julienned

Chopped

PART 2

THE WHEN WAY RECIPES

CREATE FOODS THAT FEED AND FUEL YOUR BODY WITH HEALTHY INGREDIENTS.

99

CHAPTER THREE

DIPS, SAUCES, SNACKS & APPS

ANCHO & GUAJILLO CHILI PEPPER SAUCE

PREP: 40 minutes   **COOK: 25–35 minutes**   **MAKES: 12 servings**   **SERVING SIZE: ½ cup**

Calories: 110 kcal Total fiber: 5.1 g Soluble fiber: 0 g Protein: 2.5 g Total fat: 5.8 g Saturated fat: 0.8 g
Carbohydrates: 15.8 g Sugars: 4.8 g Added sugars: 0 g Sodium: 140 mg Potassium: 436 mg Magnesium: 27 mg Calcium: 43 mg

This flavorful sauce combines dried peppers with prepared peppers, broth, and other aromatics for something much more than your typical hot sauce. It delivers great taste without excessive heat, is thicker, and is a great condiment for our Savory & Spiced Quinoa Bowl (page 79) and Egg-White Frittata (page 245), or on top of a baked sweet potato.

4 dried ancho chilies

4 dried guajillo, New Mexico, or California chilies

3 cups boiling water

3 tablespoons extra-virgin olive oil, divided

4 cups yellow onions (about 2 large), finely chopped

½ teaspoon kosher salt

6 large garlic cloves, finely chopped

2 tablespoons tomato paste

1½ cups firmly packed grilled piquillo peppers from jar, well drained

3½ cups vegetable broth

4 tablespoons Raisin Reduction (page 69)

2 tablespoons apple cider vinegar

1½ teaspoons dried oregano

1 teaspoon ground cumin

1. After detaching the stems from the chilies, lay them flat on a cutting board. Holding a chili at a time firmly with one hand, use the other hand to slit the chili lengthwise with a small paring knife from the stem end to the tip. Gently pry open the chili with the paring knife or your fingers, then remove the seeds.

2. Heat a large cast-iron skillet on medium. Place the chilies in the hot skillet and cook until light brown spots begin to appear (do not blacken or burn the chilies). Transfer to a mixing bowl. Pour 3 cups boiling water over the chilies and let stand until softened, 60 minutes. Drain well.

3. Meanwhile, in a large saucepan or pot heat 2 tablespoons olive oil over medium heat. Add the onions, season with ½ teaspoon salt, and sauté 5 minutes. Reduce heat to medium-low and continue to sauté until the onions are very tender, golden, and caramelized, stirring frequently, 20 to 25 minutes.

4. Combine the remaining 1 tablespoon olive oil with the garlic and add to the onions; stir until the garlic is aromatic and just beginning to turn color, 1 to 2 minutes. Add the tomato paste and stir 1 to 2 minutes. Transfer the onion mixture to a small bowl and set aside to cool for 5 minutes.

5. Put the drained chilies, the piquillo peppers, onion mixture, and all remaining ingredients in a blender (you may need to work in batches). Blend until the mixture is as smooth as possible. Transfer to a container and use as desired or cover and freeze up to 6 months.

What to *Know* When

To avoid bitterness, don't use the chili soaking liquid and do not overcook chili peppers or burn in pan. For less heat, remove the chili pepper veins and seeds.

JICAMA NOSH

PREP: 20 minutes   **COOK:** None   **MAKES:** 6 servings   **SERVING SIZE:** ½ cup

Calories: 7.5 kcal Total fiber: 0.4 g Soluble fiber: 0 g Protein: 0.14 g Total fat: 0.03 g Saturated fat: 0 g Healthy fats: 0.01 g
Carbohydrates: 2.3 g Sugars: 0.7 g Added sugars: 0 g Sodium: 190 mg Potassium: 37 mg Magnesium: 3 mg Calcium: 4 mg

When you're looking for a snack with a crunch, opt for jicama instead of chips. Also known as a Mexican yam bean or Mexican turnip, jicama is low in calories and high in fiber and nutrients. Its clean and crisp flavor makes for a great appetizer, addition to an antipasto, or a healthy nosh to pack for lunch. Keep a container of it in your fridge for when those chip cravings hit; the crunch of this root vegetable, paired with cilantro and a bit of heat from the jalapeño, will satisfy your snack tooth

½ cup fresh lime juice

1½ tablespoons fresh cilantro, chopped

1 teaspoon jalapeño chili, minced, roasted, peeled, and seeded*

½ teaspoon kosher salt

1 jicama (about 1 pound), trimmed, peeled, cut into 2-inch-long by ¼-inch-wide strips

1. In a medium bowl whisk first 4 ingredients to blend. Add jicama strips and toss until jicama is thoroughly coated; serve.

*__Chili preparation:__ To roast the jalapeño pepper, hold it skewered over a low flame; roast each side until blistered skin forms, then remove the jalapeño from the skewer and wrap in plastic wrap for a few minutes allowing it to "sweat" and cool. Once cool enough to handle, remove plastic wrap and use a small paring knife to gently scrape off all the blistered and blackened skin. Remove and discard the seeds from the jalapeño and finely mince.

What to *Know* When

It is best to wear vinyl or synthetic gloves or wash hands frequently while handling chili peppers. If you don't have fresh jalapeños, you can substitute the canned version. For more zing, increase the amount of lime juice or jalapeño to taste.

MINTED TAHINI SAUCE

PREP: 10 minutes   **COOK:** None   **MAKES:** 1 serving   **SERVING SIZE:** ½ cup

Calories: 376 kcal Total fiber: 3.3 g Soluble fiber: 0.1 g Protein: 11.1 g Total fat: 32 g Saturated fat: 4.5 g Healthy fats: 26 g
Carbohydrates: 18.4 g Sugars: 1.2 g Added sugars: 0 g Sodium: 506 mg Potassium: 360 mg Magnesium: 64 mg Calcium: 106 mg

Tahini is a toasted sesame seed paste popular in the Middle East, eastern Mediterranean, and parts of North Africa. It's most familiar as a key ingredient in hummus, but it's gaining popularity in North America beyond the popular dip. That makes us happy—sesame seeds are filled with When Way healthy fats that we generally don't eat enough of.

3 tablespoons fresh lemon juice (from 1 lemon)

2 garlic cloves, finely chopped

¼ cup tahini

3 to 4 tablespoons water

1½ tablespoons fresh mint, finely chopped

¼ teaspoon kosher salt

½ cup Greek yogurt (optional for tahini yogurt)

1. In a small bowl combine the lemon juice and garlic. Let stand for 10 minutes.

2. In a medium bowl combine the tahini and 3 tablespoons water. Strain the lemon juice into the tahini mixture; discard the garlic. Whisk to combine and to create a sauce. If the sauce is too thick, add more water, 1 teaspoon at a time. Stir in the mint. Season with the salt. Cover the sauce and refrigerate for 30 minutes before using.

3. If you want to make tahini yogurt, mix the tahini sauce with an equal amount of yogurt, about ½ cup, if using all the sauce.

What to *Know* When

If you've bought tahini in a jar or can from your local market, you've probably noticed that it separates into a solid layer on the bottom and an oil layer on top. Mixing it together can be challenging and messy. That's why we—and chefs—prefer tahini from Soom Foods (available on Amazon); it's high quality, much easier to work with, and delicious.

SMOKIN' BABA KALAMATA

PREP: 20 minutes   **COOK:** 20 minutes   **MAKES:** 10 servings   **SERVING SIZE:** ½ cup

Calories: 167 kcal Total fiber: 8.2 g Soluble fiber: 0.02 g Protein: 4.6 g Total fat: 10.4 g Saturated fat: 1.4 g Healthy fats: 8.5 g
Carbohydrates: 17.4 g Sugars: 5.5 g Added sugars: 0 g Sodium: 387 mg Potassium: 590 mg Magnesium: 44 mg Calcium: 46 mg

Baba ghanoush is a time-honored Middle Eastern recipe typically made with cooked eggplant, tahini, and olive oil. Our version includes kalamata olives, which even increase its heart-healthy benefits. It serves especially well as a dip for vegetables like broccoli and is excellent for breakfast, lunch, or as a snack. Roasting the eggplant in the oven works great, but roasting it over an outdoor fire adds incredible flavor that is totally worth the time and effort.

4 medium eggplants (12 ounces each; about 3 pounds total)

½ cup tahini

8 tablespoons (or more) fresh lemon juice, plus wedges for garnish (optional)

2 garlic cloves, finely chopped

1 teaspoon kosher salt

⅛ teaspoon paprika, plus 1 pinch

2 pinches cayenne pepper

½ cup fresh Italian parsley, chopped, plus 1 teaspoon

½ cup (2½ ounces) pitted kalamata olives, coarsely chopped

1 teaspoon extra-virgin olive oil

1. *On a grill:* Prep an outdoor grill with an offset lump charcoal fire. Once the coals are white and ready, place eggplants on a grill rack over the hot coals; grill until the skins begin to darken, but not burn. Rotate eggplants as needed to evenly cook on all sides. Once ready, move to the side of the grill with no coals and finish "grill roasting" with the lid down and vents open until fully cooked and soft, about 40 minutes. Or remove eggplants from the grill after darkening and finish in a 350°F oven.

   Or in an oven: Preheat the oven to 350°F. Line a baking sheet with foil. Pierce each eggplant in several places with a fork or knife. Place on a prepared sheet and bake until eggplants are tender, about 50 minutes.

2. Let eggplants rest until cool enough to handle. Cut each in half lengthwise, drain off excess liquid, and remove large seed masses. (Some little seeds will remain.) Scoop out the flesh and place in a food processor. Add tahini, lemon juice, garlic, salt, ⅛ teaspoon paprika, and cayenne. Process until smooth and well mixed.

3. Transfer mixture from processor into a mixing bowl. Add ½ cup parsley and olives and mix by hand until well combined. Place in a serving bowl and garnish with a teaspoon parsley, a pinch paprika, and a teaspoon extra-virgin olive oil. Serve with blanched or raw vegetables, whole wheat pita, or baked whole wheat pita chips.

AVOCADO TAPENADE BRUSCHETTA

PREP: 30–45 minutes   **COOK:** None   **MAKES:** 4 servings   **SERVING SIZE:** ½ cup

Calories: 345 kcal Total fiber: 10.3 g Soluble fiber: 0.2 g Protein: 4.6 g Total fat: 24.7 g Saturated fat: 3.3 g Healthy fats: 20.2 g
Carbohydrates: 30.6 g Sugars: 8 g Added sugars: 0 g Sodium: 490 mg Potassium: 528 mg Magnesium: 69 mg Calcium: 141 mg

This tapenade is jumping with the flavors and nutrients of just-picked garden tomatoes, good-quality extra-virgin olive oil, and intensifying hard-neck garlic. The perfectly ripe avocados add a luscious creaminess and healthy monounsaturated fats, which also make this an ideal snack or appetizer for women who are nursing or who want to avoid period pain or hot flashes, and for men to reduce prostate problems or who have a family history of cancer.

¾ cup pineapple juice, preferably from a jar

1 just-ripe avocado (about 6 to 7 ounces), halved, peeled, and diced

3 tablespoons extra-virgin olive oil

1 teaspoon (packed) lemon peel, finely grated

1 teaspoon garlic, finely chopped

⅛ teaspoon freshly ground black pepper

⅛ teaspoon red chili flakes, finely chopped

2 tablespoons fresh basil, very thin strips (chiffonade) cut from small leaves

1 tablespoon fresh Italian parsley, chopped, plus sprigs for garnish

1 teaspoon fresh oregano, chopped

1 teaspoon capers, drained, chopped

1 cup (about 6 ounces) cherry tomatoes, quartered

½ cup pitted Castelvetrano and kalamata olives, cut into ¼-inch dice

¼ cup oil-packed sun-dried tomatoes (about 6 pieces), patted dry, cut into ¼-inch dice

4 slices 100% whole grain bread

1. Pour the juice into a shallow bowl. Add the avocado; stir to coat.

2. In a medium bowl, whisk the oil, lemon peel, garlic, pepper, and chili flakes to blend well. Add the basil, chopped parsley, oregano, and capers; stir to combine. Mix in the cherry tomatoes, olives, and sun-dried tomatoes. Drain the avocado well. Gently mix into the tapenade.

3. Toast the bread slices. Mound ½ cup tapenade on each. Spread to cover bread completely. Cut each slice on diagonal into quarters, or if the bread is smaller, cut diagonally in half. Arrange toasts on plates. Garnish with parsley sprigs.

 **What to _Know_ When**

Soaking avocado in pineapple juice helps to keep it from browning quickly without changing the flavor. Buy avocados while still green and let them ripen at home to prevent bruises from being overly handled in the store or market. Julienne the basil from small leaves to avoid long strings in the tapenade; it makes for a better bite.

Cauliflower
Cream
(page 46)

Carrot
Crema
(page 46)

Artichoke
Cream
(page 47)

Corn Crema
(page 47)

CAULIFLOWER CREAM

PREP: 30–40 minutes   **COOK:** 25 minutes   **MAKES:** 6 servings   **SERVING SIZE:** ½ cup

Calories: 76 kcal Total fiber: 1.7 g Soluble fiber: 0.4 g Protein: 1.5 g Total fat: 4.9 g Saturated fat: 0.7 g Healthy fats: 4 g
Carbohydrates: 7.3 g Sugars: 4.1 g Added sugars: 0 g Sodium: 44 mg Potassium: 256 mg Magnesium: 13 mg Calcium: 26 mg

This is a neutral sauce most similar to a béchamel used for everything from scalloped potatoes to mac 'n' cheese. Our version skips the roux and cow's milk by utilizing the cauliflower and hemp milk. For a less creamy version, use vegetable broth instead of hemp milk.

2 teaspoons extra-virgin olive oil

1 cup sweet onion, cut into ⅓-inch dice

3 cups cauliflower, cut into 1-inch pieces

1 cup (or more) unsweetened hemp milk

1. Heat oil in a large skillet over medium-low heat. Add the onion and sauté until tender but still white, stirring often, about 10 minutes. Set aside.

2. While the onion is cooking, combine the cauliflower and 1 cup hemp milk in a medium saucepan. Bring to simmer over medium heat. Cover, reduce heat to medium-low, and cook until the cauliflower is tender (it's OK if the milk looks curdled), 10 to 12 minutes. Remove from the heat; let sit covered 5 minutes. Uncover and let cauliflower mixture cool to lukewarm, 20 to 30 minutes.

3. Scrape the cooled cauliflower mixture into a high-speed blender. Cover and puree on high until the cream is smooth, stopping occasionally to scrape down the sides, 30 to 40 seconds. Thin the cream with more hemp milk by tablespoonfuls, for desired texture.

CARROT CREMA

PREP: 10–12 minutes   **COOK:** 15–20 minutes   **MAKES:** 4 servings   **SERVING SIZE:** ⅜ cup

Calories: 170 kcal Total fiber: 5.3 g Soluble fiber: 0 g Protein: 2.7 g Total fat: 7 g Saturated fat: 1 g Healthy fats: 6 g
Carbohydrates: 24 g Sugars: 13 g Added sugars: 0 g Sodium: 60 mg Potassium: 300 mg Magnesium: 10 mg Calcium: 54 mg

This crema's beautiful orange comes from healthy beta-carotene. Add it to spinach to help prevent night vision problems—the nutrients in both veggies help preserve eye function.

3 tablespoons extra-virgin olive oil, divided

¾ pound carrots (4 medium-large), peeled, cut into ¼-inch-thick rounds

½ cup water

¼ teaspoon (or more) kosher salt

1. Heat 2 tablespoons oil in a large skillet over medium heat. Spread out the carrots in a single layer of the pan. Cook without stirring until some carrots begin to brown, about 5 minutes. Add ½ cup water. Reduce to medium-low heat; simmer until the carrots are just tender, but not too soft, 4 to 5 minutes.

2. Scrape the carrots and any juices into a Vitamix or similar quality high-speed blender. Blend in a few 30-second intervals, scraping down the bowl after each. Add the remaining 1 tablespoon oil and puree until smooth, 1 to 2 minutes. Season with salt.

ARTICHOKE CREAM (CREMA DI CARCIOFI)

PREP: 20 minutes   COOK: None   MAKES: 4 servings   SERVING SIZE: ½ cup

Calories: 240 kcal Total fiber: 8.4 g Soluble fiber: 1.1 g Protein: 2.8 g Total fat: 21.3 g Saturated fat: 3.0 g Healthy fats: 18.2 g
Carbohydrates: 11.7 g Sugars: 1 g Added sugars: 0 g Sodium: 59 mg Potassium: 279 mg Magnesium: 41 mg Calcium: 21 mg

As you read on page 21, Dr. C developed this artichoke cream recipe after stumbling across the tasty stuff in the olive oil aisle at his grocery store. Here's his go-to recipe.

1 can (13.75-ounce) quartered artichokes, drained

6 tablespoons extra-virgin olive oil

2 to 3 tablespoons water

1. Place the artichokes in a Vitamix or high-speed blender. Add olive oil. Start the blender on low speed and increase speed gradually—the mixture is very thick and may not puree if you increase the speed too quickly. Scrape down the side of the blender jar, then shake the jar, and start again as needed. Add water by tablespoonfuls (up to 3 tablespoons) and continue to blend until a very smooth puree. This may take several minutes.

CORN CREMA

PREP: 20 minutes   COOK: None   MAKES: 4 servings   SERVING SIZE: About 1 cup

Calories: 273 kcal Total fiber: 6 g Soluble fiber: 0 g Protein: 7.5 g Total fat: 8.5 g Saturated fat: 1 g Healthy fats: 6 g
Carbohydrates: 50 g Sugars: 7.5 g Added sugars: 0 g Sodium: 127 mg Potassium: 0 mg Magnesium: 0 mg Calcium: 0 mg

This crema is great with pasta, and also pairs well with fish, on top of whole grain bread, or with sautéed squash. On its own, it could even be served as a nice dessert.

6 large ears corn, husked

2 tablespoons extra-virgin olive oil

Large pinch saffron threads, crushed (optional)

1 tablespoon warm water, for saffron if used

Kosher salt to taste

1. Cut the corn kernels from the cob.

2. In a cast iron skillet or sauté pan, heat the olive oil over medium heat and add corn. Cook for about 5 minutes, season with salt, and cook for another 3 minutes to coax some of the water out of the corn. Lower the heat if it starts to cook too much; you don't want to let the corn get brown.

3. Add the cooked corn to a Vitamix. Add optional saffron and water if using. Start blender on slow to start to break down corn and then gradually turn up speed to high. If it gets stuck too often you can add a little water or olive oil. Process on high for about 2 minutes until very hot and smooth. Season again with salt to taste. Remove from the blender and use or let cool. As it cools a thin skin will form on the top; to avoid this, place piece of parchment on top.

BLUEBERRY, FIG, PRUNE & BALSAMIC DRESSING

PREP: **25 minutes** COOK: **5–7 minutes** MAKES: **12 servings** SERVING SIZE: **1½ tablespoons**

Calories: 28 kcal Total fiber: 0.8 g Soluble fiber: 0.1 g Protein: 0.3 g Total fat: 0.06 g Saturated fat: 0 g Healthy fats: 0.01 g
Carbohydrates: 6.3 g Sugars: 3.7 g Added sugars: 1.5 g Sodium: 8 mg Potassium: 33 mg Magnesium: 3 mg Calcium: 12 mg

Many salad dressings add unnecessary calories to an otherwise healthy dish. Classic vinaigrette dressings have a three parts oil to one part acid ratio. For those who are trying to reduce added sugar, oil, and salt (SOS) from their diet, this great-tasting vinaigrette is a perfect example of how you can make a salad dressing with no added SOS.

¾ cup water

3 prunes, cut in half

2 fresh or 3 dried figs, cut into quarters

½ cup fresh blueberries

½ cup balsamic vinegar (3- or 4-leaf quality)

1 tablespoon fresh Italian parsley, chopped

1 tablespoon fresh basil, chopped

2 garlic cloves, minced

1 teaspoon fresh lemon juice

¼ teaspoon freshly ground black pepper

1. In a small saucepan combine water, prunes, and figs. Bring to boil. Reduce the heat to medium and simmer uncovered until 3 tablespoons water remains, 5 to 7 minutes. If fewer than 3 tablespoons water remain, add more as needed to reach 3 tablespoons. Remove from the heat and let cool, 5 minutes.

2. Pour the prune and fig mixture into a blender. Add all the remaining ingredients and blend until the dressing is smooth.

3. Use the dressing as desired. Put the remaining dressing in a container, cover, label, date, and refrigerate. The dressing will keep refrigerated for 14 days.

Salsa Verde
(page 53)

Tomatillo
Salsa
(page 52)

(Chunky) Roasted
Tomato Salsa
(page 54)

TOMATILLO SALSA

PREP: 10 minutes   **COOK: 15 minutes**   **MAKES: 8 servings**   **SERVING SIZE: ¼ cup**

Calories: 35 kcal Total fiber: 1.6 g Soluble fiber: 0.3 g Protein: 1.6 g Total fat: 0.3 g Saturated fat: 0 g Healthy fats: 0.1 g
Carbohydrates: 8.0 g Sugars: 5.4 g Added sugars: 0 g Sodium: 75 mg Potassium: 266 mg Magnesium: 14 mg Calcium: 21 mg

Tomatillos, also known as Mexican green tomatoes or jamberries, are a great source of iron and dietary fiber. They have a thick green skin covered in a paper husk. Cooking helps soften the skin and brings out the tomatillo's flavors. They're most often used in salsas like this one, which can be used as a dip, over grilled fish, or with roasted potatoes.

4 quarts water

2 pounds tomatillos (1½ to 2 inches each), husked, rinsed well

1 small white onion (about 4 ounces), halved through root end

2 large garlic cloves, peeled

1 small jalapeño pepper (about 2 to 3 inches)

¼ cup fresh cilantro, chopped

½ teaspoon (or more) kosher salt

1 teaspoon (or more) fresh lime juice (optional)

1. In a large pot, bring 4 quarts water to a boil over high heat. Add the tomatillos, onion, garlic, and jalapeño. Adjust the heat and simmer until the ingredients are tender, 12 to 15 minutes. Drain and let stand until cool enough to handle, 20 to 30 minutes.

2. Working over the food processor bowl to prevent losing juices, cut out the small core from the top of each tomatillo and discard. Drop each tomatillo into the bowl. Peel the onion halves. Cut off the root ends and discard; add onion halves to the bowl. Remove the jalapeño stem and quarter the pepper lengthwise. For virtually no heat, scrape out the seeds and veins. To adjust the heat, add a quarter pepper at a time to taste. Add the garlic.

3. Blend in the food processor using 10 on/off turns. Taste for heat, adding more jalapeño, if desired. Continue to blend until salsa is the desired texture. Season with ½ teaspoon salt (or more). Add the cilantro; blend 1 second. Stir in lime juice, if desired.

SALSA VERDE

PREP: 20 minutes   **COOK:** None   **MAKES:** 3 servings   **SERVING SIZE:** ½ cup

Calories: 698 kcal Total fiber: 0.9 g Soluble fiber: 0 g Protein: 2.4 g Total fat: 75.5 g Saturated fat: 10.6 g Healthy fats: 65 g
Carbohydrates: 3.3 g Sugars: 0.7 g Added sugars: 0 g Sodium: 952 mg Potassium: 142 mg Magnesium: 17 mg Calcium: 47 mg

This versatile and tangy salsa has its origins in the Mediterranean, not Mexico. It can be served on top of fish, vegetables, beans, or poultry, as a dip, or spread on 100% whole grain bread. Use this recipe as a base, then add or subtract herbs and spices as you like—you really can't mess this up. It's also the perfect recipe to follow our favorite When Way tip: Make it in the evening and eat it the next day when the sun is out. It keeps well (up to four days in the fridge). To have as a dip, make it in a food processor; for other uses, chopping the herbs by hand makes for more texture.

4 anchovies packed in olive oil, drained

2 tablespoons capers

2 garlic cloves, peeled

½ cup (packed; scant ½ ounce) fresh basil leaves

½ cup (packed; scant ½ ounce) fresh cilantro leaves

½ cup (packed; scant ½ ounce) fresh Italian parsley leaves

¼ cup fresh lemon juice

1 teaspoon lemon zest, finely grated

1 cup extra-virgin olive oil

¼ teaspoon (or more) dried crushed red pepper flakes

½ to ¾ teaspoon sea salt

1. Using a sharp knife, finely mince the anchovies, capers, and garlic (or use a food processor). Transfer to a medium bowl.

2. Coarsely chop the herbs using a sharp knife, then combine with minced anchovies, caper, and garlic, or pulse in the food processor with on/off turns until the herbs are a desired size. Place in a bowl, then stir in the lemon juice and zest. Gradually whisk in the olive oil. Season with crushed red pepper flakes and sea salt to taste.

 **What to *Eat* When**

Cilantro is a great energizer, so alternate this and hummus as a snack with stress-reducing celery after hitting the gym.

(CHUNKY) ROASTED TOMATO SALSA

PREP: **20 minutes**   COOK: **12 minutes**   MAKES: **8 servings**   SERVING SIZE: **About ⅓ cup**

Calories: 91 kcal Total fiber: 1.7 g Soluble fiber: 0 g Total fat: 7.3 g Saturated fat: 1 g Healthy fats: 6.2 g
Carbohydrates: 6.1 g Sugars: 3.6 g Added sugars: 0 g Sodium: 66 mg Potassium: 296 mg Magnesium: 14 mg Calcium: 16 mg

Making salsa is really easy. Dr. C learned two authentic Mexican versions—this chunky tomato version and our Tomatillo Salsa (page 52) from his med school classmate's mom. Cooked tomatoes are a wonderful source of lycopene (much better than raw tomatoes), so enjoy this salsa for its great flavors and heart-healthy benefits. Tomatoes are also great for decreasing your risk of prostate and breast cancers.

1 to 2 tablespoons extra-virgin olive oil or avocado oil

2 pounds ripe red tomatoes, preferably plum tomatoes, unpeeled

1 medium white onion (about 6 ounces), peeled, cut in half through the root end

2 large garlic cloves, unpeeled

1 small jalapeño pepper (about 2 to 3 inches)

1 tablespoon fresh lime juice (optional)

1 to 1½ teaspoons kosher salt

⅓ cup fresh cilantro, chopped

1. Preheat the broiler. With the oil, coat the tomatoes, onion halves, garlic, and jalapeño. Arrange the vegetables on a large rimmed baking sheet.

2. Place the sheet in the broiler about 6 inches from the flames. Broil without turning until the vegetables are charred and softened, 10 to 12 minutes. Let the vegetables rest on the sheet until cool enough to handle, 30 to 40 minutes.

3. Do not peel the tomatoes (the blackened skins will add a smoky flavor). Cut out the tomato cores, then cut each into 8 chunks. Cut the root end from the onion halves, then cut each half into 8 chunks. Peel the garlic. Stem and quarter the jalapeño lengthwise. For the least heat, scrape out the veins and seeds and add only half the jalapeño to each batch. Otherwise, add the pepper a quarter at a time according to personal taste.

4. Put about half the tomatoes, onion, and garlic into a food processor; add jalapeño to taste as previously noted. Pulse with about 20 on/off turns until the salsa is in ¼- to ⅓-inch pieces. Pour the salsa into a medium bowl. Repeat with the remaining vegetables. Add the lime juice, if using, and salt to taste. Mix in the cilantro.

—What to *Know* When—

Compared to other varieties, plum tomatoes are very fleshy, with a small proportion of juices and seeds, so they make a very "meaty" salsa rather than a watery one. Let supermarket tomatoes sit at room temperature for several days to further ripen and develop their best flavor.

SWEET POTATO & BUTTERNUT SQUASH HUMMUS

PREP: 25 minutes   **COOK:** 1 hour, 12 minutes   **MAKES:** 6 servings   **SERVING SIZE:** ½ cup

Calories: 115 kcal Total fiber: 5.0 g Soluble fiber: 0.01 g Protein: 3.1 g Total fat: 0.3 g Saturated fat: 0.05 g Healthy fats: 0.1 g
Carbohydrates: 25.4 g Sugars: 9.8 g Added sugars: 0 g Sodium: 332 mg Potassium: 504 mg Magnesium: 34mg Calcium: 73 mg

Traditional hummus—a classic known throughout the world—is made with chickpeas. In this version, we use sweet potatoes, butternut squash, and great northern beans, as well as fresh parsley. Made without oil, this spread is fabulous for your blood vessels.

1 sweet potato or yam (about 1 pound)

8 ounces (about 1½ cups) butternut squash, peeled, cut into 1-inch dice

1 can (15-ounce) great northern beans, drained and rinsed

3 tablespoons fresh lemon juice

½ cup (4 ounces) roasted red peppers from jar, well drained

2 garlic cloves, minced

1 teaspoon ground cumin

½ teaspoon kosher salt

¼ teaspoon freshly ground black pepper

Pinch cayenne pepper, or more to taste

1 tablespoon fresh Italian parsley, chopped

1. Preheat the oven to 350°F. Pierce the sweet potato in several places with a fork. Place on a small baking sheet and bake until very tender, about 1 hour. Cool slightly. Scoop out the flesh and reserve; discard the peel.

2. Bring a medium saucepan of salted water to a boil. Add the butternut squash and simmer until the squash is tender, 10 to 12 minutes. Drain the squash well and let cool for 5 minutes.

3. Meanwhile, combine the beans and lemon juice in a food processor, blending until smooth with quick on/off turns. Add the butternut squash, sweet potato, and all remaining ingredients except the parsley. Process until the mixture is smooth. Transfer to a serving bowl and refrigerate at least 1 hour. Garnish with chopped parsley before serving.

WHOLE GRAIN RYE & SPELT CRACKERS

PREP: 30 minutes   **COOK:** 5–6 minutes   **MAKES:** 6 large crackers   **SERVING SIZE:** 1 cracker

Calories: 119 kcal Total fiber: 2.7 g Soluble fiber: 0.3 g Protein: 2.1 g Total fat: 7.4 g Saturated fat: 1 g Healthy fats: 6.1 g
Carbohydrates: 11.2 g Sugars: 0.2 g Added sugars: 0 g Sodium: 240 mg Potassium: 89 mg Magnesium: 11 mg Calcium: 3 mg

Finding 100% whole grain crackers without a lot of extra ingredients can be a challenge. So why not make them at home? These tasty crackers have just four ingredients. For flavored varieties, you can always add caraway seeds, flax seeds, or other spices just before baking.

½ cup (about 2.4 ounces) whole grain spelt flour (such as Arrowhead Mills)

⅓ cup (about 1.8 ounces) whole grain dark rye flour (such as Bob's Red Mill)

¾ teaspoon Diamond Crystal Kosher Salt

3 tablespoons extra-virgin olive oil, plus additional for brushing

2 to 2½ tablespoons water

1. Preheat the oven to 450°F. Place a large baking sheet in the oven to heat while preparing the dough.

2. In a medium bowl, whisk both flours and salt to blend. Add the olive oil and stir to combine (mixture will be dry and crumbly). Add water 1 tablespoon at a time until a thick but cohesive dough forms. Knead the dough in the bowl for 1 minute, then shape into a ball. Wrap in plastic wrap and let stand for 15 minutes at room temperature.

3. Divide the dough into 6 equal pieces. Roll each piece into a ball (about the size of a golf ball). Using a rolling pin, roll out each dough ball onto a very lightly floured work surface to about a 4- to 4½-inch round. Or roll the dough into a single sheet, about ¼ inch thick, and slice into 1-inch squares with a biscuit or pizza cutter. Brush each lightly on both sides with olive oil. Using a wide metal spatula, transfer to the baking sheet in the oven, spacing slightly apart.

4. Bake the crackers until cooked through, 5 to 6 minutes. When they harden and turn light golden in spots on top, remove the crackers from the baking sheet and cool to room temperature before serving.

Sweet Potato & Butternut Squash Hummus (page 55)

Beet Muhammara (page 60)

Roasted Red
Pepper
Muhammara
(page 61)

BEET MUHAMMARA

PREP: 15 minutes   **COOK: None**   **MAKES: 5 servings**   **SERVING SIZE: ¼ cup**

Calories: 113 kcal Total fiber: 1.1 g Soluble fiber: 0.34 g Protein: 1.5 g Total fat: 10.3 g Saturated fat: 1.7 g Healthy fats: 8.5 g
Carbohydrates: 4.9 g Sugars: 3 g Added sugars: 0 g Sodium: 120 mg Potassium: 136 mg Magnesium: 17 mg Calcium: 12 mg

This is a surprisingly sweet dip—made from delicious raw beets—that is great with vegetables or whole grain crackers (see page 57) or as a topping on a piece of salmon. Use it as part of your When Way Vegetable Platter (page 66). Bonus: This dip loves you back. Beets are loaded with precursors to compounds needed to dilate your arteries and keep your cardiovascular system healthy.

⅓ cup (about 1.2 ounces) walnuts, toasted

1 garlic clove, peeled

8 ounces beets (about 2 medium), peeled, cut into ¾-inch dice

2 tablespoons fresh lemon juice

3 tablespoons extra-virgin olive oil, plus more to taste

¼ teaspoon fine sea salt, plus more to taste

Fresh Italian parsley, chopped, for garnish (optional)

1. Combine walnuts and garlic in a food processor. Pulse using on/off turns until finely chopped.

2. Add beets and lemon juice, and pulse until all ingredients are incorporated and finely chopped.

3. Add 3 tablespoons oil and ¼ teaspoon salt and process until a chunky paste forms, occasionally scraping down the sides of the bowl.

4. For a thinner consistency, add additional oil by teaspoonfuls. Taste and season with more salt, if desired. Transfer to a small bowl. Garnish with parsley.

TIP: To toast walnuts, place on a parchment-lined sheet pan and cook for about 8 minutes at 350°F. They will turn a light golden brown. Don't keep toasted nuts for too long, because the heated fats turn rancid more quickly than raw nuts.

ROASTED RED PEPPER MUHAMMARA

PREP: 10 minutes   **COOK:** None   **MAKES:** 4 servings   **SERVING SIZE:** ½ cup as dip

Calories: 180 kcal Total fiber: 4.9 g Soluble fiber: 0.4 g Protein: 2.8 g Total fat: 14.5 g Saturated fat: 1.5 g Healthy fats: 12.4 g
Carbohydrates: 10.2 g Sugars: 0.5 g Added sugars: 0 g Sodium: 323 mg Potassium: 83 mg Magnesium: 28 mg Calcium: 125 mg

This attractive and colorful dip provides the red pepper polyphenols that help keep your joints young by keeping inflammation down. It is great served with toasted whole wheat pita, vegetables, or as a sandwich condiment.

⅔ cup (about 2.4 ounces) walnuts, toasted, plus more for garnish

1 garlic clove, peeled

1 jar (16-ounce; about 2 cups) roasted red peppers, well drained

1 tablespoon fresh lemon juice

1 tablespoon extra-virgin olive oil, plus more for serving

½ teaspoon smoked hot paprika

¼ teaspoon ground coriander

¼ teaspoon ground cumin

¼ teaspoon kosher salt, or more to taste

Fresh Italian parsley, chopped, for garnish (optional)

1. Combine garlic and ⅔ cup walnuts in a food processor and pulse using on/off turns until walnuts are finely chopped.

2. Add peppers and lemon juice and process until smooth, about 2 minutes.

3. Add 1 tablespoon olive oil and spices, and pulse to combine. Add ¼ teaspoon salt, or more to taste.

4. Transfer the dip to a small serving bowl. Drizzle very lightly with additional olive oil. Serve garnished with parsley and additional walnuts, if desired.

CASHEW-NAISE

PREP: **15 minutes, plus overnight**   COOK: **None**   MAKES: **¼ cup**   SERVING SIZE: **2 tablespoons**

Calories: 137 kcal Total fiber: 0.8 g Soluble fiber: 0.4 g Protein: 3.7 g Total fat: 10.7 g Saturated fat: 2.0 g Healthy fats: 8.0 g
Carbohydrates: 8.6 g Sugars: 1.5 g Added sugars: 0 g Sodium: 171 mg Potassium: 137 mg Magnesium: 62 mg Calcium: 17 mg

Chef Jim created this recipe so you'll never miss fattening, egg- and oil-heavy mayo again. In no time, you can whip up this cashew-based mayo alternative for a sandwich spread, salad dressing, or sauce.

1 cup packed raw cashews

4¼ cups water, divided

1 tablespoon apple cider vinegar

1 tablespoon fresh lemon juice

1 teaspoon Raisin Reduction (page 69)

¾ teaspoon dry mustard

½ teaspoon distilled vinegar

1 small garlic clove, minced

½ teaspoon kosher salt

Generous pinch cayenne pepper

1. Place the cashews in a medium bowl. Add 4 cups water; cover and let soak overnight in the refrigerator.

2. Drain the cashews, then place in a Vitamix or high-speed blender; add ¼ cup water and all remaining ingredients. Blend until smooth, occasionally scraping down the sides of the blender jar as needed. Transfer the Cashew-naise to a small bowl; cover and refrigerate until ready to use.

What to *Swap* When

Add freshly chopped chives, parsley, or other herbs and spices—even roasted chili pepper—for flavor variations.

Shallot, Mint &
Lemon Yogurt
(page 70)

When Way
Vegetable Platter
(page 66)

Garden Chive
Bean Dip
(page 67)

WHEN WAY VEGETABLE PLATTER

Your next event will be a big hit if you skip the raw crudité platter and serve this perfect mix of raw and cooked vegetables—with a few of your favorite sauces and dips—instead. "Non-starchy" veggies—or even starchy ones that are cooled overnight to become resistant starches, which means they won't raise your blood sugar very quickly and act more like a fiber than a starch—are key for your health because they contain so many nutrients. We encourage you to eat as many of these vegetables as you want.

Roasted

Broccoli, Cauliflower, Carrots

Blanched

String beans, Potatoes, Broccoli

Raw, sliced into batons

Cucumbers, Fennel, Peppers, Carrots, Radish

1. *For roasted vegetables:* Preheat the oven to 350°F. Cut vegetables into even-size pieces large enough to pick up and dip with your hands. (Remember they will shrink when cooking.) Toss lightly with olive oil until just coated and place on a parchment-lined sheet pan in a single layer. Roast until just cooked but still al dente, about 20 to 30 minutes. Season with salt to taste.

2. *For blanched vegetables:* Bring 4 quarts water to boil and season with kosher salt to make salty like the sea. Cut potatoes in half and boil until cooked through, fork tender but not mushy. Cut broccoli into appropriate-size florets and cook until color brightens, about 2 minutes. Cook string beans about 4 minutes. Strain vegetables and let cool.

3. Serve vegetables on a platter (or keep in the fridge) along with raw slices of cucumbers, fennel, peppers, carrots, and radishes. Serve with Garden Chive Bean Dip (page 67), Shallot, Mint & Lemon Yogurt (page 70), Fennel Bagna Cauda (page 71), or your other favorite When Way dip or sauce.

What to *Know* When

If roasting multiple types of vegetables, cook each separately because they all will cook at different rates.

GARDEN CHIVE
BEAN DIP

PREP: 30 minutes   COOK: 10 minutes   MAKES: 6 servings   SERVING SIZE: ½ cup

Calories: 226 kcal Total fiber: 6.8 g Soluble fiber: 0.3 g Protein: 9.4 g Total fat: 10.9 g Saturated fat: 1.5 g Healthy fats: 8.7 g
Carbohydrates: 24 g Sugars: 2 g Added sugars: 0 g Sodium: 524 mg Potassium: 189 mg Magnesium: 33 mg Calcium: 70 mg

When you come home hungry, you first often go for something sweet. Resist that urge and try this dip instead. It's a great filler for late afternoon or early evening cravings because it is loaded with protein and healthy fat. Have it ready to go in the refrigerator with some blanched broccoli, beans, or asparagus for dipping.

12 ounces (about 2⅓ cups) frozen lima beans, cooked according to package directions

1 cup (about 5 ounces) frozen green peas, cooked according to package directions

½ cup canned quartered artichoke hearts, well drained

½ cup tahini

5 tablespoons fresh lemon juice

2 large garlic cloves, minced

1 teaspoon kosher salt

1 teaspoon ground cumin

⅛ teaspoon freshly ground black pepper

½ cup (firmly packed) green onions, thinly sliced

¼ cup (firmly packed) fresh chives, thinly sliced

1. In the bowl of a food processor, combine all but the green onions and chives. Process until a slightly chunky puree forms, occasionally stopping to scrape down the sides of the bowl, about 2 minutes. Transfer the dip to a medium bowl.

2. Reserve a tablespoon green onions. Fold the remaining green onions and chives into the dip. Garnish the top with the reserved green onions and serve.

What to *Know* When

For a spicy version of this dip, add fresh minced jalapeños. Not only will they bring on the heat, but jalapeños are also low in calories and a good source of vitamins C and B₆.

RAISIN REDUCTION

PREP: 5 minutes   **COOL:** 15–18 minutes   **MAKES:** 32 servings (2 cups)   **SERVING SIZE:** 1 tablespoon

Calories: 73 kcal Total fiber: 1 g Soluble fiber: 0.3 g Protein: 0.8 g Total fat: 0.1 g Saturated fat: 0.04 g Healthy fats: 0.03 g
Carbohydrates: 19 g Sugars: 14.3 g Added sugars: 0 g Sodium: 5 mg Potassium: 180 mg Magnesium: 9 mg Calcium: 14 mg

Chef Jim created this recipe as a great way to sweeten recipes without adding processed sugars. You'll find it in many of our recipes, including our Heavenly Good and Fudgy Cupcakes (page 263) and Papa's Pumpkin Pie-less (page 273). This reduction has a lot of natural sugars, but paired with the raisins' fiber, the sugars are more slowly absorbed and won't raise your blood sugar as much. Raisins also contain protein and beneficial polyphenols, which may help prevent type 2 diabetes, obesity, heart disease, cancer, and dementia.

2 cups (about 9.5 ounces) golden raisins

2 cups water

1. Combine the raisins and water in a large saucepan. Bring to boil over medium-high heat. Reduce to medium-low heat and simmer uncovered until about 3 to 4 tablespoons water remain, 15 to 18 minutes. Remove from heat and let cool to lukewarm.

2. Transfer the raisin mixture to a high-speed blender or food processor. Blend until an almost smooth puree forms, stopping occasionally to scrape down the sides of the blender or bowl, about 2 minutes.

What to *Know* When

Store the Raisin Reduction in your refrigerator for up to a week, or in ½-cup measures (easier for pulling out when needed) in your freezer for up to three months.

SHALLOT, MINT & LEMON YOGURT

PREP: 30 minutes, plus overnight   **COOK:** None   **MAKES:** 4 servings   **SERVING SIZE:** ⅓ cup

Calories: 111 kcal **Total fiber:** 0.2 g **Soluble fiber:** 0 g **Protein:** 11 g **Total fat:** 1.9 g **Saturated fat:** 1.1 g **Healthy fats:** 0 g
Carbohydrates: 14.4 g **Sugars:** 5.8 g **Added sugars:** 0 g **Sodium:** 157 mg **Potassium:** 147 mg **Magnesium:** 2 mg **Calcium:** 109 mg

Greek yogurt is a healthier alternative to regular yogurt because it has less sugar, is lower in lactose, and has twice as much protein and contains gut-healthy probiotic cultures. It gets its rich, thicker texture because it is strained, eliminating some of the whey. You can make Greek yogurt even thicker by straining it overnight at home. This eliminates more whey, creating "yogurt cheese."

2 cups full-fat plain Greek yogurt

¼ cup shallot, chopped

3 tablespoons fresh lemon juice

¼ cup fresh mint or other herb of choice, chopped

⅛ to ¼ teaspoon kosher salt

⅛ to ¼ teaspoon freshly ground black pepper

1 tablespoon extra-virgin olive oil (optional)

1. Hang a large strainer over a deep bowl. Line the strainer with a smooth kitchen towel. Spoon the yogurt into the towel. Gather the towel ends and twist to enclose the yogurt, then place in the strainer. Refrigerate the strainer in the bowl for at least 18—but preferably—24 hours for more drainage and a thicker yogurt.

2. Place the shallot into a small bowl. Add the lemon juice; marinate 20 minutes.

3. Spoon 1 cup strained yogurt into a food processor (there may be some extra drained yogurt remaining). Add the shallot-lemon mixture and mint. Using 15 to 20 quick on/off turns, process until just blended (the texture will not be smooth). Transfer to a small bowl. Season with salt and pepper.

4. Drizzle with olive oil, if desired. Serve as a dip with veggies.

FENNEL BAGNA CAUDA

PREP: **15 minutes**   COOK: **10 minutes**   MAKES: **4 servings**   SERVING SIZE: **2–3 tablespoons**

Calories: 277 kcal Total fiber: 1.3 g Soluble fiber: 0 g Protein: 16.2 g Total fat: 22.3 g Saturated fat: 3.7 g Healthy fats: 17.5 g
Carbohydrates: 2.6 g Sugars: 0 g Added sugars: 0 g Sodium: 581 mg Potassium: 344 mg Magnesium: 41 mg Calcium: 94 mg

Bagna cauda means "warm bath" in Italian. This warm sauce is traditionally made with lots of anchovies and garlic and served with crunchy vegetables. Anchovies are a great source of omega-3 fats. We add leafy fennel fronds (from the top of the bulb) to our sauce for a little more body. Cut up the fennel bulb for your vegetable platter.

¼ cup extra-virgin olive oil

4 garlic cloves, minced

2 tablespoons fennel fronds, finely chopped

12 anchovy fillets packed in extra-virgin olive oil

1. In a saucepan or small sauté pan, add the olive oil, garlic, fennel fronds, and anchovy fillets. Heat over low to medium heat until the anchovies fall apart when stirred.

2. Serve warm with crunchy vegetables.

HARISSA SPICE BLEND

PREP: **10 minutes**   COOK: **None**   MAKES: **60 servings**   SERVING SIZE: **¼ teaspoon**

Calories: 20 kcal Total fiber: 1.8 g Soluble fiber: 0 g Protein: 0.9 g Total fat: 0.7 g Saturated fat: 0.01 g Healthy fats: 0.1 g
Carbohydrates: 2.8 g Sugars: 0.02 g Added sugars: 0 g Sodium: 389 mg Potassium: 15 mg Magnesium: 2 mg Calcium: 21 mg

A number of our recipes use a dry harissa, a traditional North African and Middle Eastern spice blend with lots of complex flavors. Because it may be hard to find at your grocer, Chef Jim put together this DIY version, which contains spices that help reduce inflammation throughout the body.

2 teaspoons caraway seeds

½ teaspoon red chili flakes

1 teaspoon kosher salt

4 teaspoons paprika

1 tablespoon smoked paprika

1 tablespoon ground cumin

2 teaspoons garlic powder

1. Finely grind the caraway seeds and chili flakes with a mortar and pestle or in a spice grinder. Add the salt and blend 10 seconds. Transfer the blend to a small container.

2. Mix in the remaining ingredients. Cover and store at room temperature or in the refrigerator for up to 2 months.

CARROT TOP PESTO

PREP: 15 minutes   **COOK:** None   **MAKES:** 1 cup   **SERVING SIZE:** 2 tablespoons

Calories: 858 kcal Total fiber: 1.0 g Soluble fiber: 0 g Protein: 2.6 g Total fat: 94 g Saturated fat: 12.6 g Healthy fats: 81.7 g
Carbohydrates: 2.5 g Sugars: 0 g Added sugars: 0 g Sodium: 480 mg Potassium: 6 mg Magnesium: 1 mg Calcium: 23 mg

Carrots, especially from the farmers market, often come with their green tops still attached. Don't just throw them away: Use the most delicate part of those carrot greens for this pesto, which makes a great dip for vegetables, sauce for pasta, or topper for fish.

¼ cup walnuts, toasted

½ to ¾ teaspoon kosher salt or fine sea salt, or to taste

1 large garlic clove, peeled

1 cup carrot top greens, washed and dried in a salad spinner

¾ cup extra-virgin olive oil (use the best available)

1. In a food processor (or with a mortar and pestle), combine the walnuts and salt. Process into a rough paste. Add the garlic, and process until minced. Add the carrot tops and process until they are finely chopped.

2. Transfer the carrot top mixture to a small bowl. Gradually whisk in the olive oil. Season with more salt to taste.

What to *Know* When

For a better-tasting pesto, avoid using the tough or wispy carrot stems.

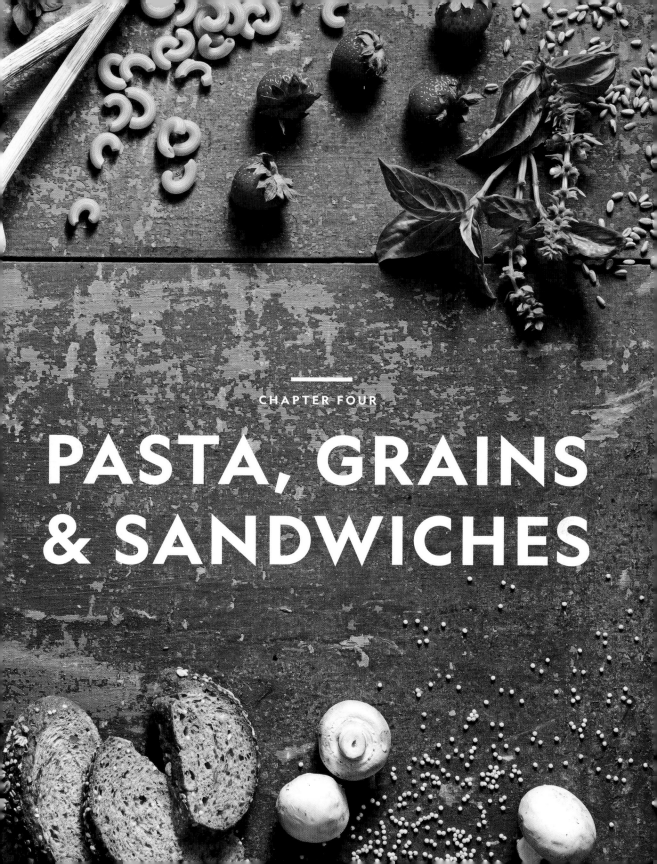

CHAPTER FOUR

PASTA, GRAINS & SANDWICHES

WHOLE GRAIN WAFFLES WITH CHIA BERRY SAUCE

PREP: 25 minutes   COOK: 30 minutes   MAKES: 6 servings

SERVING SIZE: ½ cup sauce; 1 waffle

Calories: 244 kcal Total fiber: 7.6 g Soluble fiber: 0.3 g Protein: 5.6 g Total fat: 9.6 g Saturated fat: 0.9 g Healthy fats: 7.7 g
Carbohydrates: 35.5 g Sugars: 11.2 g Added sugars: 0 g Sodium: 298 mg Potassium: 255 mg Magnesium: 30 mg Calcium: 113 mg

We love to make these egg-free waffles from scratch and always have a supply on hand in the freezer so we can have them at the ready with our morning coffee. Unlike store-bought frozen waffles, these are additive free. The chia berry sauce is a healthy alternative to maple syrup and provides beneficial nutrients (chia seeds have been used since the time of the Aztec, who carried them for survival, as a source of protein and omega-3 fatty acids).

Waffles

2 cups water, divided in half

1 tablespoon chia seeds

1⅓ cups 100% whole wheat pastry flour

2½ teaspoons baking powder

2 teaspoons ground cinnamon

½ teaspoon kosher salt

1 large ripe banana, peeled

1 tablespoon vanilla extract

¾ cup (about 3 ounces) walnuts, toasted, chopped (optional)

Canola oil cooking spray (to grease waffle iron)

Berry Sauce

2 cups (about 12 ounces) fresh strawberries, sliced

1 cup (about 5½ ounces) fresh blueberries

½ cup unsweetened orange juice

1 tablespoon chia seeds

1. In a small bowl, stir 1 cup water and chia seeds well to mix. Set aside to allow the chia seeds to plump up slightly, about 10 minutes.

2. In a large bowl, combine the pastry flour, baking powder, cinnamon, and salt; whisk to blend well and set aside.

3. In a medium bowl, coarsely mash the banana with a fork, then add the vanilla and mash until well blended.

4. To the bowl with the flour mixture, add the remaining 1 cup water, the chia seed mixture, and the banana mixture, whisking until no lumps of flour remain. Fold in the walnuts, if using. If the batter seems too thick, add water by tablespoonfuls for a slightly more pourable consistency.

5. In a medium saucepan, combine all the berry sauce ingredients. Bring to a boil over medium-high heat, then reduce to medium-low heat and simmer until the berries are softened and the sauce thickens slightly, about 10 minutes. Remove from the heat and cover with a lid to keep warm.

6. Meanwhile, coat a preheated 6- or 7-inch waffle iron with canola oil cooking spray. For a 6-inch waffle iron, pour ½ cup batter onto the iron; use ⅔ cup batter for a 7-inch iron. Close the iron and cook until the waffle is golden brown, cooked through, and beginning to crisp on top, about 3½ to 5 minutes, depending on the waffle iron. Repeat with the remaining batter. Serve with warm sauce on top.

What to *Know* When

If fresh berries aren't available, you can always use frozen berries or another favorite fruit for the sauce. For a richer batter, use almond milk or soy milk instead of water.

SAVORY & SPICED QUINOA BOWL

PREP: 35 minutes   **COOK:** 38 minutes   **MAKES:** 6 servings   **SERVING SIZE:** 1½ cups

Calories: 293 kcal Total fiber: 8.7 g Soluble fiber: 0 g Protein: 9.5 g Total fat: 7.1 g Saturated fat: 0.7 g Healthy fats: 4.1 g
Carbohydrates: 51.7 g Sugars: 8 g Added sugars: 0 g Sodium: 524 mg Potassium: 614 mg Magnesium: 30 mg Calcium: 88 mg

This one-pot meal combines red, white, and black quinoa for a colorful lunch or light dinner; leftovers taste great up to two days. The quinoa choices provide all essential amino acids needed for building and maintaining muscles (assuming you stimulate your muscles with resistance exercises). This is a great alternative to fast food lunches. If you like lunch with a bit of heat, drizzle it with our Ancho & Guajillo Chili Pepper Sauce (page 37).

2 tablespoons extra-virgin olive oil

1½ cups onion, finely chopped

3 garlic cloves, minced

2 teaspoons tomato paste

2 cups vegetable broth

3 teaspoons chili powder

2 teaspoons ground cumin

½ teaspoon smoked paprika

½ teaspoon dried oregano

¾ teaspoon kosher salt

¼ teaspoon freshly ground black pepper

2 teaspoons jalapeño chili*, peeled, seeded, minced

2 cups (11 to 12 ounces) butternut squash, peeled, seeded, cut into ½-inch dice

1 cup (about 6 ounces) sweet potato (yam), peeled, cut into ½-inch dice

1 cup red bell pepper, cut into ½-inch dice

1 cup canned diced tomatoes in juice

1 can (15-ounce) black beans, drained and rinsed

1 cup frozen corn

1 cup quinoa (preferably mixed red, black, and white), rinsed in cold water

1. In a large pot, heat the olive oil over medium heat. Add the onion and sauté until lightly caramelized, about 10 minutes.

2. Add the garlic and sauté until aromatic, 1 to 2 minutes. Add the tomato paste and stir 1 minute. Add the vegetable broth and stir with a wooden spoon to deglaze the bottom of the pot. Add all of the spices, stir 30 seconds, then add the remaining ingredients and stir to combine. Bring to a boil. Reduce to medium-low heat; cover until the quinoa is cooked through and the vegetables are tender, about 25 minutes. Turn off the heat and let stand, covered, for 20 minutes for flavors to blend.

*See Roasted Jalapeño, Bean, and Broccoli Salad (page 189) for chili preparation. We recommend preparing a bag of 6 or more jalapeños this way and freezing them in tablespoon increments. Store frozen up to 2 months.

— What to *Swap* When —

Create your own plant-forward variations by adding other vegetables, or use different grains like millet.

WHOLE BEET LINGUINE

PREP: 20 minutes   **COOK:** 20–22 minutes   **MAKES:** 4 servings   **SERVING SIZE:** 1 cup

Calories: 524 kcal Total fiber: 3.8 g Soluble fiber: 0.2 g Protein: 16.6 g Total fat: 16.8 g Saturated fat: 2.7 g Healthy fats: 3.0 g
Carbohydrates: 76.9 g Sugars: 5.6 g Added sugars: 0 g Sodium: 275 mg Potassium: 265 mg Magnesium: 73 mg Calcium: 61 mg

You may have heard of nose-to-tail eating: when every part of an animal is used instead of just the prime cuts. This recipe is about the whole vegetable—roots to stems. The dish uses beets and their greens. It's simple to make, and the bright red pasta is as striking as it is delicious. You probably never thought of beets as an aphrodisiac, but they may actually help make orgasms better because they help arteries dilate; their greens in particular aid arterial health.

Kosher salt

1 bunch small beets, with tops

¼ cup olive oil

2 anchovy fillets

2 large garlic cloves, finely chopped

12 ounces whole grain linguine

¼ to ½ teaspoon Urfa chili or dried crushed red pepper flakes, or to taste (optional)

1. Bring a large pot of water to boil. Add enough salt to make it salty like the sea.

2. Meanwhile, cut off the stems and leaves from the beets, separating the beet roots, stems, and leaves. Wash the leaves in a bowl of water until no sediment remains. Cut the stems into 1-inch pieces. Cut the leaves crosswise into 1-inch strips. Peel the beets, then cut them into matchstick-size strips, to yield about 1½ cups.

3. Heat a large skillet over medium heat and add olive oil. Add anchovies and garlic, and sauté until the anchovies break down, 2 minutes. Stir in the beet roots and sauté until softened, about 10 minutes. Turn off the heat; cover the skillet to keep warm.

4. Add pasta to the pot of boiling water and cook according to the package directions until al dente. Watch the timer carefully: When 5 minutes cooking time remains, add the beet stems to the pasta.

5. When 2 minutes pasta cooking time remains, return the skillet to medium-high and add the beet greens and Urfa chili or red pepper flakes, if using; sauté until beet greens are wilted.

6. Using a slotted spoon or spider, transfer the pasta and stems to the skillet with the beets. Toss to combine and serve.

Castelvetrano &
Kalamata Olive
Biscuits (page 84)

Eggplant El-Roma
(page 85)

CASTELVETRANO & KALAMATA OLIVE BISCUITS

PREP: **15 minutes**   COOK: **14–16 minutes**   MAKES: **13 servings**
SERVING SIZE: **1 roll (using ¼ cup batter each)**

Calories: 92 kcal Total fiber: 2.2 g Soluble fiber: 0.3 g Protein: 3.0 g Total fat: 4.1 g Saturated fat: 0.3 g Healthy fats: 3.3 g
Carbohydrates: 12.3 g Sugars: 0.2 g Added sugars: 0 g Sodium: 288 mg Potassium: 97 mg Magnesium: 32 mg Calcium: 51 mg

It's a lot of work to make a traditional loaf of olive bread given all the dough raising and punching. We've simplified the process with these fabulous biscuits that skip the labor of yeast breads. Plus, they freeze well so you can pull them out as needed, especially as the bun for our Eggplant El-Roma (next page). Olives are a great When Way food because they're low in calories and are loaded with healthy fat and potassium.

1 cup unsweetened and unflavored almond milk

1 tablespoon fresh rosemary, finely chopped

1 tablespoon apple cider vinegar

1½ cups whole wheat flour

½ cup slivered almonds, toasted, finely ground

2 teaspoons baking powder

½ teaspoon kosher salt

½ cup (packed) pitted Castelvetrano olives, coarsely chopped

½ cup (packed) pitted kalamata olives, coarsely chopped

1. Preheat the oven to 450°F. In a small bowl, combine the almond milk, rosemary, and vinegar; set aside. In a large bowl, whisk the wheat flour, ground almonds, baking powder, and salt to blend. Add the almond milk mixture to the flour mixture, gently folding together with a rubber spatula until a moist dough. Add the olives and fold in until well dispersed and blended.

2. For a sandwich-size roll, scoop the dough by ½-cup portions onto a nonstick baking sheet, spaced slightly apart. Gently flatten each a bit with your fingers. Bake until a tester inserted into the rolls comes out clean, 14 to 16 minutes. For smaller rolls, scoop the dough by ¼-cup portions and follow the same steps. Transfer to a rack and cool.

What to *Know* When

Toast your own slivered almonds, then grind in small processor or coffee grinder to a fine flour consistency (about 20 to 25 seconds). Make sure almonds are room temperature and NOT frozen before grinding.

EGGPLANT EL-ROMA

PREP: 45–50 minutes   **COOK:** 1 hour   **MAKES:** 12–14 servings   **SERVING SIZE:** 1 slider

Calories: 106 kcal Total fiber: 3.5 g Soluble fiber: 0 g Protein: 3.3 g Total fat: 2 g Saturated fat: 0.3 g Healthy fats: 1.6 g
Carbohydrates: 19.1 g Sugars: 3.1 g Added sugars: 0 g Sodium: 258 mg Potassium: 223 mg Magnesium: 25 mg Calcium: 25 mg

An unlikely combination, potatoes and chard are the perfect toppers for eggplant—a trio loaded with umami flavor. These eggplant stacks are even better when sandwiched between our Castelvetrano & Kalamata Olive Biscuits (see page 84). As a slider, it is a fabulous balance of savory, salty, and a hint of sweet.

1 eggplant (1 pound), cut into ½-inch-thick slices

2 cups canned tomato sauce with no added sugar

¾ teaspoon dried oregano

⅔ cup golden cherry tomatoes, halved lengthwise

⅓ cup kalamata olives, pitted, halved lengthwise

1 tablespoon capers

1 tablespoon extra-virgin olive oil

3 garlic cloves, minced

1 tablespoon fresh Italian parsley, chopped

1 teaspoon fresh rosemary, finely chopped

1 teaspoon kosher salt

½ teaspoon freshly ground black pepper

2 pounds (about 6 small-medium) Yukon Gold potatoes, cut into medium wedges

¾ teaspoon paprika

1½ cups cooked Swiss chard (use Chard & Roasted Butternut Squash, page 133)

1. Preheat the oven to 350°F. Arrange the eggplant slices on a parchment-lined or nonstick baking sheet, spaced apart. Top each slice with about 2 tablespoons tomato sauce, more on the larger slices and less on smaller slices (some sauce may spill out onto the baking sheet). Sprinkle evenly with oregano. Top each slice with cherry tomatoes, olives, and capers, equally divided among the slices. Bake until fork tender, 55 to 60 minutes.

2. Meanwhile, in a large mixing bowl, combine the olive oil, garlic, parsley, rosemary, salt, and pepper. Add the potato wedges and toss until well coated. Spread in an even layer on a nonstick baking sheet. Sprinkle evenly with paprika. Bake until the potato wedges are fork tender, 35 to 40 minutes. Potatoes and eggplant should be ready about the same time.

3. Follow the Chard & Roasted Butternut Squash recipe (page 133).

4. Top each eggplant slice with two potato wedges. Then top each with 1½ tablespoons warmed chard.

What to *Eat* When

Chard, like other leafy greens, has vitamins that may help prevent headaches.

ENGLISH PEA PASTA

PREP: 30 minutes   **COOK: 20–24 minutes**   **MAKES: 4 servings**   **SERVING SIZE: 1 cup**

Calories: 554 kcal Total fiber: 12 g Soluble fiber: 0.1 g Protein: 15.5 g Total fat: 16.7 g Saturated fat: 2.0 g Healthy fats: 12.1 g
Carbohydrates: 84 g Sugars: 7.7 g Added sugars: 0 g Sodium: 178 mg Potassium: 433 mg Magnesium: 14 mg Calcium: 134 mg

There is something special about using fresh peas straight out of the pod. This recipe was inspired by our root-to-stem philosophy of cooking: It always seems like such a waste to throw away the pea pods, but they are relatively inedible. To make use of the pods, we've pureed them into a spring-fresh pasta sauce. Remember: Pasta for breakfast is a great When Way choice, especially when it's loaded with healthful pea protein.

Kosher salt

1 pound fresh English peas in pods
(yields about 1 cup shelled peas
and about 3½ cups pods)

½ cup water

¼ cup extra-virgin olive oil

2 small spring onions or 2 large shallots,
chopped

2 small spring garlic (whites) or
3 garlic cloves, minced

2 tablespoons Greek yogurt (optional)

12 ounces whole grain pasta, such as
linguine, rigatoni, or small shells

Freshly ground black pepper

¼ cup fresh basil, thinly sliced

¼ cup fresh mint (peppermint
preferred), thinly sliced

Espelette pepper to taste (optional)

Grated Parmigiano Reggiano cheese
(optional)

1. Bring a large pot of water to boil and add enough salt to make it salty like the sea.

2. Meanwhile, wash the peas. Pull off the stem ends; remove the peas and place in a small bowl. Reserve the pods.

3. Fill a bowl with cold water; set aside. Add the empty pea pods to the pot of boiling water and cook for 5 minutes. Using a slotted spoon or spider, remove the pods from the boiling water and transfer to the bowl of cold water to cool quickly. Drain the pea pods and add to a Vitamix or high-speed blender. Add ½ cup water. Puree for 2 to 3 minutes.

4. Place a fine strainer over a bowl and add the pea pod puree to the strainer, pressing on the solids to release as much puree as possible into the bowl. Discard the solids in the strainer. Reserve the puree in the bowl; season to taste with salt and pepper.

5. Cook the pasta in the pot of boiling water until al dente, stirring occasionally.

6. Meanwhile, in a large skillet, heat the olive oil over medium heat. Add the onions and garlic and sauté until softened, 3 to 4 minutes. Add the peas and cook 2 minutes. Stir in the reserved pea pod puree and Greek yogurt, if using, and cook just until heated through. (Don't overcook the peas or puree as the sauce will turn brown.)

7. Using tongs or a spider, transfer the pasta to the sauce in the skillet. Toss until combined. Season to taste with salt and pepper. Transfer the pasta to a serving bowl. Add the basil and mint. Serve with Espelette pepper and grated Parmigiano Reggiano cheese, if using.

MUSHROOM "MLT"

PREP: **10 minutes**   COOK: **8 minutes**   MAKES: **1 serving**   SERVING SIZE: **1 sandwich**

Calories: **276 kcal** Total fiber: **12.6 g** Soluble fiber: **0.1 g** Protein: **7.2 g** Total fat: **14 g** Saturated fat: **1.8 g** Healthy fats: **10.1 g**
Carbohydrates: **37.6 g** Sugars: **5.4 g** Added sugars: **0 g** Sodium: **453 mg** Potassium: **302 mg** Magnesium: **115 mg** Calcium: **228.01 mg**

In 2015, the World Health Organization categorized bacon and processed meats as category 1 carcinogens, along with asbestos, tobacco smoke, and alcohol. We know everyone needs a good bacon fix, which is why we've come up with a way to satisfy those cravings without the dangers associated with the real stuff. This can't-believe-it's-not-bacon mushroom "bacon" is When Way healthy *and* makes your RealAge—your biological age instead of your calendar age—younger. Use shiitakes, which are loaded with umami flavors that release when cooked and caramelized to mimic bacon's savory notes. Combined with tomato and the delicious bitterness of arugula, you'll never think about that old-school BLT again.

2 teaspoons extra-virgin olive oil

4 fresh shiitake mushrooms, stems removed, caps sliced

⅛ teaspoon kosher salt

⅛ teaspoon freshly ground black pepper

2 slices 100% whole grain bread

4 teaspoons Cashew-naise (page 63)

2 large tomato slices

½ cup arugula

1. In a large nonstick skillet, heat the olive oil over medium heat. Add the shiitake mushrooms; season with the salt and pepper, and sauté until caramelized on both sides, about 5 minutes. Transfer the mushrooms to a plate and set aside.

2. Add the bread slices to the skillet and lightly toast on both sides, 2 to 3 minutes.

3. Assemble the sandwich by spreading 2 teaspoons Cashew-naise on both slices of the bread, top with mushroom slices, tomato slices, and arugula, then serve.

—What to *Eat* When—

Arugula is the reigning champion of dark leafy greens because it contains the highest level of nitrates. Nitric oxide dilates arteries in the body and helps reverse high blood pressure and chronic diseases.

MAC 'N' CHEESE-LESS

PREP: 40–45 minutes, starting a day before   **COOK:** 40 minutes   **MAKES:** 6 servings
SERVING SIZE: 1¼ cups

Calories: 491 kcal Total fiber: 10.8 g Soluble fiber: 0.4 g Protein: 14 g Total fat: 14.4 g Saturated fat: 2.2 g Healthy fats: 8.1 g
Carbohydrates: 79 g Sugars: 11.8 g Added sugars: 0 g Sodium: 441 mg Potassium: 1,108 mg Magnesium: 106 mg Calcium: 214 mg

Making comfort foods like mac 'n' cheese healthy can be challenging. Just remember our favorite trick: "Think about all the things you *could* have and not what you *shouldn't* have." This recipe exemplifies this perfectly. The "cheese" sauce alone has so many possibilities: Add jalapeño and you have a spicy nacho sauce, or pour it over potatoes for an au gratin. Mix in fresh diced tomatoes and mushroom "bacon" (see page 105) for a loaded version. Let your imagination run wild.

4 cups water

1 cup (5 ounces) raw cashews

12 ounces 100% whole wheat
    short elbow pasta

6 cups (about 28 ounces) sweet potato,
    peeled, cut into ½- to ¾-inch cubes

4 cups (or more) unflavored,
    unsweetened almond milk

2 teaspoons (or more) mild hot sauce
    (such as Cholula)

1 teaspoon Dijon mustard

¾ teaspoon kosher salt

¼ teaspoon freshly ground black
    pepper

¼ teaspoon ground nutmeg

1 pinch cayenne pepper

1. Combine the water and cashews in a medium bowl. Cover and refrigerate overnight. Drain the nuts and set aside.

2. Preheat the oven to 350°F. Cook the pasta in a large pot of boiling water until just tender, but still firm to the bite (al dente). Drain the pasta; rinse and drain again. Set aside in a large mixing bowl and cover.

3. In a large saucepan, bring the sweet potatoes and almond milk to a boil over medium-high heat. Reduce to medium-low heat and simmer uncovered until the potatoes are tender, about 20 minutes. Strain the sweet potatoes in a bowl, reserving the almond milk. Measure reserved almond milk and add more almond milk, if needed, to equal 3 cups.

4. Cool the 3 cups almond milk to lukewarm and place in a heavy-duty blender. Add the cashews. Blend until the sauce is smooth. Add the sweet potatoes, hot sauce, mustard, salt, pepper, and nutmeg. Process until the sauce is smooth, scraping down the container as needed.

5. Pour the sauce over the pasta and mix well. Place in a 10-by-12-inch casserole or baking pan. Bake for 40 minutes or until hot and bubbly.

What to *Know* When

To make the sauce less sweet, replace half the almond milk with unsweetened hemp or soy milk. For a crunchy topping, sprinkle with whole grain breadcrumbs.

FARRO-STUFFED PORTOBELLO MUSHROOMS

PREP: 1 hour   **COOK:** 50 minutes   **MAKES:** 4 servings   **SERVING SIZE:** 3 mushrooms

Calories: 230 kcal Total fiber: 6.8 g Soluble fiber: 0 g Protein: 7.5 g Total fat: 8.1 g Saturated fat: 1.2 g Healthy fats: 6.3 g
Carbohydrates: 31.9 g Sugars: 9.3 g Added sugars: 0 g Sodium: 459 mg Potassium: 677 mg Magnesium: 29 mg Calcium: 66 mg

We love to make this main dish at night to eat the next morning. The farro and dried tomatoes provide chewiness, while reducing the leftover juices after baking creates an intensely flavorful broth. Watercress is part of the cruciferous vegetable family, which means it's loaded with great benefits, including calcium for bone health.

1½ cups water

⅓ cup (2 ounces) farro

6 portobello mushrooms (3½- to 4-inch stuffer caps)

6 teaspoons extra-virgin olive oil, divided

2 cups onions, cut into small dice

1 cup red bell pepper, cut into small dice

½ teaspoon kosher salt

3 garlic cloves, finely chopped

¼ cup sun-dried tomatoes, diced

¼ cup Riesling wine

2 teaspoons sambal oelek chili paste

2 cups (firmly packed) spinach leaves, stemmed

1 cup low-sodium vegetable broth

½ cup watercress

1. Combine the water and farro in a large, heavy saucepan. Bring to a simmer over medium heat. Reduce to medium-low heat and cook gently until the farro is tender but still a bit chewy, 23 to 25 minutes. Drain, rinse, and drain again. Cover and set farro aside.

2. While the farro is cooking, preheat the oven to 350°F and prepare the mushrooms. Remove the stems and, using a small spoon, scrape out the gills on the underside (all of the dark portion will not come out). Grasp the white flap of skin at the top inner edge and gently pull back, peeling off some of the skin. Repeat peeling around the top. Check the underside and cut off any remaining skin. Set aside.

3. Heat 5 teaspoons oil in a large skillet over medium-high heat. Add onions, red bell peppers, and salt. Sauté until the onions begin to caramelize and turn golden, stirring often, about 15 minutes. Push vegetables to one side. Add the garlic and remaining oil to empty side. Stir until the garlic becomes aromatic, 30 to 60 seconds. Add the sun-dried tomatoes and reserved farro; stir to blend well.

4. In a small bowl, combine chili paste with Riesling wine, mix well, then pour over top of the farro and toss until well combined. Add spinach and cook, tossing with a heatproof spatula, until the spinach is just wilted, about 1 minute. Set the stuffing and skillet aside.

5. Place 1 mushroom cap, rounded side down on a clean surface. Carefully pour ½ cup stuffing into the mushroom cap, then lift the cap and press stuffing firmly into the cavity Repeat to fill all caps.

6. Arrange mushrooms, rounded side down, in a 13-by-9-by-2-inch baking dish. Pour broth around mushrooms. Cover the dish with foil; poke a hole at each end to vent steam. Bake the mushrooms until heated through and tender when pierced, about 30 minutes.

7. Divide the mushrooms among 2 wide soup or pasta dishes. Pour any juices from the baking dish into the reserved skillet. Boil over medium-high heat until the juices thicken slightly and are reduced to a light syrup (⅔ to ¾ cup), about 15 minutes. Spoon juices around mushrooms in a serving dish. Garnish with watercress.

FETTUCCINE WITH PEPPERS

PREP: **25 minutes**   COOK: **25 minutes**   MAKES: **2 servings**   SERVING SIZE: **1 cup**

Calories: 625 kcal Total fiber: 13.6 g Soluble fiber: 0.3 g Protein: 10.5 g Total fat: 40.8 g Saturated fat: 4 g Healthy fats: 25.7 g
Carbohydrates: 54.6 g Sugars: 13.1 g Added sugars: 0 g Sodium: 450 mg Potassium: 660 mg Magnesium: 37 mg Calcium: 62 mg

This is a simple pasta dish to enjoy when peppers are in season. We like to make ours with poblanos for a blend of hot and mild, but you can also use long hot Italian peppers, bell peppers, or whatever pepper you like best. By cooking the peppers in the pan undisturbed, you are essentially roasting them, adding a great depth of flavor to the pasta dish. The tomato in the sauce is minimal—you don't want it to be soupy, but the tomatoes should still stand out—and remind you that they are great for your heart and blood vessels.

1 pound (about 4 large) poblano chili peppers or other mildly spicy peppers

¼ cup extra-virgin olive oil

3 garlic cloves, crushed

½ cup canned crushed tomatoes

Kosher salt

Freshly ground black pepper

8 ounces whole grain fettuccine

¼ cup fresh basil leaves, torn

1. Cut off and discard the stem ends of the peppers. Cut the peppers lengthwise in half. Remove the seeds and scrape away the veins. Cut lengthwise into ½-inch-wide strips.

2. Heat a large skillet (with a lid) over medium heat, and add the oil when the skillet is hot. Add the peppers and cover. Cook 10 minutes without stirring.

3. Stir the peppers, then cover and cook 10 minutes more, stirring halfway through. Add the garlic, then the crushed tomatoes to the skillet. Cover and cook 5 minutes more. Season to taste with salt and pepper.

4. Meanwhile, bring a large pot of water to boil, then add salt. Add the pasta and cook until al dente according to the package directions.

5. Remove the cover from the pepper sauce and continue cooking to allow excess liquid to evaporate.

6. Using a spider, transfer the cooked pasta to the pan with the pepper sauce and stir to combine for 1 minute. Add fresh basil leaf and serve.

PASTA WITH HARISSA-ROASTED CHERRY TOMATOES & SPINACH

PREP: 50–60 minutes   **COOK:** 1 hour, 15 minutes   **MAKES:** 4 servings   **SERVING SIZE:** 1½ cups

Calories: 310 kcal Total fiber: 7.4 g Soluble fiber: 0.2 g Protein: 8.3 g Total fat: 16 g Saturated fat: 2.1 g Healthy fats: 13.3 g
Carbohydrates: 37 g Sugars: 12.8 g Added sugars: 0 g Sodium: 853 mg Potassium: 890 mg Magnesium: 42 mg Calcium: 65 mg

This recipe is ideal for practicing our favorite When Way tip: Don't stereotype food. Cook this pasta at night and then enjoy it for breakfast the next day. It's a great day-starter because it is packed with fiber, protein, and healthy fat to keep you full and energized throughout the day.

4 tablespoons extra-virgin olive oil, divided

2 teaspoons Harissa Spice Blend (page 71)

½ teaspoon kosher salt, divided

¼ teaspoon freshly ground black pepper, divided

7 cups (35 ounces; 3½ pints) red and orange cherry (or grape) tomatoes

2 cups sweet onion, cut into ⅓-inch dice

2 teaspoons garlic, finely chopped

4 cups (firmly packed; 5½ to 6 ounces) spinach leaves, stemmed

2½ canned anchovies, mashed to a paste (about 1 teaspoon)

1 teaspoon drained capers, finely chopped

1 tablespoon Raisin Reduction (page 69)

¼ teaspoon red chili flakes, finely chopped

¼ cup fresh basil, cut into thin strips, then small dice, plus sprigs for garnish

2 tablespoons fresh Italian parsley, chopped

1 teaspoon dried oregano

1 tablespoon mild hot sauce (such as Cholula; optional)

8 ounces (2⅓ cups) whole grain short pasta (such as penne or rotini), cooked and drained

1. Preheat the oven to 350°F. Coat a large rimmed baking sheet with nonstick spray.

2. In a medium bowl, combine 2 tablespoons oil, Harissa Spice Blend, and half the salt and pepper. Add the tomatoes and toss to coat. Scrape tomatoes with the oil mixture onto the prepared sheet; spread out evenly. Roast until the tomatoes are soft, wrinkled, splitting open, and the juices are browning, 55 to 60 minutes. Set aside until lukewarm, about 15 minutes.

3. Meanwhile, heat 1 tablespoon oil in a large skillet, over medium-low heat. Add the onions and sauté until golden and lightly caramelized, 25 to 30 minutes. Push onions to one side. Add the remaining 1 tablespoon oil and the garlic to the bare side of the skillet. Stir until the garlic is fragrant, 30 to 60 seconds; mix with the onions. Add the spinach. Toss until the spinach just wilts, about 1 minute. Set the skillet aside.

4. Scrape the roasted tomatoes and any juices into a food processor. Add the anchovies, capers, Raisin Reduction, and chili flakes. Using 5 on/off turns, blend to a chunky sauce consistency.

5. Set the skillet with the onion mixture over medium heat. Add the tomato sauce, basil, parsley, and oregano. Stir until the sauce is heated. Add hot sauce, if using. Add pasta to the sauce, tossing until the pasta is heated through.

6. Divide pasta among bowls. Garnish with basil sprigs.

What to *Know* When

To freeze this sauce, skip adding the spinach, and store for up to three months—add spinach when reheating. For pasta, we recommend short shapes that capture and hold the sauce's ingredients.

Orecchiette
(page 98)

ORECCHIETTE

PREP: 40 minutes   **COOK:** 13-15 minutes   **MAKES:** 4 servings   **SERVING SIZE:** 19 orecchiette

Calories: 160 kcal **Total fiber:** 4.0 g **Soluble fiber:** 0.7 g **Protein:** 5.0 g **Total fat:** 4.4 g **Saturated fat:** 0.7 g **Healthy fats:** 3.6 g

Carbohydrates: 27 g **Sugars:** 0.2 g **Added sugars:** 0 g **Sodium:** 2 mg **Potassium:** 136 mg **Magnesium:** 52 mg **Calcium:** 14 mg

Cooking can be a luxurious way to celebrate. For Dr. C, nothing says celebration like making fresh pasta. This orecchiette is a labor of love that you'll only tackle for special occasions (it's a great way to blow away dinner guests). Even better, it's fun to make together with your friends and family like Dr. C does every year.

Orecchiette is a very special pasta that originates from Puglia, the heel of the boot of Italy. Dr. C learned to make it at The Awaiting Table Cookery School. Orecchiette means "little ears" for its shape. This recipe uses whole wheat durum flour, which is high in resistant starch. You can order freshly milled whole wheat durum flour from *breadtopia.com*.

1¼ cups (about 7 ounces) whole wheat durum flour, plus more as needed

½ cup water

1 tablespoon extra-virgin olive oil

1. On a large wooden board or other work surface, make a mound of the flour, then gently spread it out, making a large well in the center and forming a wall of flour around the outside.

2. Gradually pour the water into the well, a few tablespoons at a time, and add the olive oil. Using a fork, slowly mix the flour from the inside of the well into the water. Be careful not to break the walls or the water will spill out. Continue incorporating the flour into the water from the inside of the well until most of the flour is mixed in (all the flour will not yet be mixed—that will happen as you knead it).

3. After forming the dough into a ball, knead it on the wooden board or work surface, incorporating all the remaining flour until the dough is elastic but not at all sticky, about 10 minutes; add more flour if dough is too sticky and is sticking to the table. Wrap the dough in plastic, and let rest for 30 minutes.

4. To make the orecchiette, lightly flour the work surface and roll out a strip of the dough into a rope about ½ inch thick. Keep the rest of the dough covered with plastic to prevent it from drying out. Using a non-serrated table knife, cut a ½-inch-long piece of dough from the rope and roll it into a ball. Place the table knife on the dough ball with the flat side down at about 45 degrees to the table. Push down into the ball of dough and drag the knife along the work surface until you've pulled it through the dough ball. Gently remove the pasta from the knife and flip it inside out, so it looks like a little ear—or orecchiette. Place on a wire rack to dry completely overnight. Repeat until all the dough is used up.

ORECCHIETTE WITH CABBAGE

PREP: 15 minutes   **COOK: 13 minutes cabbage; 12 minutes pasta**   **MAKES: 6 servings**

SERVING SIZE: 1 generous cup

Calories: 346 kcal Total fiber: 6.8 g Soluble fiber: 0.3 g Protein: 9.5 g Total fat: 11.3 g Saturated fat: 1.3 g Healthy fats: 8.1 g

Carbohydrates: 52 g Sugars: 3.3 g Added sugars: 0 g Sodium: 138 mg Potassium: 449 mg Magnesium: 14 mg Calcium: 100 mg

Your homemade orecchiette is really the star of this simple dish of pasta and cabbage. In Puglia, they might make this with some cured pork belly, but with our veggie-forward approach we promise you won't miss the meat! The trick is to get a little color on the cabbage to help bring out some umami flavor.

½ small head green cabbage, or cabbage of your choice (about 16 ounces)

¼ cup extra-virgin olive oil

¾ teaspoon kosher salt

¾ teaspoon dried crushed red pepper flakes (or more to taste)

14 ounces orecchiette

Fresh Italian parsley, chopped (optional garnish)

1. Bring a large pot of water to a boil.

2. Cut the cabbage lengthwise into wedges about 1½ inches wide. Then cut the wedges crosswise into 1½-inch pieces. Separate all the layers into individual pieces to ensure the cabbage pieces cook evenly.

3. Heat a 12-inch skillet over medium heat. Add the olive oil and, when hot, add the cabbage. Cook until the cabbage starts to brown, stirring frequently, 6 to 7 minutes. Add the salt and red pepper flakes. Continue to sauté until the cabbage is slightly softened, but still has some texture, about 6 minutes more.

4. Meanwhile, generously salt the boiling water. Add the pasta and cook until al dente. Using a spider or large slotted spoon, transfer the pasta to the skillet with the cabbage; stir to mix thoroughly. Increase to medium-high heat and stir until heated through, about 2 minutes. Season with more salt and crushed red pepper, if desired, and serve garnished with parsley.

— **What to *Eat* When** —

Cabbage is a great choice when you need a testosterone boost (it helps lower estrogen levels, thereby raising testosterone, in turn).

CAULIFLOWER MASALA WITH LEMON-SCENTED MILLET

PREP: 40 minutes   **COOK:** 40–45 minutes   **MAKES:** 8 servings
SERVING SIZE: 1½ cups cauliflower; ⅔ cup millet

Calories: 190 kcal Total fiber: 5.3 g Soluble fiber: 0.9 g Protein: 4.8 g Total fat: 9.5 g Saturated fat: 1.3 g Healthy fats: 7.5 g
Carbohydrates: 22.5 g Sugars: 8.4 g Added sugars: 0 g Sodium: 364 mg Potassium: 458 mg Magnesium: 33 mg Calcium: 66 mg

Some meals are genuinely worth the effort. This Cauliflower Masala is one of them. The lemon-scented millet pairs perfectly with gently spiced cauliflower. Millet is a wonderful grain to choose before you have a test or big day to face. This whole grain gives you a steady drip of energy to help you function at your top level.

2 cups low-sodium vegetable broth

1 cup (6½ ounces) millet, rinsed well and drained

4 tablespoons Italian parsley, chopped, divided

2 teaspoons (packed) lemon peel, finely grated

3 tablespoons extra-virgin olive oil, plus 1 teaspoon, divided

8 cups (22 ounces) cauliflower florets, cut into 1-inch pieces with some stem attached

¾ teaspoon kosher salt, divided

1 cup sweet onion, cut into small dice

2 teaspoons garlic, finely chopped

1 teaspoon fresh ginger, peeled, finely chopped

1 tablespoon ground cumin

1 teaspoon paprika

½ teaspoon smoked paprika

½ teaspoon ground turmeric

⅛ teaspoon red chili flakes, finely chopped

⅛ teaspoon freshly ground black pepper

1¾ cups canned crushed tomatoes

⅔ cup (5.5 ounces) tomato juice

1 tablespoon Raisin Reduction (page 69)

1½ cups Cauliflower Cream (page 46)

1. Bring broth to a boil in a medium saucepan; stir in millet. Cover, adjust heat to low, and simmer until all the broth is absorbed and the millet is tender, 23 to 25 minutes. Mix in 2 tablespoons parsley and the lemon peel. Fluff with a fork and set aside.

2. Meanwhile, heat 2 tablespoons oil in a large skillet over medium heat; swirl to cover the bottom. Add cauliflower, season with ¼ teaspoon salt, and toss to coat. Continue to toss and stir until the florets are brown in spots and just tender, 18 to 20 minutes. Remove to a bowl and set aside. (Note: If the florets are tinged with brown spots but still not tender, stop cooking and set aside as directed so they do not burn. They can be simmered until tender when added to the sauce.)

3. Wipe skillet clean, if necessary. To the same skillet, add 1 tablespoon oil and the onions. Sauté over medium heat until the onions are lightly caramelized, about 10 minutes. Push onions to one side. Add garlic, ginger, and remaining 1 teaspoon oil to the bare side of the skillet. Stir until the garlic is fragrant, 30 to 60 seconds; mix with the onions. Stir in cumin, paprika, smoked paprika, turmeric, red chili, black pepper, and remaining ½ teaspoon salt. Stir 30 seconds. Mix in the crushed tomatoes, tomato juice, and the Raisin Reduction; simmer 3 minutes to blend flavors. Add the Cauliflower Cream and simmer until heated through, stirring occasionally, about 3 minutes. Add the cauliflower florets to the sauce. Reduce to low heat. Simmer until the sauce reduces to the desired consistency and the masala is heated, stirring occasionally.

4. While the cauliflower is simmering, cover the millet and rewarm in a microwave or in a double boiler.

5. Spoon the cauliflower on top of the millet. Sprinkle with the remaining 2 tablespoons of parsley.

PUMPKIN RYE BREAD

PREP: 30–40 minutes, plus 2 hours rising time   **BAKE:** 35 minutes
MAKES: 2 loaves, 28 servings   **SERVING SIZE:** 1 slice

Calories: 106 kcal Total fiber: 4 g Soluble fiber: 0.3 g Protein: 4.4 g Total fat: 1 g Saturated fat: 0.1 g Healthy fats: 0.5 g
Carbohydrates: 22 g Sugars: 2.8 g Added sugars: 2.6 g Sodium: 107 mg Potassium: 157 mg Magnesium: 26 mg Calcium: 17 mg

We love the flavor, density, and texture of this bread. It's great with almond or peanut butter spread on top, but you can also eat it plain with your morning coffee. It freezes well for up to four months.

2½ cups warm water (105–115°F), divided

3 packages (7 grams or ¼ ounce each) active dry yeast

1 teaspoon sugar

4 cups whole wheat flour, divided

1½ cups whole grain rye flour

1 cup unsweetened canned pumpkin

⅓ cup Raisin Reduction (page 69)

1½ teaspoons kosher salt

Olive oil to grease bowl and bread pans

1. In a small bowl, combine 1 cup warm water, yeast, and sugar; stir to blend. Let stand until the yeast dissolves and mixture is bubbly and doubled in size, about 10 minutes.

2. Meanwhile, in a large bowl of an electric mixer fitted with a dough hook, combine 2 cups whole wheat flour and rye flour.

3. In a medium bowl, combine 1½ cups warm water, pumpkin, maple syrup, and salt; whisk until well blended.

4. Add the yeast mixture to the flour mixture, then add the pumpkin mixture. Mix on low speed until the flour is incorporated, occasionally scraping down the sides and bottom of the bowl with a rubber spatula, then beat on medium speed until well blended. Add the remaining whole wheat flour, mixing well on medium speed, again occasionally scraping the bowl sides and bottom, until a very moist dough forms.

5. Turn the dough out onto a floured work surface and knead briefly just until the dough is smooth (dough will be very sticky). Grease a large bowl with olive oil. Place the dough in the bowl and spray the top of the dough with olive oil. Cover the bowl with plastic wrap, then a clean kitchen towel. Place on top of the stove and let rise in a warm draft-free area until doubled in volume, about 2 hours.

6. Position the oven rack in the center of the oven and preheat to 350°F. Grease a couple 9-by-5-inch glass loaf pans with olive oil. Turn the dough out onto a lightly floured work surface and divide into 2 equal pieces. Form each piece into a loaf shape and transfer to a prepared loaf pan. Place the pans on top of the stove and cover with a kitchen towel. Let the dough rise in a warm draft-free area for 30 minutes.

7. Bake the breads until lightly brown on top and firm to the touch (when tapped, they will sound hollow), 35 to 40 minutes. Transfer to a cooling rack and let cool in pans for 15 minutes. Turn breads out onto a rack and cool completely.

LINGUINE WITH MUSHROOM "BACON," ONION & TOMATO (WHEN WAY AMATRICIANA)

PREP: 25 minutes   **COOK:** 22–24 minutes   **MAKES:** 2 servings   **SERVING SIZE:** 1 cup

Calories: 361 kcal Total fiber: 7.8 g Soluble fiber: 0 g Protein: 7.2 g Total fat: 28.8 g Saturated fat: 4 g Healthy fats: 24.4 g
Carbohydrates: 22.8 g Sugars: 4.1 g Added sugars: 0 g Sodium: 253 mg Potassium: 701 mg Magnesium: 42 mg Calcium: 33 mg

Amatrice is a small town in Italy not too far from Rome. It is famous for its eponymous bucatini pasta made with guanciale (cured pork jowl), onion, and tomato. The When Way version of Amatriciana swaps the bacon for shiitake mushrooms. Trust us: You won't miss the bacon at all! The umami created by sautéing the mushrooms is equally delicious in flavor, but without the saturated fat.

12 ounces fresh plump shiitake mushrooms

¼ cup extra-virgin olive oil

¾ teaspoon kosher salt

½ teaspoon freshly ground black pepper

1 small red or yellow onion (6 to 7 ounces), halved lengthwise, thinly sliced crosswise

3 large garlic cloves, minced

½ cup crushed tomatoes

¼ to ½ teaspoon crushed red pepper flakes, to taste

8 ounces whole grain linguine

Grated pecorino or Parmigiano Reggiano cheese (optional)

1. Wipe the shiitake mushrooms clean with a damp paper towel. Cut off the stems and discard. Cut the caps into ⅛-inch-thick slices.

2. Heat a large skillet over medium-high heat. Add the olive oil, then the mushroom slices. Season with salt and pepper. Sauté until the mushrooms are brown and begin to crisp, stirring frequently, 10 to 12 minutes.

3. Add the onions to the skillet and sauté over medium heat until very tender, 10 to 12 minutes. Add the garlic and stir 2 to 3 minutes. Add the crushed tomatoes and red pepper flakes and cook for 1 minute longer. Remove from the heat; cover to keep warm.

4. Meanwhile, bring a large pot of water to boil (large enough to hold the linguine without breaking). Add salt to the boiling water, then add the linguine and cook until al dente according to the package directions.

5. Using tongs, transfer the pasta from the cooking water to the skillet with the mushroom mixture. (You want to bring some of the pasta cooking water with you, so don't drain it in a colander.) If more moisture is desired, add more of the pasta cooking water by table-spoonfuls until the sauce is the desired consistency.

6. Toss the pasta in the sauce and cook for 1 minute more. Transfer the pasta to a large serving bowl. Add a dusting of grated pecorino or Parmigiano Reggiano cheese, if using, and stir to combine and serve.

What to Swap When

The sauce in this recipe is traditionally served with bucatini, a spaghetti-like noodle with a hole down the center, but it's often hard to find whole grain versions. Linguine, fettuccine, or another long noodle are good substitutes.

FARRO WITH LEFTOVER PESTO

PREP: 10 minutes   **COOK: 26–32 minutes**   **MAKES: 4 servings**   **SERVING SIZE: 1 cup**

Calories: 429 kcal Total fiber: 7 g Soluble fiber: 0 g Protein: 13.2 g Total fat: 22.2 g Saturated fat: 4.8 g Healthy fats: 15.7 g
Carbohydrates: 41.5 g Sugars: 1.9 g Added sugars: 0 g Sodium: 248 mg Potassium: 185 mg Magnesium: 25 mg Calcium: 258 mg

You will find a lot of different styles of pesto beyond the traditional basil version in this book. One is our Root-to-Stem Kohlrabi Salad (page 205), which also makes for a great side dish to this recipe. Use the leftover pesto from the salad to toss with farro. If you make another pesto, freeze any extra for when you need a breakfast or lunch in a hurry. Farro is a wonderfully fiber-rich grain that will fill you up easily and is rich in nutrients like magnesium and zinc.

2 tablespoons extra-virgin olive oil

1 medium shallot (about ⅓ cup), finely chopped

2 large garlic cloves, minced

1 cup (about 6 ounces) pearled farro

½ cup dry white wine

2½ cups water

½ cup leftover pesto, thawed if frozen

Kosher salt, to taste

Freshly ground black pepper, to taste

1. Heat the olive oil in a heavy large saucepan over medium-high. Add the shallot and garlic, and sauté until softened, 3 to 5 minutes. Add the farro and sauté until lightly browned, 3 to 4 minutes. Add the wine and cook until evaporated, 2 to 3 minutes. Add the water and bring to a boil. Reduce to medium heat and simmer until the farro is tender and the water is absorbed, 18 to 25 minutes. (If the water is absorbed/evaporated before the farro is tender, add more water, ¼ to ½ cup at a time, depending on how well cooked the farro is.)

2. Add the pesto to the farro and stir to coat. Season to taste with salt and pepper, then serve.

VEGETABLE FARRO

PREP: 50-60 minutes   **COOK:** 30 minutes   **MAKES:** 4 servings   **SERVING SIZE:** 1½–2 cups

Calories: 329 kcal Total fiber: 12.4 g Soluble fiber: 0.1 g Protein: 13.2 g Total fat: 3.4 g Saturated fat: 0.1 g Healthy fats: 0.2 g
Carbohydrates: 61.8 g Sugars: 9.3 g Added sugars: 0 g Sodium: 683 mg Potassium: 726 mg Magnesium: 36 mg Calcium: 101 mg

The best—and healthiest—way to moisten whole grains is with a lot of vegetables. This farro is a great way to learn how to do just that, with loads of flavor to boot. Learn the basics of this recipe and you can come up with variations of your own to make this a favorite go-to meal, swapping in your favorite veggies or changing farro out for millet, sorghum, or quinoa. This is also a great potluck dish—it can be made ahead and serves a ton of people as a vegetable side or salad.

1 cup (6 ounces) farro

4 cups water

4 tablespoons extra-virgin olive oil, divided

3 cups (15 ounces) red and orange cherry or grape tomatoes, halved

¾ teaspoon kosher salt, divided

½ teaspoon freshly ground black pepper, divided

12 garlic cloves, finely chopped, divided

4 cups (firmly packed; 5½ to 6 ounces) spinach leaves, stems removed

1½ cups onion, cut into ⅓-inch dice

1½ cups red bell pepper

2½ cups (about 7 ounces) crimini (baby bella) mushrooms, sliced

1½ cups (about 6 ounces) zucchini, cut into ⅓-inch dice

1 cup (5 to 6 ounces) frozen green peas, blanched in boiling water 30 seconds

1 cup green beans, cut into ⅓-inch dice, blanched in boiling water 2 to 3 minutes

2½ tablespoons fresh lemon juice

1½ teaspoons (packed) lemon peel, finely grated

¼ teaspoon smoked paprika

1. In a heavy medium saucepan, combine farro and water. Bring to simmer over high heat. Reduce to medium-low heat and cook gently until the farro is tender but still a bit chewy, 23 to 25 minutes. Drain, rinse, and drain again. Set aside in the saucepan.

2. Meanwhile, in a large skillet, heat 1 tablespoon oil until it shimmers. Add the tomatoes; season with ⅛ teaspoon salt and ⅛ teaspoon pepper. Sauté until the tomatoes soften, 3 to 4 minutes. Transfer to a bowl and set aside.

3. In the same skillet, heat 1 tablespoon oil over high heat. Add 1 tablespoon garlic and stir until the garlic is fragrant, 30 to 60 seconds. Add the spinach. Season with ⅛ teaspoon salt and ⅛ teaspoon pepper. Toss until the spinach is just wilted, about 1 minute. Scrape spinach into a bowl and set aside.

4. In the same skillet, heat 1 tablespoon oil over high heat. Add onion and bell pepper. Sauté until the onion is translucent, about 3 minutes. Push vegetable mixture to one side. Add remaining 1 tablespoon oil and all remaining garlic to the bare side of the skillet. Sauté until the garlic is fragrant, 30 to 60 seconds; mix into the vegetables. Add the mushrooms and zucchini. Sauté until the onions begin to caramelize and mushrooms begin to brown, 3 to 4 minutes. Add peas, green beans, lemon juice, lemon peel, smoked paprika, and remaining salt and pepper; toss to blend. Mix in farro and tomatoes. Add spinach; toss gently until heated through, about 1 minute longer.

What to *Eat* When

Mushrooms, a key ingredient in this dish, may help fight infections by supporting your immune cells. They also are good sources of selenium, which is linked to lower rates of cancer in some studies.

PASTA WITH RAMPS & BEANS

PREP: 20 minutes　　**COOK: 15–18 minutes**　　**MAKES: 2 servings**　　**SERVING SIZE: 1½ cups**

Calories: 595 kcal　Total fiber: 13.6 g　Soluble fiber: 0 g　Protein: 12.5 g　Total fat: 30 g　Saturated fat: 4 g　Healthy fats: 24 g
Carbohydrates: 70.2 g　Sugars: 5.5 g　Added sugars: 0 g　Sodium: 443 mg　Potassium: 100 mg　Magnesium: 0 mg　Calcium: 121 mg

This dish is only possible in the spring when ramps—a wild spring leek with a pungent aroma and flavor that's a cross between garlic and onions—are in season. When we see ramps in the month or two they are available, we have to have them. And so should you. Here's a great way to use them in pasta for a dish that loves you back. When ramps aren't in season, you can make this pasta with young garlic and other spring favorites like asparagus or fiddlehead ferns.

2 cups of short whole grain pasta (6½ to 8 ounces), such as penne, rigatoni, or orecchiette*

Kosher salt

12 fresh ramps

¼ cup extra-virgin olive oil

¼ to ½ teaspoon dried crushed red pepper flakes

1 cup cooked small white beans (like Alubia Blanca from Rancho Gordo or cannellini beans)

Freshly ground black pepper

Toasted fresh breadcrumbs

1. Bring a large pot of water to boil. Add a generous amount of salt, then the pasta, and cook until al dente according to the package directions.

2. Meanwhile, clean the ramps well by cutting off the roots and removing any debris. Wash and dry well. Separate the white and green parts of the ramps; cut the white parts into small pieces and the greens into wide strips.

3. In a large skillet over medium-low heat, add the olive oil, then the ramp whites and crushed red pepper flakes. Gently sauté to soften ramp whites slightly, 2 to 3 minutes. Add the beans and cook until heated through, about 2 minutes. Season to taste with salt and pepper.

4. Using a large slotted spoon or a spider, transfer the pasta to the skillet with the ramps and beans. Add the ramp greens and sauté until just wilted. Serve topped with toasted breadcrumbs.

*If you're not using beans in this recipe, opt for a long pasta like linguine.

JAMAICAN JERK JACK

PREP: 20 minutes   COOK: 21–23 minutes   MAKES: 4 servings   SERVING SIZE: ½ cup

Calories: 254 kcal Total fiber: 2.2 g Soluble fiber: 0.2 g Protein: 2 g Total fat: 0.6 g Saturated fat: 0.07 g Healthy fats: 0.14 g
Carbohydrates: 63.3 g Sugars: 20.6 g Added sugars: 0 g Sodium: 436 mg Potassium: 418 mg Magnesium: 40 mg Calcium: 106 mg

This is a great swap for a pork BBQ sandwich when those cravings hit, without the added sugars or unhealthy meat. Swapping in the Raisin Reduction for sugar in the barbecue sauce extends your energy levels because the natural sugars paired with fiber are more slowly absorbed in the body.

3 cups (24 ounces) unsweetened pineapple juice

3 tablespoons Raisin Reduction (page 69)

2 large garlic cloves, minced

1 tablespoon low-sodium gluten-free tamari sauce

2 teaspoons apple cider vinegar

1 teaspoon dried thyme leaves

½ teaspoon fresh ginger, peeled, finely chopped

½ teaspoon smoked paprika

½ teaspoon kosher salt

½ teaspoon jalapeño chili pepper, minced, seeded

¼ teaspoon ground allspice

¼ teaspoon ground cloves

¼ teaspoon ground cinnamon

¼ teaspoon ground cumin

¼ teaspoon ground nutmeg

¼ teaspoon crushed red pepper flakes

2 teaspoons water

2 teaspoons cornstarch

1 can (20-ounce; about 2 cups) jackfruit pieces in water, well drained, then shredded

1. Combine all ingredients except the 2 teaspoons water, cornstarch, and jackfruit in a medium saucepan. Bring to a boil over medium-high heat. Reduce to medium heat and simmer until the liquid is reduced to 2 cups, 15 to 17 minutes.

2. Meanwhile, in a small bowl whisk water and cornstarch until the cornstarch is dissolved. Add the cornstarch mixture to the liquid in the saucepan and cook 1 minute, whisking vigorously until the mixture thickens slightly. Add the shredded jackfruit and simmer for 5 minutes to blend flavors.

3. Serve on 100% whole grain bread as a sandwich or over your choice of cooked whole grains.

What to *Swap* When

This sauce also complements tofu, tempeh, grains, and vegetables. Make a large batch and freeze it for up to three months.

CORN MUFFINS

PREP: 25 minutes   **BAKE:** 19–20 minutes   **MAKES:** 14 muffins   **SERVING SIZE:** 1 muffin

Calories: 73 kcal Total fiber: 2.6 g Soluble fiber: 0.2 g Protein: 2.2 g Total fat: 0.8 g Saturated fat: 0.1 g Healthy fats: 0.2 g
Carbohydrates: 15 g Sugars: 0.2 g Added sugars: 0 g Sodium: 214 mg Potassium: 65 mg Magnesium: 19 mg Calcium: 35 mg

You probably love corn muffins, but not all the fat—loads of butter and sugar—added to them. These 100% whole grain corn muffins have a great When Way substitution to keep the moisture you love, without those ingredients that don't love you back: Swap fresh grated apple or pear. Plus our Raisin Reduction (page 69) replaces sugar for a healthier touch of sweetness. Using this trick and whole grains, you'll have a great burst of flavor in every bite that is nutritious and low in calories.

1¼ cups unsweetened almond milk

½ cup Raisin Reduction (page 69)

2 teaspoons apple cider vinegar

2 teaspoons lemon zest, finely grated

1½ cups whole wheat flour

¾ cup cornmeal

1½ teaspoons baking powder

1½ teaspoons baking soda

1 teaspoon kosher salt

1 cup apple (1 to 1½ apples depending on size), unpeeled, freshly grated on the large holes of a box grater

1. Preheat the oven to 350°F. Have ready 14 silicone muffin cups, or line a muffin pan with paper liners.

2. In a large mixing bowl whisk almond milk, Raisin Reduction, vinegar, and lemon zest to blend; set aside. In a medium bowl, mix flour, cornmeal, baking powder, baking soda, and salt, and set aside.

3. Add the grated apple to the almond milk mixture, then add the flour mixture, mixing by hand until a batter forms and the ingredients are well mixed.

4. Spoon the batter into the prepared muffin cups, dividing equally and filling them about three-quarters full.

5. Bake until a tester inserted into the muffins comes out clean, 19 to 20 minutes. Before removing muffins from the pan, let cool, 5 minutes or when cool enough to touch. You can freeze these muffins for up to 2 months.

What to *Swap* When

If you have pears on hand, you can swap them in place of apples.

PENNE WITH CHERRY TOMATOES & BASIL

PREP: 20 minutes   **COOK:** 8–10 minutes   **MAKES:** 2 Servings   **SERVING SIZE:** 1½ cups

Calories: 601 kcal Total fiber: 10 g Soluble fiber: 0 g Protein: 12.3 g Total fat: 30.7 g Saturated fat: 4 g Healthy fats: 24.3 g
Carbohydrates: 70 g Sugars: 7 g Added sugars: 0 g Sodium: 263 mg Potassium: 719 mg Magnesium: 23 mg Calcium: 66 mg

We are sure you've seen lots of recipes for pasta with tomato and basil, but this is not your typical version. This sauce has only four ingredients—and it's not cooked. It's great either hot or cold and is the perfect summertime lunch or simple breakfast (remember the third When Way commandment: Don't stereotype foods). Get the best cherry tomatoes you can find, like tangy orange Sungolds or mixed heirloom varieties often sold at farmers markets, to add loads of flavor to this dish.

1 pint cherry tomatoes or Sungolds, preferably multicolored, quartered

½ to ¾ teaspoon kosher or fine sea salt

¼ cup extra-virgin olive oil

½ cup (packed) fresh basil, chopped

2 cups (8 ounces) whole grain penne or orecchiette pasta

Freshly ground black pepper (optional)

1. Put the cherry tomatoes in a large bowl and season with salt to taste. Let stand for 10 to 20 minutes.

2. Add the olive oil and the basil to the tomatoes and stir gently to blend.

3. Meanwhile, bring a large pot of water to boil. Add enough salt to make the water salty like the sea. Add the pasta and cook until al dente according to package directions.

4. Drain the pasta and add to the bowl with the tomatoes. Toss gently. If desired, season with freshly ground pepper to taste. Serve immediately or let cool and refrigerate for another time.

What to *Know* When

It's important to have a sharp knife on hand when dealing with tomatoes—a sharp blade means you can cut the tomatoes without crushing them. If you want to up the lycopene you get from the tomatoes, cook this sauce about 1 minute in a pan over medium heat before adding the pasta and then for 30 seconds more.

CARCIOFI E PEPE

PREP: 20 minutes   **COOK: 10 minutes**   **MAKES: 4 servings**   **SERVING SIZE: ½ cup**

Calories: 422 kcal Total fiber: 10 g Protein: 9.6 g Total fat: 22 g Saturated fat: 3.2 g Healthy fats: 18.2 g
Carbohydrates: 48.7 g Sugars: 3 g Added sugars: 0 g Sodium: 61 mg Potassium: 350 mg Magnesium: 68 mg Calcium: 30 mg

Roman *cacio e pepe* is a simple yet delicious dish of just-cooked pasta served with freshly grated pecorino cheese and a healthy dose of freshly ground pepper. Of course, on the When Way, we recommend limiting your cheese intake, so we came up with this version made with a creamy artichoke sauce (crema di carciofi) rather than cheese. This is a pasta dish we prefer warm, so just make as many servings as you are going to eat immediately.

1 can (13.75-ounce) quartered artichokes, drained

6 tablespoons extra-virgin olive oil

2 to 3 tablespoons water

4 quarts water

Salt

8 ounces whole grain linguine

Freshly ground black pepper

1. Place the artichokes in a Vitamix or high-speed blender. Add olive oil. Start the blender on low speed and increase speed gradually—the mixture is very thick and may not puree if you increase the speed too quickly. Scrape down the side of the blender jar, then shake the jar, and start again as needed. Add water by tablespoonfuls (up to 3 tablespoons), and continue to blend until a very smooth puree. This may take several minutes.

2. Bring a large pot of water to boil. Add salt until it's salty like the sea. Add the pasta and cook until al dente according to package directions. Drain the pasta, then transfer to a large bowl. Add the crema di carciofi (page 47) and toss to coat. Add a generous amount of freshly ground black pepper and additional salt to taste.

What to *Know* When

Dr. C was a reluctant user of ground pepper until he found the Tellicherry Whole Black Peppercorns sold online by The Reluctant Trading Experiment *(reluctanttrading.com)*. It's a worthwhile investment for a more flavorful, fragrant, and spicy pepper.

CHAPTER FIVE

VEGETABLES

ESQUITES

PREP: 45–50 minutes   COOK: 10–15 minutes   MAKES: 6 servings
SERVING SIZE: 1½ cups

Calories: 256 kcal Total fiber: 4.1 g Soluble fiber: 0 g Protein: 7.2 g Total fat: 13.5 g Saturated fat: 2 g Healthy fats: 10.1 g
Carbohydrates: 30.5 g Sugars: 6 g Added sugars: 0 g Sodium: 96 mg Potassium: 138 mg Magnesium: 8 mg Calcium: 25 mg

This recipe was inspired by a Mexican wedding Dr. C attended, which included an elaborate lunch at 1 p.m. (the perfect When Way time for the largest meal of the day). The wedding went on until 3 a.m., and included several snacks brought out throughout the night (this was a perfect excuse for some When Way celebration foods). One of those snacks was the famous Mexican corn in a cup known as *esquites*. In this version, we made a few changes to make it healthier, including swapping mayo with a version of our Cashew-naise. Remember: It's best to soak the cashews overnight, but we have a shortcut in case you forget.

4¼ cups of water, divided

1 cup cashews

6 tablespoons fresh lime juice, divided

½ cup, plus 2 tablespoons fresh cilantro, chopped, divided

1½ teaspoons kosher salt

1 container cherry tomatoes (1 pint), quartered

2 tablespoons white onion, chopped

1 to 2 tablespoons jalapeño pepper, chopped

4 large ears of corn, husked

2 tablespoons extra-virgin olive oil

1. Combine 4 cups water and the cashews in a medium bowl. Cover and refrigerate overnight.

2. Drain the cashews and place in a Vitamix or other high-speed blender and add 5 tablespoons lime juice and the remaining ¼ cup water. Process on high until smooth. Add ¼ cup cilantro; blend 30 seconds. Add ½ teaspoon salt and remaining 1 tablespoon lime juice, if desired, and blend for another 30 seconds. Transfer to a small bowl.

3. Combine the tomatoes, onion, 1 tablespoon jalapeño pepper, and ¼ cup cilantro in a medium bowl. Toss to blend well. Season the tomato salsa (*pico de gallo*) with ½ teaspoon salt and more jalapeño, if desired.

4. Cut the corn off the cobs (about 4 cups). Heat the oil in a medium skillet over medium heat. Add the corn and sauté until tender, stirring often, about 5 minutes; season with ¼ to ½ teaspoon salt. Mix in ½ cup of the cilantro cashew cream.

5. Divide the corn mixture into four shallow bowls, then top with ⅓ cup salsa and sprinkle with remaining chopped cilantro.

—What to *Know* When—

You can do a quick cashew soak by bringing water to a boil, removing it from the heat, and soaking the cashews in the water covered for 1 hour.

TOMATO-BRAISED SWISS CHARD

PREP: **15 minutes**   COOK: **23 minutes**   MAKES: **2 servings**   SERVING SIZE: **1 cup**

Calories: 191 kcal Total fiber: 2.4 g Soluble fiber: 0 g Protein: 2.6 g Total fat: 14.2 g Saturated fat: 2 g Healthy fats: 12.1 g
Carbohydrates: 9.1 g Sugars: 4.2 g Added sugars: 0 g Sodium: 633 mg Potassium: 358 mg Magnesium: 84 mg Calcium: 96 mg

In this recipe, we cook Swiss chard twice—first blanching, then braising—to bring out maximum flavor and texture. Leafy greens like Swiss chard and spinach are loaded with oxalic acid, which combines with calcium in your mouth and can create a weird chalky sensation. By blanching the chard first and disposing the water, you can get rid of the oxalic acid and make the vegetable much more enjoyable.

4 quarts water

Kosher salt

1 large bunch Swiss chard (13 to 14 ounces)

1 can (14.5-ounce) diced or crushed tomatoes in juice

½ cup wine (red or white)

¼ cup extra-virgin olive oil

3 large garlic cloves, whole

Freshly ground black pepper

1. In a large pot, bring the water to a boil. Add enough salt to make it salty like the sea.

2. Meanwhile, cut the tips off the Swiss chard stems and discard. Thoroughly wash the Swiss chard in a large bowl of cold water. Discard this water, then repeat washing in clean, cold water until no sand or dirt remains at the bottom of the bowl.

3. Add the chard to the pot of boiling water and cook about 3 minutes or until the water returns to a boil for about a minute. Drain the chard in a colander, then shake off any excess water. Rinse and wipe dry the pot.

4. Return the chard to the pot, then add the tomatoes, wine, olive oil, and garlic. Cook over medium heat until the sauce has thickened and both the chard stems and leaves are very soft, stirring occasionally, about 20 minutes. (Because the chard is cooked to death, you can't overdo it.) Season to taste with salt and pepper and serve.

LEFTOVER CELERY SICILIAN STYLE

PREP: **15 minutes**   COOK: **9–11 minutes**   MAKES: **4 servings**   SERVING SIZE: **½ cup**

Calories: 123 kcal Total fiber: 0.7 g Soluble fiber: 0 g Protein: 0.8 g Total fat: 11.6 g Saturated fat: 1.2 g Healthy fats: 8.3 g
Carbohydrates: 5.2 g Sugars: 2.5 g Added sugars: 0 g Sodium: 220 mg Potassium: 102 mg Magnesium: 13 mg Calcium: 14 mg

It seems there is always a bunch of celery in the back of the refrigerator. This dish is a nice way to use up those leftover stalks. Celery helps prevent periodontal disease, thanks to its fibrous, abrasive texture, which scrapes away yellowing plaque and bits of food stuck in your teeth. All that chomping revs up the production of cleansing saliva and turns your mouth into a mini-cleaning machine.

1 tablespoon dark raisins

¼ cup water

2 tablespoons extra-virgin olive oil

1 bunch celery, leafy tops removed, stalks cut into ¼-inch-thick slices on sharp diagonal

2 large garlic cloves, minced

⅛ teaspoon dried crushed red pepper flakes

⅓ cup pitted olives, such as kalamata or Castelvetrano, sliced

2 tablespoons pine nuts

2 tablespoons fresh Italian parsley, chopped

¼ teaspoon kosher salt

⅛ teaspoon freshly ground black pepper

1. Put the raisins in a small bowl; add water and let soak 15 minutes. Drain.

2. In a large skillet over medium heat, add the olive oil, then the celery, garlic, and red pepper flakes. Sauté until the celery starts to soften, stirring occasionally, 6 to 8 minutes.

3. Add the drained raisins to the skillet along with the olives and pine nuts. Sauté another 3 minutes to blend flavors. Stir in parsley. Season with the salt and pepper, and serve.

What to *Eat* When

Women should try to eat celery, especially paired with hummus, to help reduce period pain. Because it's water filled, celery is hydrating, which helps beat back symptoms associated with menstrual cycles, including cramps, bloating, and acne.

Butternut Squash
Dumplings (page 128)
& Vegetable Ragout
(page 129)

BUTTERNUT SQUASH DUMPLINGS

PREP: 25 minutes   **COOK:** 20–25 minutes   **MAKES:** 4 servings   **SERVING SIZE:** 6–8 dumplings

Calories: 124.67 kcal Total fiber: 5.01 g Soluble fiber: 0.41 g Protein: 3.53 g Total fat: 0.64 g Saturated fat: 0.11 g Healthy fats: 0.34 g
Carbohydrates: 27.25 g Sugars: 4.25 g Added sugars: 0 g Sodium: 521.51 mg Potassium: 266.48 mg Magnesium: 48.67 mg Calcium: 76.30 mg

These delicious vegan dumplings have all the flavor of traditional dumplings that some crave—without any of the added fats or simple carbs of traditional dumplings. These squash dumplings are a great addition in soups, but Chef Jim especially loves them in our Vegetable Ragout (page 129). These dumplings are quick and easy to make and freeze well for up to two months.

6 cups (or more) vegetable broth

1½ cups butternut squash (from 1 small squash), peeled, cut into ½-inch dice

¾ cup whole wheat flour

½ teaspoon baking powder

½ teaspoon kosher salt

¼ teaspoon ground cumin

⅛ teaspoon freshly ground black pepper

1. In a large pot, bring broth to a boil over medium-high heat. Add the squash and cook until soft, about 10 minutes. Using a spider or large slotted spoon, transfer the squash to a food processor. Reserve the broth in the pot.

2. Using on/off turns, pulse the squash in the processor until smooth. Add the flour, baking powder, salt, cumin, and pepper. Puree until well blended and smooth; the dough will be wet and sticky. Scrape the dough into a medium bowl.

3. Measure the broth in the pot and add enough water to equal 6 cups liquid. Return to the same pot and bring to a gentle boil. Working with half the dough at a time and using 2 teaspoons—one to scoop the dough and one to scrape the dough into the boiling broth— drop the dough into the broth and gently simmer the dumplings until cooked through, about 10 minutes. Using a spider or large slotted spoon, transfer the dumplings to a strainer and drain well, then rinse under cold water.

4. Repeat the procedure with the second half of the dough, adding more water or vegetable broth to the pot as necessary. Reserve any leftover broth for the Vegetable Ragout (page 129).

What to *Swap* When

You can swap the butternut squash for cooked carrots, sweet potato, or lentils (see our Lentil Dumplings recipe, page 154).

VEGETABLE RAGOUT

PREP: 45–55 minutes   COOK: 50–60 minutes   MAKES: 4 servings   SERVING SIZE: 2 cups

Calories: 250 kcal Total fiber: 9.2 g Soluble fiber: 1.5 g Protein: 6.7 g Total fat: 11.7 g Saturated fat: 1.7 g Healthy fats: 9.8 g
Carbohydrates: 31 g Sugars: 12.8 g Added sugars: 0 g Sodium: 660 mg Potassium: 758 mg Magnesium: 56 mg Calcium: 130 mg

If you're looking for a delicious and satisfying plant-based meal, turn to this Vegetable Ragout. Enjoy it with the Butternut Squash Dumplings (page 128) for a hearty meal—remember, the dumplings can be made a day or weeks ahead and frozen. To foster your health, you can have virtually unlimited non-starchy veggies at any meal—more before 2 p.m., though, please, so cook this favorite at night or on a free day and enjoy during the week and early in the day.

3 cups (or more) vegetable broth

2 cups rutabaga, peeled, cut into ½-inch dice

3 tablespoons extra-virgin olive oil, divided

2 cups small cauliflower florets (about ½ medium head; 8 to 9 ounces)

1 cup (about ½ pint) cherry tomatoes, halved lengthwise

¾ teaspoon kosher salt, divided

1 cup yellow onion (about 1 small), finely chopped

½ cup red bell pepper (about ½ medium pepper), cut into ½-inch dice

3 large garlic cloves, finely chopped

1 cup leek (about 1 large), white and light green parts only, finely chopped

2 cups (about 6 ounces) small broccoli florets

1 cup canned fire-roasted tomatoes

1 cup (about 6 ounces) frozen peas

2 teaspoons chia seeds

½ teaspoon dried crushed red pepper flakes

1. In a large pot, bring 3 cups vegetable broth (use reserved broth from Butternut Squash Dumplings if available) to a gentle boil over medium heat. Add the rutabagas; cover and cook until tender, about 20 minutes. Using a slotted spoon or spider, transfer the rutabagas to a medium bowl. Reserve the broth in the pot.

2. Meanwhile, in a large skillet over medium heat, add 1 tablespoon olive oil and the cauliflower; season with ¼ teaspoon salt and sauté until cauliflower begins to brown in spots, 6 to 7 minutes (cauliflower will not yet be tender). Transfer to the bowl with the rutabagas.

3. In the same skillet over medium heat, add 1 teaspoon olive oil and the cherry tomatoes, and sauté until tomatoes start to soften, 3 to 4 minutes. Transfer to the bowl with cauliflower.

4. Again, in same skillet on medium heat, add 1 tablespoon plus 1 teaspoon olive oil with the onion and bell pepper; scrape the bottom of the skillet with a rubber spatula to deglaze any reduced juices from the tomatoes. Sauté until onion begins to lightly brown and caramelize, 7 to 8 minutes.

5. Add the remaining 1 teaspoon olive oil and garlic to the same skillet and sauté until aromatic, 1 to 2 minutes. Add the leek and cook for about 5 minutes to soften slightly, then add the broccoli florets, fire-roasted tomatoes, peas, chia seeds, red pepper flakes, the reserved rutabagas, cauliflower, and cherry tomatoes to the skillet. Add enough additional broth to the reserved vegetable broth to measure 3 cups total. Add to the skillet and simmer over medium heat until the vegetables are crisp-tender, about 10 minutes. Season with remaining salt, if desired. Add the dumplings, if desired, and heat through, about 5 minutes. Serve hot.

WHOLE ROASTED CAULIFLOWER WITH WARM VINAIGRETTE

PREP: 50–60 minutes   **COOK:** 1 hour, 5 minutes   **MAKES:** 4–6 servings
SERVING SIZE: ½ pound cauliflower

Calories: 407 kcal Total fiber: 4 g Soluble fiber: 0.2 g Protein: 11.6 g Total fat: 21.2 g Saturated fat: 3 g Healthy fats: 18.1 g
Carbohydrates: 53 g Sugars: 13 g Added sugars: 0 g Sodium: 527 mg Potassium: 460 mg Magnesium: 5 mg Calcium: 51 mg

Not only does serving a whole roasted cauliflower make for a beautiful presentation, it also makes for delicious textures and flavors. By blanching the cauliflower before roasting in a very hot oven, you'll develop a striking color on the vegetable, as well as great nutty notes. We've offered two variations of a vinaigrette to pair with this dish, too.

Cauliflower

1 head (2¼- to 2½-pound) cauliflower, with leaves intact (if possible)

3½ teaspoons kosher salt, divided

1 tablespoon extra-virgin olive oil

Mustard Caraway Vinaigrette

4½ tablespoons extra-virgin olive oil, divided

3 tablespoons shallot, finely chopped

3 garlic cloves, finely chopped

1½ teaspoons caraway seeds

1½ tablespoons coarsely ground Dijon mustard

3 tablespoons white balsamic vinegar

½ teaspoon kosher salt

Lemon Caper Jalapeño Vinaigrette

4½ tablespoons extra-virgin olive oil

3 tablespoons shallot, finely chopped

1 tablespoon (or more) jalapeño chili pepper, finely chopped

3 garlic cloves, finely chopped

1½ tablespoons drained capers

1½ teaspoons (packed) lemon peel, finely grated

3 tablespoons fresh lemon juice

½ teaspoon kosher salt

1. For the cauliflower, bring a large pot of water to boil over high heat. Add 3 teaspoons salt. Put the cauliflower, bottom side up, into the pot. Boil until the cauliflower is barely tender, testing the core with a narrow pin (like a turkey lacer) or skewer, about 8 to 9 minutes—be sure not to overcook. Using a spider or large scoop, lift out the cauliflower and place on a kitchen towel, right side up. Let cool and dry for at least 30 minutes and up to 1 hour. Wipe off any moisture around the bottom.

2. Preheat the oven to 450°F. Line a small, 12-by-8-inch baking sheet with foil and place the cauliflower on top. Brush cauliflower all over with 1 tablespoon oil, and season with ½ teaspoon salt. Roast until deeply browned, 30 to 45 minutes.

3. Meanwhile, for the Mustard Caraway Vinaigrette, heat 1½ tablespoons oil in a medium skillet over medium heat. Add shallot and garlic. Sauté until soft, about 3 minutes. Add the caraway seeds; stir 30 seconds. Add the mustard; stir 30 seconds. Remove the skillet from heat, then whisk in the vinegar, followed by the remaining oil. Season with ½ teaspoon salt. Transfer to a small bowl.

4. For the Lemon Caper Jalapeño Vinaigrette, heat 1½ tablespoons oil in a medium skillet over medium heat. Add the shallot, jalapeño, and garlic. Sauté until soft, about 3 minutes. Mix in capers and lemon peel; stir 30 seconds. Remove skillet from heat, then whisk in the lemon juice, then the remaining oil. Season with ½ teaspoon salt. Transfer to a small bowl.

5. Place the cauliflower on a platter. Cut into wedges and serve with the vinaigrettes.

CHARD & ROASTED BUTTERNUT SQUASH

PREP: 30 minutes   **COOK:** 40 minutes   **MAKES:** 8 servings   **SERVING SIZE:** Generous ½ cup

Calories: 84 kcal Total fiber: 3.3 g Soluble fiber: 0g Protein: 2.5 g Total fat: 3.7 g Saturated fat: 0.5 g Healthy fats: 3.1 g
Carbohydrates: 13 g Sugars: 2.5 g Added sugars: 0 g Sodium: 275 mg Potassium: 722 mg Magnesium: 98 mg Calcium: 88 mg

Chef Jim and his wife love Swiss chard, and this quick and easy recipe is their favorite way to prepare it. The key is to spin-dry the chard after washing, otherwise the excess water that clings to the chard dilutes the flavors. You'll also want to cook the chard slow enough that it releases enough of its own moisture to thoroughly cook it until tender. The roasted butternut squash is a wonderful and healthy way to sweeten greens without adding sugar.

4 cups (1¾ to 2 pounds) butternut squash, peeled, seeded, cut into ⅓-inch cubes

6 large garlic cloves, minced, divided

2 tablespoons extra-virgin olive oil, divided

½ teaspoon kosher salt, divided

½ teaspoon fresh, coarsely ground black pepper, divided

2 large bunches (1¼ to 1½ pounds) Swiss chard, center ribs removed, leaves cut crosswise into ⅓- to ½-inch-thick strips

1. Preheat the oven to 350°F. In a large mixing bowl, combine squash, half the garlic, 1 tablespoon olive oil, and ¼ teaspoon each salt and pepper. Toss to mix well. Spread out on a rimmed baking sheet. Bake until squash is tender, stirring occasionally, about 35 minutes. Remove from the oven and set aside.

2. In a large, deep nonstick skillet, heat remaining olive oil over medium heat. Add the remaining garlic and sauté until aromatic, 30 seconds to 1 minute. Add the chard to the skillet; season with the remaining salt and pepper, and stir frequently until the chard is tender, 5 to 7 minutes. Add the squash to the chard, and stir until well mixed and heated through, 2 to 3 minutes.

3. Transfer the mixture a large bowl and serve.

─ **What to *Know* When** ─

You can also add the chard ribs to this recipe, if you like the texture and flavor. Slice them super thin and simmer the ribs in vegetable broth to make them tender because they take longer to cook.

JAPANESE TURNIPS WITH GREENS

PREP: **15–20 minutest**   COOK: **8–10 minutes**   MAKES: **4 servings**   SERVING SIZE: **½ cup**

Calories: 123 kcal Total fiber: 0.9 g Soluble fiber: 0.3 g Protein: 1.5 g Total fat: 12.3 g Saturated fat: 1.5 g Healthy fats: 10.5 g
Carbohydrates: 2.9 g Sugars: 0.8 g Added sugars: 0 g Sodium: 131 mg Potassium: 75 mg Magnesium: 15 mg Calcium: 17 mg

Japanese turnips are a common find at the farmers market. They are small, round, and white, and look a little bit like radishes. They have a mild, sweet, and earthy turnip flavor and are usually sold with the green attached, which we use in this root-to-stem recipe.

1 bunch small Japanese turnips with greens

3 garlic cloves, finely chopped

½ to ¼ teaspoon kosher salt, to taste

8 walnuts, toasted

2 tablespoons extra-virgin olive oil

½ teaspoon freshly ground black pepper, to taste

⅛ teaspoon dried crushed red pepper flakes, to taste

1. Cut off the turnip tops and cut the leaves at the stem base. Halve or quarter the turnip bulbs so all the pieces are about the same size. Wash and spin-dry the turnip greens.

2. On a cutting board, chop the garlic with ½ teaspoon salt. Then add the walnuts to the garlic mixture and finely chop. Place the turnip greens over the garlic-walnut mixture and finely chop (you are making a quick turnip top pesto).

3. In a medium skillet over medium heat, add the olive oil and turnip bulbs, and sauté until light golden brown and crisp-tender, turning halfway through cooking, 6 to 8 minutes. Add the turnip top pesto mixture, stirring to combine, and season to taste with salt, pepper, and the red pepper flakes, if using. Sauté for 1 minute more.

GRILLED BROCCOLI RABE

PREP: 5–10 minutes, plus overnight   **COOK:** 8–10 minutes   **MAKES:** 4–6 servings
SERVING SIZE: 6 stalks

Calories: 69 kcal Total fiber: 0 g Soluble fiber: 0 g Protein: 3.1 g Total fat: 4.8 g Saturated fat: 0.7 g Healthy fats: 4 g
Carbohydrates: 4.4 g Sugars: 1 g Added sugars: 0 g Sodium: 105 mg Potassium: 6 mg Magnesium: 1 mg Calcium: 42 mg

Broccoli rabe, or rapini, looks like baby broccoli but is actually related to the turnip. Like most vegetables, it is nutritious and low in calories, but still helps you feel full. People are often afraid to use broccoli rabe because it can taste bitter, and its toughness sometimes requires par cooking first. But this recipe involves almost no work—aside from starting the night before to help cut down that bitter flavor and toughness. Dr. R loves to make this simple preparation and eat it with a salad just before sundown.

1 large bunch (17 to 18 ounces) broccoli rabe

2 garlic cloves, smashed

Kosher or fine sea salt

¼ teaspoon dried, crushed red pepper flakes (optional)

1 teaspoon extra-virgin olive oil, plus 2 tablespoons, divided

1. Trim the tough lower stalks of the broccoli rabe, then wash and dry the broccoli rabe thoroughly in a salad spinner. Place the broccoli rabe and garlic cloves in a large resealable plastic bag. Sprinkle with salt and crushed red pepper flakes. Add 1 teaspoon olive oil, seal the bag, and shake vigorously to combine. Refrigerate overnight.

2. If grilling, prepare the grill for direct cooking over medium heat (350°F). Add the broccoli rabe to the grill and cook until crisp-tender, turning occasionally, 8 to 10 minutes. Remove from the grill. Transfer to a serving dish and toss with the remaining 2 tablespoons olive oil. Season with more salt, if desired.

3. If roasting, preheat the oven to 350°F. Line a large rimmed baking sheet with parchment paper. Remove the broccoli rabe from the bag and toss with 2 tablespoons olive oil. Arrange on the prepared baking sheet, spaced apart. Roast until crisp-tender, about 15 minutes.

SOUTHWEST SQUASH & BEAN MEDLEY

PREP: 55 minutes   COOK: 1 hour, 24 minutes   MAKES: 4 servings   SERVING SIZE: 2¼–2½ cups

Calories: 147 kcal Total fiber: 5.4 g Soluble fiber: 0 g Protein: 4.5 g Total fat: 3.4 g Saturated fat: 0.4 g Healthy fats: 2.5 g
Carbohydrates: 26 g Sugars: 7 g Added sugars: 0 g Sodium: 497 mg Potassium: 436 mg Magnesium: 40 mg Calcium: 92 mg

We're lucky to have so many different cultures' cuisines in America's melting pot. This squash and bean medley incorporates the iconic flavors of the American Southwest—a blend of American, southern, and Mexican tastes. And like many similar preparations, it is great—if not better—the next day. A true When Way dish, this is worth making a double batch to have for lunch throughout the week. It also goes great over our Lentil Dumplings (page 154).

2 tablespoons extra-virgin olive oil, divided

6 large garlic cloves, finely chopped, divided

½ teaspoon kosher salt, divided

½ teaspoon freshly ground black pepper, divided

6-cups butternut squash (about 2 pounds), peeled, seeded, cut into ½-inch dice

1 cup red bell pepper, cut into ½-inch dice

2 cups sweet onion (from 1 large), finely chopped

1½ teaspoons dried oregano

1¼ teaspoons ground cumin

¾ teaspoon chipotle chili in adobo sauce, finely chopped

½ teaspoon smoked paprika

½ teaspoon chili powder

½ teaspoon ground cinnamon

1 cup canned crushed tomatoes, preferably fire-roasted

6 cups vegetable broth

1 bag (10-ounce) frozen lima beans, thawed

1. Preheat the oven to 350°F. In a large bowl, combine 1 tablespoon olive oil, and half the garlic, salt, and pepper. Add the squash and toss until well coated. Spread the squash mixture evenly on a large rimmed baking sheet (setting the bowl aside). Roast until the squash is tender when pierced with a fork or wooden skewer, stirring occasionally, 55 to 60 minutes. Set aside.

2. In the same bowl, toss the bell pepper with 1 teaspoon olive oil to coat. Spread on a rimmed baking sheet and roast in the oven until tender, about 30 minutes. Set aside.

3. Meanwhile, in a large heavy pot, combine the onion, and remaining 2 teaspoons olive oil, salt, and pepper. Sauté over medium-low heat until the onion is light golden and slightly caramelized, 12 to 14 minutes.

4. Add the remaining garlic to the pot and sauté until aromatic, 1 to 2 minutes. Add all the spices and chipotle chili, and stir for 30 seconds to 1 minute to toast the spices. Add the crushed tomatoes and vegetable broth, deglazing the bottom of the pot with a wooden spoon. Bring to a boil. Add the lima beans, roasted squash, and bell pepper. Reduce to medium-low heat and simmer uncovered to blend flavors, 10 to 15 minutes. Serve hot.

What to *Swap* When

Try this recipe with other squashes like acorn, delicata, or pumpkin to create new flavors.

ASPARAGUS WITH CASHEW BASIL "AIOLI"

PREP: 25–30 minutes, plus overnight soaking for cashews **COOK:** 5–15 minutes
MAKES: 4 servings **SERVING SIZE:** 4 asparagus; ¼ cup aioli

Calories: 260 kcal Total fiber: 3.7 g Soluble fiber: 0.02 g Protein: 9 g Total fat: 18.7 g Saturated fat: 3 g Healthy fats: 14 g
Carbohydrates: 16 g Sugars: 5 g Added sugars: 0 g Sodium: 250 mg Potassium: 264 mg Magnesium: 21 mg Calcium: 65 mg

This dish is a great choice to replace fries or similarly unhealthy but addictive side dishes. Asparagus is loaded with nutrients that help keep type 2 diabetes at bay, and cashews have a ton of heart-healthy fats.

Aioli

1 cup raw cashews

4 cups water

¼ cup fresh lemon juice
(from 1 large lemon)

¼ cup water (or more)

¼ cup (packed) fresh basil leaves,
chopped

2 anchovies, chopped (optional)

1 large garlic clove, chopped

¼ teaspoon (generous) kosher salt

Asparagus

¼ cup raw cashews

1 bunch (1 pound) asparagus,
tough ends trimmed

1 tablespoon extra-virgin olive oil

¼ teaspoon kosher salt

⅛ teaspoon freshly ground
black pepper

¼ cup fresh basil, chopped

1. **For the aioli:** Put cashews in a large bowl and pour the water over top. Cover and let soak in the refrigerator overnight.

2. Drain and place the cashews in a high-speed blender or a Vitamix. Add the lemon juice and ¼ cup water. Blend, slowly at first, then gradually increase the speed to create a very smooth puree, occasionally stopping to scrape down the sides of the blender. If the mixture gets "stuck" and is too thick to blend, add more water, 1 teaspoon at a time, until smooth. Add the basil, anchovies, if using, and garlic. Blend until well incorporated. Season with the salt. Refrigerate until ready to use.

3. **For the asparagus:** Preheat the oven to 350°F. Place the ¼ cup cashews on a parchment-lined baking sheet and bake until toasted and light golden, about 8 to 10 minutes. Cool, then coarsely chop. Set aside.

4. Prepare a grill for cooking over direct medium heat (350° to 400°F) or warm a 12-inch cast-iron skillet over medium heat. Toss the asparagus with the olive oil to coat. Season with salt and pepper. Place the asparagus on the grill grates or in the skillet and cook until lightly browned and crisp-tender, turning occasionally, 3 to 5 minutes.

5. On a serving platter, evenly spread about half of the aioli. Top with the asparagus. Sprinkle with the toasted cashews and chopped basil. Cover and refrigerate the remaining "aioli" for another use, like a sauce for salmon or crudités. (The aioli will keep for 5 days in the refrigerator.)

ROASTED ROSEMARY PERUVIAN POTATOES

PREP: 10–12 minutes COOK: 30 minutes MAKES: 4 servings SERVING SIZE: ¼ cup (loosely packed)

Calories: 131 kcal Total fiber: 1.64 g Soluble fiber: 0 g Protein: 2.9 g Total fat: 3.6 g Saturated fat: 0.5 g Healthy fats: 3 g
Carbohydrates: 21.2 g Sugars: 0.03 g Added sugars: 0 g Sodium: 248 mg Potassium: 19 mg Magnesium: 2 mg Calcium: 12 mg

These tiny potatoes have a *lot* of flavor and make a bright addition to any meal. Dr. R loves to eat 'em cold at 10:30 in the morning (when Dr. C is digging into cold pasta). At that time and served cold, potatoes contain resistant starch, working more as fiber *for* you than calories and starch *against* you. Make a meal of it by pairing these potatoes with our Chard & Roasted Butternut Squash recipe (page 133).

3 large garlic cloves, minced

1 tablespoon extra-virgin olive oil

1 tablespoon fresh Italian parsley, chopped

1½ teaspoons fresh rosemary, finely chopped

½ to ¾ teaspoon kosher salt

¼ teaspoon freshly ground black pepper

1 pound Peruvian purple potatoes, unpeeled, cut into 1-inch pieces

1. Preheat the oven to 350°F. In a medium bowl, combine garlic, olive oil, parsley, rosemary, salt, and pepper. Add the potatoes and toss until well coated.

2. Spread the potato mixture in a single layer on a rimmed baking sheet. Bake until tender when pierced with a fork, stirring occasionally, about 30 minutes. Serve warm.

Loaded Roasted
Potatoes
(page 144)

Tangy Heirloom Beans
(page 145)

Broccoli Gremolata
(page 146)

LOADED ROASTED POTATOES

PREP: 45 minutes   COOK: 30–40 minutes   MAKES: 6 servings   SERVING SIZE: 1 generous cup

Calories: 179 kcal Total fiber: 6.9 g Soluble fiber: 1.2 g Protein: 4.7 g Total fat: 0.8 g Saturated fat: 0.1 g Healthy fats: 0.2 g
Carbohydrates: 38.5 g Sugars: 2.1 g Added sugars: 0 g Sodium: 218 mg Potassium: 896 mg Magnesium: 49 mg Calcium: 57 mg

This recipe turns a basic roasted potato recipe into much more by adding spices, lemon zest, and sautéed vegetables. The wilted spinach adds moisture, and the carrots add sweetness. These potatoes are great just slightly warm or even cold from the fridge in the morning. Just as with the Roasted Rosemary Peruvian Potatoes (page 141), that overnight refrigeration turns the starch in the potatoes into a resistant starch, which means they won't raise your blood sugar very quickly and act more like a fiber than a starch.

2 pounds mixed baby potatoes (gold, red, and purple, about 1-inch diameter), rinsed and dried

4 tablespoons extra-virgin olive oil, divided

4 large garlic cloves, finely chopped, divided

½ teaspoon chili powder

½ teaspoon kosher salt, divided

½ teaspoon freshly ground black pepper, divided

¼ teaspoon ground turmeric

¼ teaspoon ground cumin

1½ cups red onion, cut into ⅓-inch dice

1½ cups red bell pepper, cut into ½-inch pieces

1½ cups carrots, cut into ⅓-inch dice

1½ teaspoons (packed) lemon peel, finely grated

3 cups (firmly packed; about 4½ ounces) spinach leaves,

2 tablespoons fresh Italian parsley, chopped

1. Preheat the oven to 350°F. Coat a large rimmed baking sheet with nonstick spray. Cut the potatoes in half or thirds, making ½- to ¾-inch pieces. Place the potatoes in a large bowl. Add 1½ tablespoons oil and 1 tablespoon garlic; toss to blend. In a small bowl or cup, stir together the chili powder, half the salt and pepper, and the turmeric and cumin. Gradually sprinkle the spice mixture over the potatoes, tossing to coat evenly. Scatter the potatoes onto the prepared baking sheet in a single layer. Roast until tender, without stirring, 45 to 50 minutes.

2. Meanwhile, warm 1½ tablespoons oil in a large skillet over medium heat. Add the onion, bell pepper, and carrot; season with remaining salt and pepper. Sauté until the vegetables are just tender and beginning to brown, stirring occasionally and reducing heat if vegetables are coloring too quickly, 18 to 20 minutes.

3. Push the vegetables to one side of the pan. Add the remaining ½ tablespoon oil and ½ tablespoon garlic to the other side. Stir until the garlic is fragrant, 30 to 60 seconds, and stir into the vegetables. Mix in the lemon peel, then add the spinach. Toss until the spinach just wilts, about 1 minute. Add the roasted potatoes and parsley. Toss until blended and heated through, about 1 minute. Serve hot or at room temperature.

What to *Swap* When

For a variation on this dish, swap in arugula or kale for the spinach to add a hint of bitterness.

TANGY HEIRLOOM BEANS

PREP: 30 minutes **COOK: 1½ hours** **MAKES: 4 servings** **SERVING SIZE: ¼ cup**

Calories: 158 kcal Total fiber: 11.9 g Soluble fiber: 0 g Protein: 6.3 g Total fat: 1.2 g Saturated fat: 0 g Healthy fats: 0 g
Carbohydrates: 30 g Sugars: 0 g Added sugars: 0 g Sodium: 1,767 mg Potassium: 65 mg Magnesium: 11 mg Calcium: 186 mg

Here is another way to get beans into your diet. And you should get as many in as possible: Beans are a super longevity food enjoyed in great quantities in all five Blue Zones (the five regions of the world where people live the longest). You can make this dish with a variety of different heirloom beans; we prefer the Rio Zape variety (available from Rancho Gordo).

1½ cups (9½ ounces) heirloom beans, kidney beans, or pinto beans

12 cups water, divided

1 tablespoon kosher salt, plus 1 teaspoon

⅓ cup shallot, cut into ¼-inch dice

¼ cup white balsamic vinegar (6% acid)

2 garlic cloves, sliced paper thin

½ teaspoon Urfa pepper flakes

2 dried bay leaves

¼ cup fresh basil, sliced

1. Stir 6 cups water and 1 tablespoon salt in a large bowl until salt dissolves. Add beans and soak overnight.

2. Before cooking the beans, combine the shallot, vinegar, garlic, and Urfa pepper in a small bowl. Let marinate until the garlic loses its harshness, about 2 hours.

3. Drain the beans well. Place beans in a 3-quart saucepan. Add the bay leaves, remaining 6 cups water, and 1 teaspoon salt. Bring the beans to a gentle simmer over medium-low heat. Adjust the heat as needed to maintain the barest simmer. Cook until the beans are tender, about 1 hour and 20 to 30 minutes. Remove from heat and set beans aside in their liquid for at least 30 minutes to cool and firm up.

4. Drain the beans over a deep bowl, reserving the cooking liquid. Place the beans into a serving bowl. Mix in the shallot relish and enough of the reserved cooking liquid to just about cover. Garnish with the basil. Season with salt to taste.

What to *Eat* When

This recipe is a great choice for women's health. It helps to increase fertility with a high folate content and is a great source of iodized salt when breast-feeding an infant.

BROCCOLI GREMOLATA (WITH LEMON & HAZELNUTS)

PREP: 45 minutes **COOK:** 15 minutes **MAKES:** 4 servings **SERVING SIZE:** 1 cup

Calories: 145 kcal Total fiber: 4.7 g Soluble fiber: 0.5 g Protein: 5.0 g Total fat: 10.1 g Saturated fat: 1.2 g Healthy fats: 8.3 g
Carbohydrates: 12.1 g Sugars: 3 g Added sugars: 0 g Sodium: 209 mg Potassium: 509 mg Magnesium: 48 mg Calcium: 110 mg

This is a quick and easy way to prepare broccoli. Gremolata is a traditional Italian herb topping for meat that is made with parsley, lemon, and garlic. This version adds hazelnuts and skips the meat. Be sure to keep the stems on your florets—they're the most nutrient-concentrated part of the broccoli. Serve this as a side, or mix it with whole grain pasta for a delicious breakfast or lunch.

2 large heads of broccoli with stalks (1¼ pounds)

2½ teaspoons kosher salt (or more)

12 hazelnuts

1½ teaspoons (packed) lemon peel, finely grated

1 tablespoon parsley, chopped

1 clove garlic, minced

2 tablespoons extra-virgin olive oil

3 tablespoons fresh lemon juice

Freshly ground black pepper

1. Preheat the oven to 350°F. Cut the crowns off the broccoli stems, chopping into approximately 1½-inch florets. Peel the stems; cut them into ⅓-inch-thick disks.

2. Bring a large saucepan of water to a boil. Gradually add 2½ teaspoons salt. Add the broccoli and blanch for 2 minutes. Drain well and transfer the broccoli to a towel to cool, at least 15 minutes and up to an hour.

3. Meanwhile, scatter the hazelnuts on a small, rimmed baking sheet. Roast in the oven until golden brown, 10 to 12 minutes. Set aside to cool. Once cool enough to handle, wrap the nuts in a small cloth and rub briskly to loosen and remove any skins. Place the nuts in a plastic bag. Using a rolling pin or the bottom of a small saucepan, crush the nuts into small pieces. Combine the nuts, lemon peel, parsley, and garlic in a small bowl. Stir to blend. Set aside.

4. Add oil to a large nonstick skillet and heat over high until the oil shimmers. Add the broccoli. Toss to coat. Then cook, turning only occasionally, until the broccoli browns well in spots, about 4 minutes. Sprinkle with the lemon juice. Toss as the lemon juice evaporates, about 30 seconds. Season with salt and pepper. Arrange the broccoli in a shallow dish and sprinkle with the hazelnut mixture before serving.

TWICE-BAKED EGGPLANT STACKS WITH TOMATO BASIL PESTO

PREP: 25 minutes   **COOK:** 70 minutes   **MAKES:** 4 servings   **SERVING SIZE:** ¼ eggplant stack

Calories: 338 kcal Total fiber: 11 g Soluble fiber: 0.2 g Protein: 6 g Total fat: 26.6 g Saturated fat: 3.6 g Healthy fats: 22.6 g
Carbohydrates: 23.2 g Sugars: 8.4 g Added sugars: 0 g Sodium: 334 mg Potassium: 669 mg Magnesium: 50 mg Calcium: 60 mg

Toward the end of summer, eggplants fill the market. They are delicious enough simply sliced and grilled, but by adding a tomato-basil pesto to these slices, we've really amped up the flavor profile—not to mention the nutrition. First, you'll get fiber from eggplants, which are a nightshade vegetable and great to start the day. Then, cooked tomatoes offer lycopene, and basil has vitamin K for an extra boost to brain, heart, and bones.

1 large eggplant or 2 medium eggplants, sliced into ⅜-inch rounds

½ teaspoon salt (plus more)

¼ cup walnuts

2 to 4 tablespoons extra-virgin olive oil, divided

2 garlic cloves, whole, peeled

1 tablespoon capers (preferably packed in salt, then soaked in water to remove salt)

1 large bunch basil

12 semidried tomatoes

1. Preheat the oven to 350°F. Line a baking sheet with paper towels. Rub salt on the eggplant slices and place them on the paper towels in a single layer, using multiple sheet pans if necessary. Place paper towels on top of the salted eggplant and a second sheet pan on top. Let sit for about 30 minutes to draw out some moisture from the eggplants.

2. Meanwhile, toast the walnuts on a small sheet pan in the oven for about 7 minutes. Remove and let cool.

3. Remove the paper towels and eggplants from the baking sheets. Line the baking sheets with parchment paper, then place the eggplant slices in a single layer on the pans. Lightly coat the slices with 2 tablespoons olive oil. Bake until soft, about 30 minutes. Remove and let cool.

4. While the eggplant cooks, add garlic and salt to a food processor and pulse until combined. Add the toasted walnuts, capers, and basil. Process until the basil is broken down, then add the tomatoes and process again until well incorporated. Slowly add 2 tablespoons olive oil and process until a thick pesto. Add oil by teaspoonfuls as necessary for a thick, spreadable texture. Taste and season with salt, if needed.

5. When eggplants are cool enough to handle, place a slice on a plate, top with a tablespoon pesto, then another slice of eggplant. Repeat until all eggplant slices and pesto are used in a tower.

6. Wrap the eggplant tower in parchment paper and make a tight package. Place the parchment package on a baking sheet in the oven for 25 to 30 minutes.

7. Carefully open the parchment. Cut into slices to serve.

PESTO GREEN BEANS

PREP: 45–50 minutes   **COOK:** 5 minutes   **MAKES:** 12 servings   **SERVING SIZE:** ½ cup

Calories: 248 kcal Total fiber: 3.3 g Soluble fiber: 0.4 g Protein: 3.9 g Total fat: 23.8 g Saturated fat: 2.8 g Healthy fats: 20.4 g
Carbohydrates: 7.3 g Sugars: 2.3 g Added sugars: 0 g Sodium: 167 mg Potassium: 107 mg Magnesium: 26 mg Calcium: 66 mg

There are many variations of pesto, most of which include cheese. This version is just as delicious as the traditional kinds but skips the cheese that doesn't love your body back. Rather than just pine nuts and basil, we've also changed this pesto to use heart-healthy walnuts and pecans, as well as arugula, parsley, and spinach. Combine this delicious sauce with small, fresh, cut green beans, and eat cold for a WTEW breakfast, packed lunch, or to nosh on when you get home from work. The green beans also make a great side for our grilled and roasted salmon recipes (pages 221 and 227).

2 pounds fresh green beans, trimmed, cut into ½-inch pieces

¾ cup (about 3 ounces) pecans, toasted

¾ cup (about 2.8 ounces) walnuts, toasted

1 cup (packed; about 1 ounce) fresh arugula leaves

1 cup (packed; about 1 ounce) fresh basil leaves

1 cup (packed; a generous ½ ounce) fresh Italian parsley leaves

1 cup (packed; about 1 ounce) fresh baby spinach leaves

2 garlic cloves, minced

1 teaspoon kosher salt

¼ teaspoon freshly ground black pepper

¾ cup extra-virgin olive oil

1. Bring a large pot of water to boil. Add the beans and cook just until the beans are tender when pierced with a fork, stirring often, about 5 minutes. Drain well in a colander (do *not* rinse with cold water).

2. Line a large baking sheet with several layers of paper towels. Spread the beans out onto the prepared baking sheet to cool and dry.

3. Meanwhile, combine the pecans and walnuts in a food processor bowl. Pulse, using on/off turns, until the nuts are finely chopped. Add the arugula, basil, parsley, spinach, garlic, salt, and pepper; process until the greens are coarsely chopped. Gradually add the olive oil through the feed tube, and process until all the ingredients are finely chopped and the pesto is well blended.

4. In a large mixing bowl, combine the green beans and pesto. Toss until beans are well coated with the pesto.

What to *Know* When

This pesto freezes exceptionally well (up to three months), so don't be afraid to make big batches when you have robust basil plants in the fall. Pro tip: Freeze the pesto in an ice cube tray so you can portion out servings as needed.

ROASTED CAULIFLOWER WITH ROMESCO SAUCE

PREP: 25 minutes   **COOK: 25–30 minutes**   **MAKES: 24 servings**   **SERVING SIZE: 1 cup**

Calories: 251 kcal Total fiber: 5.8 g Soluble fiber: 0.2 g Protein: 4.6 g Total fat: 20.5 g Saturated fat: 2.6 g Healthy fats: 17.7 g
Carbohydrates: 13.3 g Sugars: 3.3 g Added sugars: 0 g Sodium: 286 mg Potassium: 453 mg Magnesium: 18 mg Calcium: 87 mg

Between broccoli and cauliflower power, we should really reduce our chances of getting the most common cancers—breast, prostate, colon, and lung. Romesco is traditional Spanish pepper sauce used to top vegetables or fish. Its bright red color turns this cauliflower recipe into a bold-tasting and -looking dish.

Romesco Sauce

10 walnuts (about ¼ cup), toasted

2 whole roasted red peppers from a jar, drained well

1 large garlic clove

½ teaspoon smoked paprika

½ teaspoon balsamic vinegar

¼ teaspoon kosher salt

Cauliflower

1 head cauliflower (about 1¼ pounds), trimmed, cut into bite-size florets

1 tablespoon extra-virgin olive oil

⅛ teaspoon kosher salt

⅛ teaspoon freshly ground black pepper

¼ cup fresh basil, thinly sliced

1. **For the Romesco sauce:** In a food processor or a high-speed blender, combine all the sauce ingredients. Blend until the mixture is as smooth as possible. Transfer to small bowl. (You can prepare the sauce a day ahead; cover and refrigerate.)

2. **For the cauliflower:** Preheat the oven to 400°F. Line a rimmed baking sheet with parchment paper.

3. In a medium bowl, toss the cauliflower florets with the olive oil to coat. Spread the cauliflower florets on the prepared baking sheet and roast until tender and browned in spots, 25 to 30 minutes. Season with the salt and pepper.

4. Spread the Romesco sauce on a platter and arrange the cauliflower on top. Sprinkle with the basil and serve. You can also toss the cauliflower in the sauce and garnish with basil before serving.

GRILLED LITTLE GEM LETTUCE WITH AVOCADO DRESSING

PREP: 10 minutes   **COOK:** 5–6 minutes   **MAKES:** 4 servings   **SERVING SIZE:** 1 cup

Calories: 117 kcal Total fiber: 7.8 g Soluble fiber: 0.02 g Protein: 4.3 g Total fat: 7.1 g Saturated fat: 1 g Healthy fats: 5.5 g
Carbohydrates: 12.9 g Sugars: 4.2 g Added sugars: 0 g Sodium: 147 mg Potassium: 875 mg Magnesium: 50 mg Calcium: 707 mg

Little Gem lettuces are a chef's favorite. They look like baby romaine but are actually their own variety. You'll likely find them at a farmers market, but if you can't spot them, feel free to make this recipe using any baby lettuce you can find.

½ avocado, peeled and pitted

3 to 4 tablespoons fresh lemon juice (from 1 lemon)

¼ teaspoon (heaping) kosher salt

⅛ teaspoon freshly ground black pepper, plus more for serving

2 heads Little Gem lettuces, halved lengthwise, washed and patted dry

1 tablespoon extra-virgin olive oil

1. Prepare a grill for direct cooking over medium heat (350° to 400°F), or use a large cast-iron skillet on medium heat.

2. Using a fork, mash together the avocado and the lemon juice in a large bowl to form a paste. If the mixture is too thick, add more lemon juice by teaspoonfuls and whisk until almost smooth. Season with the salt and pepper. Set aside.

3. Brush the surface of the lettuce halves with the olive oil. Place, cut side down, on the grill grates or in the preheated cast-iron skillet. Grill or cook until the lettuce starts to brown and soften, about 3 minutes. Turn the lettuce halves over and cook 2 to 3 minutes more. Remove from the grill or skillet.

4. Toss the lettuce halves in the dressing to coat. Transfer to a plate. Sprinkle with pepper to taste and serve warm.

What to *Eat* When

We use avocado in this dressing, which is a great source of healthy plant-based fat. Healthy fats help to improve bone density and joint health, and can help lower the risk of type 2 diabetes.

LENTIL DUMPLINGS

PREP: 25–30 minutes   **COOK:** 34–37 minutes   **MAKES:** 6 servings   **SERVING SIZE:** 6 dumplings

Calories: 241 kcal Total fiber: 9.2 g Soluble fiber: 0.6 g Protein: 13 g Total fat: 1.5 g Saturated fat: 0.14 g Healthy fats: 0.5 g
Carbohydrates: 45.3 g Sugars: 2.8 g Added sugars: 0 g Sodium: 433 mg Potassium: 404 mg Magnesium: 45 mg Calcium: 57 mg

Dumplings are a favorite comfort food, and these are the healthiest version we can imagine. Traditional dumplings are made with white flour and eggs; ours are composed of plant-base protein, fiber, and nutrient-packed lentils. They are a great addition to vegetable ragouts (see ours on pages 129 and 162), soups, or the Southwest Squash & Bean Medley recipe (page 137).

1 cup (about 6 ounces) dried red lentils

1¾ cups water, plus more for rinsing lentils

¾ cup whole wheat flour

¾ teaspoon kosher salt

¾ teaspoon ground cumin

½ teaspoon harissa (see our Harissa Spice Blend on page 71)

½ teaspoon baking powder

⅛ teaspoon freshly ground black pepper

6 cups (or more) vegetable broth or water

1. In a medium bowl, cover the lentils with cold water and swirl with your hands to rinse, then drain in a strainer. Return the lentils to the bowl and add enough clean water to cover the lentils. Rinse and drain the lentils two more times.

2. In a medium saucepan, combine the lentils and 1¾ cups water. Bring to a boil. Reduce to medium-low heat and simmer, partially covered, for 10 to 15 minutes. Turn off the heat, cover, and let stand for 5 minutes. Uncover the saucepan and allow the lentils to cool for 5 minutes more (all the water will be absorbed, and lentils will be mushy).

3. Meanwhile, in a small bowl combine the flour, salt, cumin, harissa, baking powder, and pepper. Whisk to blend well.

4. In a food processor, puree the lentils until smooth, 20 to 30 seconds. Add the dry ingredients to the processor and mix until well blended, 10 to 15 seconds. Transfer the dumpling dough to a medium bowl.

5. In a large pot, bring 6 cups broth (or water) to a boil. Scoop out the dumpling dough by scant tablespoonfuls, leveling off the dough with a silicone spatula. Working in three batches, drop the dumplings into the boiling broth until cooked through in the center, 8 to 9 minutes a batch. Using a slotted spoon or spider, transfer the dumplings to a rimmed baking sheet or tray. Add more broth or water to the pot, as needed, and repeat with each batch. After all the dumplings are cooked and cooled, cover with plastic wrap and refrigerate until needed. Or label, date, and freeze up to 2 months.

What to *Know* When

If your dumpling dough disappears in the broth or doesn't keep its shape, then it is too wet. An easy fix: Add a little more flour a teaspoon at a time to tighten dough.

FENNEL WITH CORIANDER & CUMIN SCENTED TOMATO SAUCE

PREP: 10 minutes   COOK: 16–20 minutes   MAKES: 4 servings   SERVING SIZE: ½ cup

Calories: 197 kcal Total fiber: 5.8 g Soluble fiber: 0 g Protein: 3.2 g Total fat: 14.6 g Saturated fat: 2 g Healthy fats: 12.2 g
Carbohydrates: 16.1 g Sugars: 4.6 g Added sugars: 0 g Sodium: 312 mg Potassium: 776 mg Magnesium: 40 mg Calcium: 96 mg

Fennel is a delicious and versatile vegetable that adds a hearty component to any dish. This preparation is great on its own, as a side, or served under fish. We sauté the fennel in a tomato sauce, which loads your plate with flavonoids. These compounds, found in high concentrations in cooked tomatoes, decrease the risk of cardiovascular disease, including stroke and maybe even prostate cancer.

2 teaspoons whole coriander seeds

½ teaspoon cumin seeds

1 large fennel bulb (or two medium), fronds removed

¼ cup extra-virgin olive oil

1 can (14 to 15 ounces) crushed tomatoes

¼ teaspoon dried crushed red pepper flakes

¼ teaspoon kosher salt

1. In a small skillet, stir the coriander and cumin seeds until fragrant and slightly darker in color, about 2 minutes. Remove from the heat. Cool slightly. Finely grind the spices in a spice or coffee grinder.

2. Trim the bottom of the fennel bulb so it will sit flat on the work surface. Starting at one end, cut the bulb into ¼-inch-wide sections across the narrower part of the bulb, so that you end up with pieces that are held together by the root. The end pieces will fall apart, but try to keep the layers together.

3. In a heavy saucepan large enough to hold the fennel slices in a single layer, heat the olive oil over medium-high heat. (You may need to work in batches to fit the fennel in a single layer in the saucepan—do not overcrowd the pan.) Cook the fennel until browned on both sides, about 3 to 5 minutes a side. Transfer the fennel to a plate.

4. Add the crushed tomatoes to the saucepan along with the ground spices, red pepper flakes, if using, and salt. Return the fennel to the saucepan, arranging it in a single layer as much as possible. Bring the sauce to a boil. Reduce to medium-low heat and simmer, stirring often, until the sauce reduces slightly and the fennel is very tender, about 10 minutes. Add water by tablespoonfuls if the sauce becomes too thick.

BROCCOLI WITH GINGER TAHINI SATAY SAUCE

PREP: 30 minutes   **COOK:** 12–15 minutes   **MAKES:** 2 servings
SERVING SIZE: 1 cup broccoli; ¼ cup sauce

Calories: 220.28 kcal Total fiber: 2.44 g Soluble fiber: 0.27 g Protein: 7.00 g Total fat: 13.37 g Saturated fat: 2.43 g Healthy fats: 10.47 g
Carbohydrates: 18.96 g Sugars: 13.41 g Added sugars: 0 g Sodium: 562.73 mg Potassium: 267.79 mg Magnesium: 36.10 mg Calcium: 38.48 mg

Broccoli is the favorite vegetable of all three of us. As a When Way yes food, it's also great for preventing cancer if you have a family history. So it's good to have a supply of broccoli recipes in your arsenal. This recipe uses ginger (great for treating nausea) in the tahini satay sauce, which can be frozen up to three months and used again for another day or with other healthy veggies.

1 cup water

½ cup (firmly packed; 3 ounces) golden raisins

1½ cups low-sodium vegetable broth, divided

6 tablespoons creamy all-natural peanut butter (made only with peanuts and salt)

4 tablespoons tahini (stir to blend if separated)

4 tablespoons balsamic vinegar

2½ tablespoons low-sodium, gluten-free tamari

2 or 3 teaspoons sambal oelek chili paste, depending on taste

2 teaspoons fresh ginger, peeled, finely chopped

2 cups (5 to 6 ounces) broccoli florets, cut into 1- to 1½-inch pieces

1. In a small saucepan, bring the water and raisins to a boil. Reduce to medium-low heat and simmer until the raisins are very soft, 12 to 14 minutes. Cover and set aside 15 minutes.

2. Drain the raisins well, and place them in a blender. Add 1¼ cups broth, peanut butter, tahini, vinegar, tamari, chili paste to taste (less for more mild flavors, more for spicier flavors), and ginger. Blend until the sauce is smooth, about 2 minutes. If desired, thin the sauce with more broth by tablespoonfuls. Reserve ½ cup of the sauce in a small bowl. Cool, cover, and refrigerate or freeze the remaining sauce (up to 4 days in the fridge; 3 months in the freezer).

3. Bring a medium saucepan of water to boil over high heat. Add the broccoli and cook until just crisp-tender, 3 minutes. Drain the broccoli well. Lay florets on a plate, blot with paper towels, and allow to cool 10 minutes.

4. Stir the ½ cup reserved sauce in a medium skillet over medium heat until bubbles form at the edges. Add the broccoli; toss until the broccoli is well coated and heated through, 1 to 2 minutes. Transfer the broccoli to plates.

―What to *Know* When―――――――――――

This sauce needs to be reheated slowly at a low temperature because of the peanut butter and tahini. High temperatures and overheating will reduce the sauce too quickly, making it overly thick and stiff.

ANYTIME CAULIFLOWER RISSOLE

PREP: 20 minutes   COOK: 25 minutes   MAKES: 4 servings   SERVING SIZE: 1 cup

Calories: 318.3 kcal Total fiber: 11.6 g Soluble fiber: 11.6 g Protein: 12.8 g Total fat: 18.9 g Saturated fat: 2.1 g Healthy fats: 16 g
Carbohydrates: 29.6 g Sugars: 10.9 g Added sugars: 0 g Sodium: 337 mg Potassium: 134 mg Magnesium: 35 mg Calcium: 132 mg

The ascension of cauliflower as an alternative to potatoes has been impressive. Chef Jim's recipe doesn't mash it, rice it, or turn it into a pizza crust. Instead, it showcases centuries-old aromatic and enticing spices, chewy toasted walnuts, and umami from reduced tomato in an amazing dish that is great warm or cold.

1 tablespoon garam masala

1 teaspoon ground cumin

½ teaspoon chili powder

½ teaspoon ground turmeric

Pinch of cayenne pepper

2 tablespoons extra-virgin olive oil

1 head cauliflower (about 2 pounds), trimmed, cut into small florets

¼ teaspoon kosher salt

1½ cups vegetable broth

3 tablespoons tomato paste

1 tablespoon almond butter

½ cup (about 2 ounces) walnuts, toasted, coarsely ground

1. In a small bowl, combine the first 5 ingredients and set aside.

2. In a large skillet over medium heat, swirl the oil to cover the bottom, then add the cauliflower and toss. Sprinkle with salt and mix well. Continue to toss and stir frequently until the cauliflower florets become golden brown and crisp-tender, 15 to 18 minutes. Transfer the cauliflower to a medium bowl and set aside.

3. To the hot skillet, add the reserved spices, stir until lightly toasted, 5 seconds, then quickly add the vegetable broth and whisk to blend. Add the tomato paste and whisk until incorporated and smooth. Add the almond butter and whisk until smooth. Return the cauliflower to the skillet and toss until all the florets are well coated. Add the walnuts and toss to coat.

4. Allow the cauliflower mixture to cool 10 minutes, then transfer to a bowl and serve.

—What to *Know* When—

Organic vegetable broth from a carton often contains some salt so do not add any more than the ¼ teaspoon salt called for in the recipe. The tomato paste also has some salt.

SLOW-COOKED POLE BEANS

PREP: 25–30 minutes   **COOK:** 1½ hours   **MAKES:** 4 servings   **SERVING SIZE:** ½ cup

Calories: 271 kcal Total fiber: 9.5 g Soluble fiber: 0.2 g Protein: 4.2 g Total fat: 14.1 g Saturated fat: 1.9 g Healthy fats: 12.1 g
Carbohydrates: 28.8 g Sugars: 11.8 g Added sugars: 0 g Sodium: 206 mg Potassium: 121 mg Magnesium: 10 mg Calcium: 100 mg

Usually we favor lightly cooking vegetables, but on occasion we like to cook them to death. What do we mean by that? Cooking pole beans (romano beans, green beans, or yellow wax beans) slow and low until they melt. You should eat green beans when you want extra energy or after a workout to build muscle; a cup and a half contain almost 30 percent of your daily protein requirement.

¼ cup extra-virgin olive oil

4 small spring onions (about 3 cups whites and greens), chopped, or 1 cup shallots (about 2 very large) or leeks, chopped

6 large garlic cloves, coarsely chopped

1 bunch small carrots (about 10; reserve any tops for Carrot Top Pesto, page 73), scrubbed

3 large carrots, peeled, cut into medium-size pieces

1½ pounds romano beans, green beans, or yellow wax beans, or a mixture, stem ends trimmed

⅓ cup dry white wine

¾ teaspoon kosher salt

½ teaspoon freshly ground black pepper

1 to 2 tablespoons fresh lemon juice

¼ cup fresh basil, chopped

1. In a heavy Dutch oven (preferably enameled cast iron), heat the olive oil on medium. Add the onions and garlic, and sauté until soft, 3 to 5 minutes.

2. Add the carrots, then beans, and wine. Season with salt and pepper. Cover the pot; reduce to medium-low heat and cook until the beans are meltingly tender, stirring frequently to make sure they are not browning or sticking to the bottom of the pot, about 1½ hours. The ingredients should be gently cooking. If the mixture becomes dry, add water by ¼ cupfuls to moisten and prevent sticking.

3. Taste the bean mixture and season with lemon juice and additional salt and pepper, if desired. Transfer to a serving dish. Sprinkle with basil and serve.

HARISSA VEGETABLE RAGOUT WITH LEMON-SCENTED MILLET

PREP: 40 minutes   COOK: 40 minutes   MAKES: 4 servings
SERVING SIZE: 1½ cups ragout; 2⅛ cups with millet

Calories: 378 kcal Total fiber: 14.8 g Soluble fiber: 10.9 g Protein: 14.6 g Total fat: 3.5 g Saturated fat: 0.5 g Healthy fats: 1.6 g
Carbohydrates: 75 g Sugars: 15.4 g Added sugars: 0 g Sodium: 878 mg Potassium: 508 mg Magnesium: 97 mg Calcium: 68 mg

Here's a complex-flavored ragout that will leave you satisfied and forgetting all about meat. The harissa marries perfectly with creamy lima beans, fire-roasted tomatoes, and mellow green beans. Make this in the evening, store in the fridge overnight, then eat it for breakfast the next day. The majority of these vegetables are great for combating inflammation.

2 cups water or low-sodium vegetable broth

2 teaspoons lemon peel, finely grated

1 cup (6½ ounces) millet

4 tablespoons extra-virgin olive oil, divided

2 cups onions, cut into ⅓-inch dice

¼ teaspoon kosher salt, divided

¼ teaspoon freshly ground black pepper, divided

1½ cups orange bell pepper, cut into 1½- x ¼-inch strips

3 large cloves garlic, finely chopped

2 cups fire-roasted canned crushed tomatoes

⅔ cup (5½ ounces) tomato juice

2 teaspoons Harissa Spice Blend (page 71)

¼ teaspoon red chili flakes, finely chopped

1 cup green beans, cut into 1-inch pieces, cooked 3 minutes

1 cup slender asparagus stalks, cut into 1-inch pieces, cooked 2 minutes

1 cup (5 ounces) frozen baby lima beans, thawed, blanched 6 minutes

¼ cup (2½ ounces) roasted red pepper from a jar, cut into ⅓-inch dice

2 tablespoons fresh Italian parsley, chopped

1 tablespoon thin fresh basil strips, cut into small dice, plus sprigs

1. Bring the broth or water and lemon peel to a simmer in a medium saucepan over medium heat. Add millet; swirl pan to distribute. Reduce heat to low. Partially cover pan, leaving the lid ⅓ inch ajar. Cook gently until the liquid is absorbed, 18 to 20 minutes. Remove from the heat. Cover fully and let the millet stand 10 minutes.

2. Meanwhile, heat two tablespoons oil in a large skillet over medium heat. Add the onions, and half the salt and pepper. Sauté until the onions are translucent, stirring often, 8 to 10 minutes. Add the bell pepper; sauté until just tender, 6 to 8 minutes. Push the vegetable mixture to one side. Add 1 tablespoon oil and garlic to the other side. Stir until the garlic is fragrant, 30 to 60 seconds. Add crushed tomatoes, tomato juice, harissa, and chili flakes; stir to blend. Add the green beans, asparagus, lima beans, and roasted red pepper. Reduce to low heat. Cook until the ragout is heated through, stirring occasionally, 2 to 3 minutes. Turn off the heat; let stand.

3. In another large skillet on medium-high, heat the remaining 1 table-spoon oil until the oil just begins to shimmer. Add 3 cups of the cooked millet, parsley, and 1 tablespoon diced basil. Toss to rewarm millet and blend, about 2 minutes.

4. Spoon ¾ cup millet into each of four shallow bowls, making a well in the center. Mound 1½ cups ragout into each well. Garnish with basil sprigs.

What to *Swap* When

If you don't have millet on hand, you can also make this ragout with other 100% whole grains like quinoa, farro, or sorghum. It also makes for a great pasta sauce over whole grain noodles. Or try it served with our Lentil Dumplings (page 154).

TSO GOOD BROCCOLI

PREP: 20–25 minutes   **COOK: 10 minutes**   **MAKES: 4 servings**   **SERVING SIZE: 1 cup**

Calories: 88 kcal Total fiber: 0.6 g Soluble fiber: 0 g Protein: 1.2 g Total fat: 4 g Saturated fat: 0.6 g Healthy fats: 3 g
Carbohydrates: 11 g Sugars: 3.1 g Added sugars: 3.8 g Sodium: 534 mg Potassium: 26 mg Magnesium: 2 mg Calcium: 8 mg

This is an example of Chef Jim revising a traditional Chinese "General Tso Sauce" to have less sodium, sugar, and fat. He combines it with our favorite vegetable, broccoli. It is especially filling and a rock star ingredient for cancer prevention.

Water

4 cups (lightly packed) broccoli florets (1½-inch pieces) and stalks (¼-inch slices on the diagonal)

1½ teaspoons toasted sesame oil

1 large garlic clove, finely chopped

1½ teaspoons fresh ginger, peeled, finely chopped

½ cup low-sodium vegetable broth

¼ cup white grape juice

1½ tablespoons Raisin Reduction (page 69)

1½ tablespoons low-sodium gluten-free tamari

1½ teaspoons apple cider vinegar

1 teaspoon sambal oelek chili paste

½ teaspoon tomato paste

1½ teaspoons cornstarch

Pinch of freshly ground black pepper

1. Bring a large pot of water to a boil. Once water is boiling, reduce to a simmer and add the broccoli florets and stalks; blanch until al dente, about 2 to 3 minutes. Strain the broccoli in a colander, then place on paper towels or a kitchen towel to absorb moisture and cool. (The drier the broccoli, the better to absorb the Tso Good sauce flavors.)

2. Meanwhile, in a 4-quart saucepan, add sesame oil, garlic, and ginger. Cook on medium heat until garlic becomes aromatic, about 1 minute. Add vegetable broth, grape juice, Raisin Reduction, tamari, apple cider vinegar, chili paste, and tomato paste. Stir until mixed well and bring to a simmer.

3. Combine cornstarch with 2 teaspoons cold water and mix with a clean fingertip to create a smooth lump-free slurry. Whisk slurry slowly into simmering sauce. Turn off heat and set aside.

4. When broccoli is dry, pour the Tso Good sauce into a 12-inch skillet. Warm on medium heat until just beginning to bubble on the sides of the pan. Add the broccoli and toss until well coated and warmed through.

—**What to *Know* When**—

Keeping the broccoli as dry as possible is important for stir-fries, where extra moisture from the florets can thin the sauce. Don't skip drying your florets on paper towels or kitchen towels. And don't shock the broccoli in cold water after it's blanched, which can lead to more water absorption. Let it cool in the air instead.

WHEN WAY BAKED BEANS

PREP: **40 minutes, plus overnight soaking**   COOK: **30–35 minutes**   MAKES: **6 servings**
SERVING SIZE: **1 cup**

Calories: 121 kcal Total fiber: 5.2 g Soluble fiber: 0.1 g Protein: 8 g Total fat: 4 g Saturated fat: 0.5 g Healthy fats: 3.1 g
Carbohydrates: 14.9 g Sugars: 2.5 g Added sugars: 0 g Sodium: 1096 mg Potassium: 339 mg Magnesium: 33 mg Calcium: 142 mg

Beans are a wonderful love-you-back When Way food, but they lose their benefits when they're coated in pork fat and sugar, like in typical baked beans. Our take on the classic dish is loaded with as much flavor, but skips the unhealthy ingredients. Spoon a plate of this for lunch or a breakfast prepared the night before. In this particular recipe, we use flageolet beans, which are a mild and creamy small French bean. You can also try this with navy beans or black-eyed peas.

Soaking Beans

4 cups water

1 cup dried flageolet beans (about 6.4 ounces)

1 tablespoon kosher salt

Precooking Beans

4 cups water

2 dried bay leaves

1 teaspoon kosher salt

Vegetable Sauté

2 tablespoons extra-virgin olive oil, plus additional for drizzling

2 celery stalks (about 1⅓ cups), cut into ⅓-inch dice

1 large carrot (about 1 cup), cut into ⅓-inch dice

½ large fennel bulb (about 1½ cups), cut into ⅓-inch dice

½ large leek (about 1 cup), cut crosswise into thin strips

3 large garlic cloves, minced

Kosher salt

Freshly ground black pepper

16 cherry tomatoes, quartered

1 cup plain Greek yogurt (2%)

½ cup (packed; about 10 very large leaves) fresh basil, thinly sliced, plus additional for garnish

½ cup fresh whole grain breadcrumbs (about 1 large bread slice)

1. Combine 4 cups water, beans, and 1 tablespoon salt in a heavy large pot. Cover and let soak overnight.

2. Drain and rinse the beans and return to the same pot. Add 4 cups fresh water, bay leaves and 1 teaspoon salt. Bring to a boil. Reduce heat and simmer until the beans are tender, about 30 minutes (cooking time may vary based on beans). Drain the beans and reserve.

3. Preheat the oven to 350°F. Heat 2 tablespoons olive oil in a large skillet on medium. Add the celery, carrot, fennel, and leek, and sauté until the vegetables are tender and lightly brown, 12 to 15 minutes. Add the garlic and stir 2 to 3 minutes. Remove from the heat. Season to taste with salt and pepper.

4. Meanwhile, in a small bowl combine the tomatoes with ¼ teaspoon salt; let stand 10 minutes.

5. In a large bowl combine the beans, cooked vegetables, tomatoes, yogurt, and ½ cup basil. Gently stir until well combined. Transfer to an 11-by-7-inch or a 13-by-9-inch oval or rectangular baking dish. Sprinkle the breadcrumbs over and drizzle with a little olive oil (about 2 tablespoons). Bake until the vegetables are heated through, the juices are starting to lightly bubble, and the top is crisp. Serve warm with basil garnish.

Sautéed Beet Greens
(page 169)

Naturally Sweet Roasted Beets (page 168)

Pickled Beet Stems (page 169)

NATURALLY SWEET ROASTED BEETS

PREP: **25 minutes**   COOK: **25–35 minutes**   MAKES: **4 servings**   SERVING SIZE: **½ cup**

Calories: 94 kcal Total fiber: 1.9 g Soluble fiber: 0.5 g Protein: 1.2 g Total fat: 7.1 g Saturated fat: 1 g Healthy fats: 6.1 g
Carbohydrates: 7 g Sugars: 4.2 g Added sugars: 0 g Sodium: 170 mg Potassium: 219 mg Magnesium: 16 mg Calcium: 17 mg

These beets are great in a salad (see our kale version on page 187), as an antipasto, or on sandwiches for great texture and considerable health benefits: Beets are rich in the precursors to nitric oxide, which helps your arteries dilate and feed your organs.

2 tablespoons extra-virgin olive oil

3 large garlic cloves, minced

1½ tablespoons fresh Italian parsley, chopped, divided

1 teaspoon fresh ginger, peeled, minced

¼ teaspoon kosher salt

¼ teaspoon freshly ground black pepper

3 very large beets (about 1⅓ pounds without stems and leaves), peeled, halved lengthwise, cut crosswise into ⅛-inch-thick slices

1. Preheat the oven to 350°F. In a medium bowl, whisk the olive oil, garlic, 1 tablespoon parsley, ginger, salt, and pepper. Smash the garlic in the bowl to increase infusion of flavors. Add the beets and toss until well coated.

2. Spread the beets in a single layer on a rimmed nonstick baking sheet. Bake until the beet slices are fork tender, stirring once or twice, 25 to 35 minutes (beet slices will shrink while roasting).

3. Transfer the beets to a platter. Sprinkle with the remaining ½ tablespoon parsley and serve.

 **What to *Know* When**

Cutting beets in half first will make them more manageable to slice; you can slice by hand with a chef's knife, on a box grater, or with a mandoline.

PICKLED BEET STEMS

PREP: **15 minutes**   COOK: **None**   MAKES: **3 servings**   SERVING SIZE: **¼ cup**

Calories: 115 kcal Total fiber: 3.6 g Soluble fiber: 0.9 g Protein: 2.2 g Total fat: 0.3 g Saturated fat: 0.1 g Healthy fats: 0.1 g
Carbohydrates: 28.7 g Sugars: 14.2 g Added sugars: 0 g Sodium: 618 mg Potassium: 446 mg Magnesium: 30 mg Calcium: 25 mg

After buying a bunch of fresh beets, try to use the whole vegetable—root to stem. These pickled stems are a healthy addition to salads because they are loaded with great-for-you amino acids, phytonutrients, and minerals (they add loads of crunch, texture, and flavor, too).

¼ cup apple cider vinegar

1 tablespoon fresh ginger, peeled, cut into 1½-inch-long by ⅛-inch-wide strips

2 teaspoons Raisin Reduction (page 69)

1 teaspoon dry mustard

¼ teaspoon paprika

¼ teaspoon kosher salt

¾ cup beet stems, finely chopped into ⅛-inch dice

1. In a small bowl, combine all the ingredients except the beet stems. Whisk until well blended. Add the beet stems and stir until well coated. Cover and refrigerate for at least an hour before serving—eat within a couple days.

SAUTÉED BEET GREENS

PREP: **10 minutes**   COOK: **6–9 minutes**   MAKES: **2 servings**   SERVING SIZE: **¼ cup**

Calories: 108 kcal Total fiber: 4.3 g Soluble fiber: 0.7 g Protein: 3.9 g Total fat: 7.4 g Saturated fat: 1 g Healthy fats: 6.2 g
Carbohydrates: 9 g Sugars: 0.9 g Added sugars: 0 g Sodium: 469 mg Potassium: 132 mg Magnesium: 99 mg Calcium: 170 mg

This recipe pairs the fabulous lushness of the greens with garlic and a subtle touch of ginger, and is a good way to use an entire bunch of beets.

1 tablespoon extra-virgin olive oil

2 large garlic cloves, minced

½ teaspoon fresh ginger, peeled, minced

2 cups (packed) beet greens (from one large bunch beets), center ribs removed, very thinly sliced

⅛ teaspoon kosher salt

⅛ teaspoon freshly ground black pepper

1. In a 12-inch skillet, combine the olive oil, garlic, and ginger. Stir over medium heat until the garlic is aromatic and just begins to turn light golden, 1 to 2 minutes. Add the beet greens and toss until the garlic and ginger are mixed in to keep the garlic from overbrowning. Season with salt and pepper, and stir frequently until the greens are tender, 5 to 7 minutes.

What to *Know* When

Look for fresh beets with greens that are fresh, not limp or rusty, and vibrant in their colors.

NO-FUSS ROASTED BRUSSELS SPROUTS

PREP: 25–30 minutes   **COOK:** 35 minutes   **MAKES:** 8 servings   **SERVING SIZE:** ½ cup

Calories: 83 kcal Total fiber: 4.4 g Soluble fiber: 2.3 g Protein: 4 g Total fat: 4 g Saturated fat: 0.5 g Healthy fats: 3.2g
Carbohydrates: 10.7 g Sugars: 2.5 g Added sugars: 0 g Sodium: 209 mg Potassium: 446 mg Magnesium: 26 mg Calcium: 50 mg

We've had roasted brussels sprouts many ways, and less is more in our opinion. We find more enjoyment from simple preparations where the naturally occurring nutty flavor of the sprouts is the star of the show. This simple preparation is one the whole family will enjoy. For the best texture, be sure to score the core of this cabbage-like vegetable so it cooks evenly with the leafy part.

2 pounds medium brussels sprouts

2 tablespoons extra-virgin olive oil

3 large garlic cloves, finely chopped

¾ teaspoon kosher salt

¼ teaspoon freshly ground black pepper

1 teaspoon paprika

1. Preheat the oven to 350°F. Clean and trim the brussels sprouts by pulling off any ragged outer leaves, then cut a thin slice off the bottom of each. Cut the brussels sprouts lengthwise in half. Carefully score the length of the core only with the tip of small knife.

2. In a large mixing bowl, combine the olive oil, garlic, salt, and pepper. Add the brussels sprouts and toss until well coated. Spread them evenly on a large rimmed baking sheet (preferably nonstick). Sprinkle evenly with paprika. Bake until the brussels sprouts are fork tender, about 35 minutes.

What to *Eat* When

Like all cruciferous veggies, brussels sprouts are loaded with sulfur-containing compounds that have been linked to prostate health and to reducing the risk of cancer in both men and women.

CREAMED CORN

PREP: 25 minutes   **COOK:** 25 minutes   **MAKES:** 4 servings   **SERVING SIZE:** 2 cups

Calories: 270 kcal Total fiber: 4.2 g Soluble fiber: 0 g Protein: 5.2 g Total fat: 15 g Saturated fat: 2 g Healthy fats: 12 g
Carbohydrates: 34 g Sugars: 5.4 g Added sugars: 0 g Sodium: 255 mg Potassium: 22 mg Magnesium: 5 mg Calcium: 14 mg

When you think of creamed corn, you probably picture the sugary substance found in a can. Our take is the exact opposite. It's made with gently cooked fresh corn right off of the cob, and skips any butter, heavy cream, or added sugar. This simple recipe is great as a summer side or served under a piece of fish.

4 large ears corn

4 cups water

¼ cup extra-virgin olive oil

¼ cup chopped red onion

½ teaspoon kosher salt

⅛ teaspoon freshly ground black pepper

¼ cup fresh herbs, like basil and/or mint, finely chopped

1. Set a box grater on a large plate. Using the large holes of the box grater, grate the corn kernels off the cobs. (You want to shred the corn and collect it along with its liquid. You should have about 2 cups.)

2. Break the four bare corncobs in half and place in a 4-quart pot with enough water to cover. Bring the water to a boil, then turn off the heat and let the cobs soak for 10 to 15 minutes to make corn broth.

3. When a 10-inch skillet over medium heat is hot, add the olive oil, then the onion. Sauté until the onion is soft, about 5 minutes. Add the reserved corn with any corn liquid, plus ¼ cup corn broth to the skillet. Cook until the corn is softened and the mixture thickens, stirring occasionally, 5 to 6 minutes (the corn should still have some bite). If the mixture gets too thick, add a little more corn broth. Season with salt and pepper. Stir in the chopped herbs and serve.

CHAPTER SIX

SOUPS & SALADS

SUGAR SNAP PEA & AVOCADO SOUP

PREP: 25–30 minutes   **COOK:** 5 minutes   **MAKES:** 4 Servings   **SERVING SIZE:** 1¼ cups

Calories: 365 kcal Total fiber: 6 g Soluble fiber: 0 g Protein: 4.6 g Total fat: 31.7 g Saturated fat: 4.5 g Healthy fats: 27 g
Carbohydrates: 14.7 g Sugars: 6.2 g Added sugars: 0 g Sodium: 281 mg Potassium: 14 mg Magnesium: 20 mg Calcium: 120 mg

Snap peas are nutritious, delicious, and only available for a short time. Dr. C loves to use them in a variety of ways, like in this recipe, which can be as simple or as extravagant as you like. Serve this soup hot or cold, as is, or made more luxurious topped with mint oil and crab, which usually doesn't increase inflammatory trimethylamine N-oxide production.

4 quarts water

Kosher salt

Mint Oil

½ cup extra-virgin olive oil

1 bunch fresh mint (about 1 ounce; peppermint preferred)

Soup

1½ pounds sugar snap peas, strings removed

½ avocado, peeled, diced

Ice cubes

Freshly ground black pepper

Jumbo lump crab (optional)

1. In a large pot, bring 4 quarts water to a boil and season to make it salty like the sea.

2. *For the mint oil:* Fill a medium bowl with cold water; set aside. Remove the mint leaves from the sprigs, add them to the boiling water, and blanch for 10 seconds. Using a slotted spoon or spider, transfer the mint leaves to a bowl of cold water to cool. Drain, then spin the leaves dry. (Keep the pot of water boiling.)

3. Blend the mint and olive oil on high speed until only tiny flecks of mint remain. Transfer the mint oil to a small bowl and reserve.

4. *For the soup:* Add the trimmed snap peas to the boiling water and cook 2 minutes. Using a slotted spoon or a spider, transfer the snap peas to a colander. Run cold water over the snap peas to cool.

5. Chop 8 snap peas and set aside. Add the remaining snap peas to a high-speed blender. Add 1 cup cold water plus a few ice cubes, and puree. Add more ice cubes as needed for a smooth puree. Add the diced avocado and puree until as smooth as possible. Season the soup to taste with salt and pepper.

6. In a medium saucepan, warm the pea soup until just warm. In another saucepan, warm the crab, if using.

7. Ladle the soup into bowls. Add the reserved chopped snap peas to the bowls. Place the crab in the center of each bowl. Spoon the mint oil off the top (the mint should have settled to the bottom) and lightly drizzle over each serving.

What to *Know* When

Make sure you puree the soup with ice, not water. You don't want to "cook" the puree more in the blender and darken the beautiful green color.

ROASTED WHOLE GRAIN PANZANELLA SALAD

PREP: 45–50 minutes   **COOK:** 45 minutes   **MAKES:** 6 servings   **SERVING SIZE:** 1⅓ cups

Calories: 276 kcal **Total fiber:** 11.4 g **Soluble fiber:** 0 g **Protein:** 7.6 g **Total fat:** 13.7 g **Saturated fat:** 1.8 g **Healthy fats:** 10.3 g **Carbohydrates:** 36.1 g **Sugars:** 8.6 g **Added sugars:** 0 g **Sodium:** 415 mg **Potassium:** 389 mg **Magnesium:** 95 mg **Calcium:** 238 mg

This is a When *In Season* recipe—only make this salad when you can pick fresh tomatoes from your garden or the farmers market. Wonderful varieties, such as plum, heirloom, and "Sun Gold Cherry," are supersweet. Roasting them with harissa will intensify flavors, and combining them with whole grain bread and chia seeds will add fiber, protein, and nutrients.

4 cups (6 to 7 ounces) whole grain bread, cut into 1-inch cubes

4 cups (20 ounces; 2 pints) cherry or grape tomatoes

4 tablespoons extra-virgin olive oil, divided

¾ teaspoon freshly ground black pepper, divided

½ teaspoon Harissa Spice Blend (page 71)

3½ tablespoons red wine vinegar (5% acid)

1 tablespoon Raisin Reduction (page 69)

5 canned anchovies, mashed to paste (about 2 teaspoons)

1 teaspoon white chia seeds

1 teaspoon garlic, finely chopped

½ to ¾ teaspoon kosher salt

½ teaspoon Dijon mustard (preferably whole grain)

4 cups (about 20 ounces) plum tomatoes, cut into ½-inch dice

1½ cups cucumber (5-inch), peeled, quartered, seeded, thinly sliced

½ cup red onion, thinly sliced

1½ cups (firmly packed; about 2 ounces) baby wild arugula

1½ cups (firmly packed; about 2 ounces) watercress tops or leaves

1 cup fresh basil leaves, cut into thin strips, then small dice

¼ cup (1 ounce) raw unsalted pepitas (pumpkin seeds)

1. Preheat oven to 350° degrees. Spray a large rimmed baking sheet with nonstick coating. Scatter the bread on the prepared sheet. Bake until the croutons are crisp, firm, and lightly colored, 12 to 14 minutes. Transfer to a plate and cool.

2. In a medium bowl, combine the tomatoes with 2 teaspoons oil, ¼ teaspoon pepper, and Harissa Spice Blend; toss to coat evenly. Scrape the tomatoes with their seasonings onto the same baking sheet. Roast the tomatoes until soft, wrinkled, and perhaps with split skin, about 30 minutes.

3. Meanwhile, in a large (4- to 6-quart or larger) bowl, combine the vinegar, Raisin Reduction, anchovy paste, chia seeds, garlic, salt, mustard, and remaining ½ teaspoon pepper. Gradually add the remaining oil, whisking until the dressing is well blended.

4. Stir the hot roasted tomatoes into the dressing. Cool 15 minutes. Add the diced tomatoes, cucumber, and red onion; toss to blend. Mix in the arugula, watercress, basil, and pepitas, then the croutons.

5. Serve immediately so croutons remain crisp.

What to *Know* When

Use day-old 100% whole grain bread to make croutons, or set fresh cubed bread out to dry the day before baking.

SNAP PEA SALAD

PREP: **30 minutes**   COOK: **2 minutes**   MAKES: **4 servings**   SERVING SIZE: **1 cup**

Calories: 117 kcal Total fiber: 3.0 g Soluble fiber: 0.02 g Protein: 2.9 g Total fat: 7.4 g Saturated fat: 1 g Healthy fats: 6 g
Carbohydrates: 9 g Sugars: 4.2 g Added sugars: 0 g Sodium: 158 mg Potassium: 14 mg Magnesium: 11 mg Calcium: 97 mg

Sugar snap peas are a delicious sign of late spring. When at their peak, these tender pods should be available at your local farmers market. Look for ones that are bright green, not too fat, and unscarred. You can eat them raw, but their flavor and color are enhanced by a quick blanch. Save this recipe only for the spring: We don't recommend buying sugar snap peas out of season because they can be too tough to enjoy with this simple preparation.

1 pound sugar snap peas

4 quarts water

Kosher salt

2 tablespoons fresh lemon juice

2 tablespoons extra-virgin olive oil

1 teaspoon poppy seeds (optional)

⅛ teaspoon crushed red pepper flakes

2 tablespoons fresh mint, finely chopped

Freshly ground black pepper

1 teaspoon lemon zest, finely grated

Pecorino cheese, finely grated (optional)

1. Bring a large pot of water to a boil. Add enough salt to the boiling water to make it salty like the sea.

2. Meanwhile, remove the strings from the snap peas by pulling the pointy ends toward the inside curve of each snap pea.

3. Add the snap peas to the boiling water and cook 2 minutes. Using a slotted spoon or spider, transfer the snap peas to a colander. Rinse with cold water to cool. Set aside to dry for a few minutes.

4. Using a sharp knife, thinly slice the snap peas on a deep diagonal. Transfer to a medium bowl.

5. In a small bowl, whisk the lemon juice, olive oil, poppy seeds (if using), and crushed red pepper until the dressing is emulsified.

6. Pour the dressing over the snap peas and toss to coat. Season to taste with salt and pepper. Sprinkle with the lemon zest, mint, and the pecorino cheese, if using, and serve as soon as it is prepared—it should be served bright green.

What to *Know* When

If you're following the When Way to a tee, skip adding the pecorino cheese; this salad tastes delicious without it. But if you've gone a quarter or two without the stuff, you can make it a special day and grate a bit of well-aged pecorino on top.

"ADDICTIVE" QUINOA SALAD

PREP: 30–45 minutes   **COOK: 35 minutes**   **MAKES: 9–10 servings**   **SERVING SIZE: 1 cup**

Calories: 240 kcal Total fiber: 7.8 g Soluble fiber: 0.8 g Protein: 9.1 g Total fat: 7.8 g Saturated fat: 1.1 g Healthy fats: 6 g
Carbohydrates: 35 g Sugars: 6.9 g Added sugars: 0 g Sodium: 286 mg Potassium: 520 mg Magnesium: 87 mg Calcium: 62 mg

We prefer this flavorful salad as a late meal choice, in that 5 to 7 p.m. window—your last for eating before the sun goes down. It has enough fiber and protein to keep you satisfied till the next a.m.—eat it even earlier in the evening the next day for a longer window of intermittent fasting. This dish is the perfect balance of sweet and spicy, with a great contrast of heat from the sambal chili paste and the earthy sweetness of currants.

2 cups low-sodium vegetable broth

1 cup tricolor quinoa (6½ ounces), rinsed, drained

1 teaspoon sambal oelek chili paste

4 teaspoons toasted sesame oil, divided

1 cup onion, cut into ¼-inch dice

1 cup carrot, cut into ¼-inch dice

1 cup red bell pepper, cut into ¼-inch dice

2 cloves garlic, finely chopped

½ teaspoon ground cumin

½ teaspoon ground cinnamon

½ teaspoon kosher salt

¼ teaspoon ground turmeric

¼ teaspoon ground ginger

⅛ teaspoon freshly ground black pepper

1 cup cucumber, seeded, peeled, cut into ¼-inch dice

1 cup (about 5 ounces) green bean pieces, cut into ⅓-inch dice, blanched 5 minutes

¼ cup currants, dark raisins, or figs

1 cup (5½ ounces) grape tomatoes, each quartered, then halved

¼ cup (1 ounce) raw unsalted pepitas (pumpkin seeds)

½ cup watercress, chiffonade

1. Bring the broth, quinoa, and chili paste to a simmer in a medium saucepan over medium-high heat, stirring occasionally. Reduce to low heat. Cover and cook the quinoa 15 minutes. Turn off the heat. Let the quinoa sit, covered, 20 minutes.

2. Meanwhile, heat 3 teaspoons oil in a large skillet over medium-low. Add onion, carrots, and bell pepper. Sauté until the vegetables are just tender, stirring occasionally, about 18 minutes. Push the vegetables to one side. Add the remaining one teaspoon oil to the other side. Add garlic and stir until the garlic is fragrant, 30 to 60 seconds; stir into the vegetables. Add cumin, cinnamon, salt, turmeric, ginger, and pepper; blend well. Sauté until the vegetables are completely tender, 2 to 3 minutes longer. Add cucumber, green beans, and currants. Stir gently for 2 minutes to blend the flavors.

3. Remove the skillet from the heat. Mix in the tomatoes and pepitas, then the quinoa. Garnish with ½ tablespoon watercress.

4. Serve warm, at room temperature, or refrigerate and serve cold.

What to *Know* When

This dish is a natural for a party or as a hostess gift. It's delicious and can be served either as a side or main. It is a great way to introduce party guests to the When Way of eating—shared only when the sun is up.

CUCUMBER & SQUASH SALAD

PREP: 15 minutes   **COOK:** None   **MAKES:** 4 servings   **SERVING SIZE:** 1 cup

Calories: 84 kcal Total fiber: 5 g Soluble fiber: 0.2 g Protein: 5.6 g Total fat: 0.7 g Saturated fat: 0.2 g Healthy fats: 0.2 g
Carbohydrates: 16.7 g Sugars: 10.9 g Added sugars: 0 g Sodium: 136 mg Potassium: 537 mg Magnesium: 37 mg Calcium: 96 mg

We're used to eating cumbers raw, but not usually squash. In this salad (it's great for dinner), we treat our fresh vegetables the same and think you'll be pleasantly surprised by the results. The farmers market often has interesting varieties of squash and cucumbers, and we recommend trying them all, especially yellow squash that makes this dish more colorful. Squash is rich in calcium and potassium, great for your nervous system, and low in calories.

4 small or 2 large cucumbers

4 small or 2 large zucchini or
     summer squash

Kosher salt

Red pepper flakes, to taste

1 garlic clove

1 lemon, juiced

2 tablespoons chopped fresh mint

1. Cut the cucumbers in half and remove the seeds with a spoon. Then cut each half in half again on a slight angle into ⅛-inch pieces.

2. Cut the squash the same way, but don't worry about removing the seeds.

3. Place the cut cucumbers and squash in a bowl, and season with salt and red pepper flakes to taste. Let sit for at least an hour and up to four in the refrigerator. Stir occasionally. A lot of liquid will accumulate in the bowl.

4. Rub a serving bowl with the clove of garlic. Slice the garlic finely, then place it in a small bowl with the lemon juice and let sit for 15 minutes.

5. Drain the cucumbers and squash from the liquid. Place in the seasoned bowl and toss with the lemon-garlic mixture and mint.

HEIRLOOM TOMATO & PEACH SALAD

PREP: 15 minutes   COOK: None   MAKES: **8 servings**   SERVING SIZE: **1¼ cups**

Calories: 103 kcal Total fiber: 2.9 g Soluble fiber: 0 g Protein: 1.9 g Total fat: 4.1 g Saturated fat: 0.5 g Healthy fats: 3.2 g
Carbohydrates: 33.6 g Sugars: 13.6 g Added sugars: 0 g Sodium: 67 mg Potassium: 452 mg Magnesium: 14 mg Calcium: 15 mg

Tomatoes and peaches often come into season at about the same time, and it turns out they go very well together. Here we marinate peaches with a little vinegar and Urfa chili to create a sweet, sour, and spicy flavor combination, great for taste and health. This makes for a simple When Way dinner, low on calories, but filling enough to keep you going after the sun sets.

2 pounds large peaches, rubbed dry to de-fuzz

2 tablespoons white balsamic vinegar (6% acid)

½ teaspoon dried Urfa pepper flakes

½ teaspoon kosher salt, divided

2 pounds heirloom tomatoes of various colors

2 tablespoons extra-virgin olive oil

2 tablespoons tiny basil leaves (from a sprig's center)

1. Cut each peach in half. Remove the pit. Cut each half into 4 wedges, then cut wedges in half crosswise, making 8 chunks. Place the peaches in a large bowl. Stir vinegar, pepper, and ¼ teaspoon salt in a small bowl to dissolve the salt. Add to the peaches and toss to coat. Let marinate 30 minutes, tossing occasionally.

2. Meanwhile, core the tomatoes. Cut each into ¾-inch wedges. If tomatoes are very large, cut in half horizontally and cut each round into wedges (like cutting a pizza). Place tomatoes in another bowl. Toss with ¼ teaspoon salt.

3. Add the tomatoes, oil, and most basil leaves to the peaches and blend. Sprinkle with the remaining basil.

—**What to *Swap* When**—

For another dinner option, serve the marinated peaches with arugula. Dr. R loves to serve this salad as dinner when vacationing in a warm spot in the winter.

KALE, AVOCADO & TOMATO SALAD

PREP: 30 minutes   **COOK: None**   **MAKES: 2 servings**   **SERVING SIZE: 2 cups salad; 2 tablespoons dressing**

Calories: 217 kcal Total fiber: 6.1 g Soluble fiber: 0.7 g Protein: 6.8 g Total fat: 12.6 g Saturated fat: 1.8 g Healthy fats: 9.7 g
Carbohydrates: 24 g Sugars: 7.2 g Added sugars: 0 g Sodium: 590 mg Potassium: 717 mg Magnesium: 54 mg Calcium: 139 mg

We hear a lot of complaints about eating raw kale. This salad will change your mind. Not only is it loaded with flavors and textures, it's also packed with calcium and potassium, as well as heart-healthy polyphenols. Unlike most unhealthy dressings, the oil in this vinaigrette comes from healthy tahini (though you can skim the oil off the top if you're going oil free). Pair this salad with salmon for a main course.

Salad

4 cups (about ½ large bunch) red or regular curly kale, center ribs and stems removed, torn

1 ripe avocado, peeled, pitted, diced

½ cup grape tomatoes, halved

½ cup red onion, thinly sliced

Blueberry, Lemon, Tahini & Balsamic Dressing

½ cup fresh blueberries

½ cup fresh lemon juice

½ cup tahini, oil drained off

½ cup balsamic vinegar (3- or 4-leaf quality)

¼ cup low-sodium, gluten-free tamari

2 garlic cloves, minced

1 teaspoon Dijon mustard

1. **For the salad:** For chewy kale, combine the kale, avocado, tomatoes, and onion in a large bowl. Add the vinaigrette and toss to coat well. For less chewy and more tender kale, massage the kale with clean hands for about 2 to 3 minutes before combining with other ingredients.

2. **For the dressing:** Combine all the ingredients in a blender and blend until smooth. The dressing will keep in the fridge for up to 2 weeks; whisk before serving.

3. Toss salad with ½ cup dressing.

─ **What to *Swap* When** ─

Instead of blueberries, you can try other fruits such as fresh figs, or even balsamic-marinated cherries.

ROASTED JALAPEÑO, BEAN & BROCCOLI SALAD

PREP: 25 minutes **COOK:** 10 minutes **MAKES:** 4 servings **SERVING SIZE:** 1 cup

Calories: 143.79 kcal Total fiber: 7 g Soluble fiber: 0.2 g Protein: 6.9 g Total fat: 7.3 g Saturated fat: 1 g Healthy fats: 6.1 g
Carbohydrates: 18.8 g Sugars: 2.9 g Added sugars: 0 g Sodium: 786 mg Potassium: 502 mg Magnesium: 15 mg Calcium: 66 mg

Beans and broccoli are filled with great protein, fiber, and key sulfur ingredients that help prevent cancer. To cut back the amount of oil in this salad, we mash part of the beans into our dressing as a thickening agent. Beans add great flavor to dressing and make it cling to the broccoli better. Pro tip: Keep the broccoli dry after blanching—it will let the dressing adhere better.

1 medium jalapeño chili pepper*

3 cups (firmly packed; from 11- to 12-ounce head) broccoli, cut into bite-size florets, including ¼-inch-thick slices of the tender stems

2 tablespoons fresh lemon juice

2 tablespoons extra-virgin olive oil

2 garlic cloves, minced

1 tablespoon fresh parsley, finely chopped

¾ teaspoon kosher salt

¼ (heaping) teaspoon freshly ground black pepper

1 can (15-ounce) great northern beans, rinsed, well drained

1. Skewer the jalapeño on the end of a long metal skewer to hold it over an open flame on the stovetop, turning occasionally to blister on all sides. (If you have an electric stove, char the jalapeños under your broiler on high.) Follow the remaining instructions for the chili preparation below. After the chili is skinless, seedless, deveined, and chopped, measure 1 teaspoon and reserve for the salad. Freeze the remaining chili for another use, such as guacamole.

2. Bring a medium saucepan of water to a boil. Add the broccoli and simmer just until crisp-tender, about 2 minutes. Drain. Transfer the broccoli to a double layer of paper towels to drain.

3. Pour the lemon juice into a medium mixing bowl. Gradually add the olive oil, whisking vigorously until well blended (dressing will not thicken/emulsify and will be rather thin). Add the jalapeño, garlic, parsley, salt and pepper; whisk to blend.

4. Using a fork, lightly mash about a third of the beans to thicken the dressing. Add the broccoli and toss to coat. Serve at room temperature.

*Chili preparation: It is best to wear vinyl or synthetic gloves, or wash hands frequently while handling chili peppers. Using a skewer and a low flame, hold the jalapeño pepper over the flame, roasting each side until a blistered skin forms. Once fully roasted and blistered, turn off flame, remove jalapeño from skewer, and wrap jalapeño in plastic for a few minutes, allowing the chili to "sweat" and cool. Remove plastic wrap, and using a small paring knife, gently scrape off all the blistered and blackened skin without rinsing (to preserve roasted pepper juice/flavor). Remove the seeds from the jalapeño and finely mince.

What to *Swap* When

Canned jalapeño chilies can be substituted if needed. But we must say, fresh jalapeños are worth the extra work—bag and freeze chopped jalapeños so you always have them on hand.

ROASTED VEGETABLE RIBOLLITA

PREP: 45 minutes **COOK: 1 hour** **MAKES: 8 servings** **SERVING SIZE: 2 cups**

Calories: 288 kcal Total fiber: 15.8 g Soluble fiber: 0.8 g Protein: 10 g Total fat: 7.7 g Saturated fat: 1.1 g Healthy fats: 6.3 g
Carbohydrates: 46.1 g Sugars: 12.2 g Added sugars: 0 g Sodium: 598 mg Potassium: 578 mg Magnesium: 59 mg Calcium: 232 mg

Ribollita is a classic Italian bread soup recipe. We roasted some of the vegetables to create that rich, umami flavor you're used to from meat. This soup is even better the next day after the flavors have a chance to intensify and marry.

2 cups (11 to 12 ounces) rutabaga, peeled, cut into ½-inch dice

1½ cups carrots (about 3 medium), peeled, cut into ½-inch dice

4 tablespoons extra-virgin olive oil, divided

½ teaspoon kosher salt

½ teaspoon freshly ground black pepper

2 cups (11 to 12 ounces) butternut squash, peeled, seeded, cut into ½-inch dice

1½ cups (1 medium, about 8 ounces) yellow onion, cut into ¼-inch dice

3 large garlic cloves, minced

1 large leek (about 1½ cups), white and light green parts only, cut into ¼-inch dice

1 cup celery (about 3 stalks), cut into ¼-inch dice

1 can (14-ounce) crushed tomatoes

1 tablespoon sherry vinegar

¾ teaspoon smoked paprika

¼ teaspoon red pepper flakes

10 cups vegetable broth

2 cans (15-ounce each) small white beans or great northern beans, rinsed and drained

2 cups packed Tuscan kale, ribs removed (about ½ bunch), coarsely chopped

4 slices stale 100% whole grain bread, coarsely chopped

1. Preheat the oven to 350°F. In a medium mixing bowl, combine the rutabaga and carrot, and add 1½ tablespoons olive oil. Toss until well coated. Season lightly with salt and pepper, and spread evenly onto an 18-by-13-inch rimmed baking sheet. Roast, stirring and turning occasionally, until vegetables are fork tender, 35 to 40 minutes.

2. In the same medium mixing bowl, combine butternut squash and ½ tablespoon olive oil. Season lightly with salt and pepper. Spread onto another rimmed baking sheet. Roast, stirring and turning occasionally, until squash is fork tender, about 30 to 40 minutes.

3. Meanwhile, heat 1 tablespoon olive oil in a heavy large pot on medium. Add the onion and sauté until golden and lightly caramelized, 12 to 15 minutes. Add the garlic; sauté until aromatic but not brown, about 1 minute. Add the remaining ½ tablespoon oil; stir in the leeks and celery, then the crushed tomatoes, vinegar, paprika, and red pepper flakes. Cook over medium-high heat, stirring frequently for about 5 minutes to cook the crushed tomatoes and to intensify flavors.

4. Add the vegetable broth to the pot, and bring to a simmer over medium-high heat. Add the roasted vegetables, reduce heat to medium, and simmer for 15 minutes.

5. Add the beans and kale, simmer 5 minutes, then add bread and simmer 5 more minutes. Taste and add more salt, pepper, and crushed red pepper, if desired. Ladle into soup bowls and serve.

WTEW VEGETABLE SOUP

PREP: 45 minutes   **COOK: 1 hour, 15 minutes**   **MAKES: 10 servings**   **SERVING SIZE: 2 cups**

Calories: 187 kcal Total fiber: 8.7 g Soluble fiber: 0.8 g Protein: 5.4 g Total fat: 1.5 g Saturated fat: 0.2 g Healthy fats: 1.2 g
Carbohydrates: 37.1 g Sugars: 12.1 g Added sugars: 0 g Sodium: 353 mg Potassium: 609 mg Magnesium: 32 mg Calcium: 114 mg

This soup is one of Chef Jim's favorites because it's loaded with rutabagas—he was raised on the vegetable and regularly fed them to his kids and grandchildren. Rutabagas add sweetness to soups unequaled by other root vegetables. Leeks are the aristocrats of the allium family, providing their own incredible flavors, but like onions, taste better when cooked before being added to the broth to release their sulfur compounds. Chia seeds add body and healthy fat, fiber, and protein to this soup. This is a hearty and satisfying winter soup that you can enjoy for several days, or make to feed a crowd.

2 teaspoons extra-virgin olive oil

2 cups (about 12 ounces) yellow onions, cut into ¼-inch dice

1 cup leek (about 1 large leek), white and light green parts only, cut into ¼-inch dice

1 cup celery (about 2 large stalks), cut into ¼-inch dice

4 quarts vegetable broth

3 cups (about 16 ounces) rutabagas, peeled, cut into ½-inch dice

11 ounces low-sodium V8 juice (two 5.5-ounce cans)

1½ cups carrots (about 2 large), peeled, cut into ¾-inch dice

2 cups (10 to 12 ounces) sweet potatoes, peeled, cut into ½-inch dice

2 cups (10 to 12 ounces) Yukon Gold potatoes, peeled, cut into ½-inch dice

1½ cups (about 7 ounces) green beans, cut into ¾-inch pieces

1 cup white turnip (about ½ large), peeled, cut into ¾-inch dice

1¼ cups (6 ounces) frozen baby lima beans

1 tablespoon chia seeds

½ teaspoon freshly ground black pepper

1¼ cups (6 ounces) frozen peas

1 teaspoon hot sauce, such as Cholula

1. In a heavy large pot or Dutch oven, heat the olive oil on medium. Add the onion and sauté until transparent, about 8 to 10 minutes. Add the leek and celery and sauté until slightly softened, about 5 minutes. Add the vegetable broth, and bring to a low boil, then add the rutabagas and simmer until just tender, about 25 minutes.

2. Add the V8 juice and carrots to the pot, and simmer until the carrots are crisp-tender, about 10 minutes. Stir in both potatoes, green beans, turnip, lima beans, chia seeds, and pepper. Simmer until the vegetables are tender, about 25 minutes. Add frozen peas and the hot sauce. Turn off the heat and let stand for 15 minutes. Season with more salt and pepper, if desired, and serve.

What to *Know* When

For more protein, add your favorite 100% whole grain to the soup. Always make a double batch of this soup. As a key principle of the When Way—make the night before, enjoy later—you can eat this soup for up to three days when stored in the fridge (longer if you freeze a batch).

CUCUMBER, ORANGE & MINT SALAD

PREP: 20 minutes   **COOK:** None   **MAKES:** 4 servings   **SERVING SIZE:** 1 cup

Calories: 30 kcal Total fiber: 1.7 g Soluble fiber: 0 g Protein: 1.07 g Total fat: 0 g Saturated fat: 0 g Healthy fats: 0 g
Carbohydrates: 6.5 g Sugars: 4.8 g Added sugars: 0 g Sodium: 241 mg Potassium: 10 mg Magnesium: 1 mg Calcium: 34 mg

Pair this light and fresh salad with our Orange Sesame Meatballs (page 219). The citrus and mint balance out the heat from the crushed red pepper, and the cucumber is high in anti-oxidants and low in calories—the perfect mid-afternoon snack.

1 large English cucumber

½ teaspoon kosher salt

1 large navel orange

¼ cup (packed) fresh mint leaves, finely chopped

⅛ teaspoon dried crushed red pepper flakes

1. Cut the cucumber lengthwise in half. Using a small measuring spoon, scrape out the seeds and discard. Cut the cucumber crosswise into ¼-inch-thick half-moon slices. Place in a medium bowl; sprinkle with salt and let stand for 15 minutes.

2. Meanwhile, cut off both the top and bottom end of the orange. Using a sharp knife and following the contour of the fruit, cut off all the peel and white pith from the orange, revealing the flesh. Working over a bowl and using a small sharp knife, cut the orange segments between the membranes, releasing the segments and any juices into the bowl. Cut the orange segments crosswise in half. Reserve the membranes and any juices in the bowl.

3. Drain and discard all the liquid from the cucumbers. In a medium bowl, combine the cucumber slices, orange pieces, mint, and crushed red pepper. Add the juice reserved from the orange, and squeeze the juice from the orange membranes over the cucumber mixture. Let stand for 10 minutes before serving.

WHEN WAY BLACK LENTIL SOUP

PREP: 35 minutes   **COOK:** 1 hour, 10 minutes   **MAKES:** 10 servings   **SERVING SIZE:** 1 cup

Calories: 88 kcal Total fiber: 1.8 g Soluble fiber: 0.3 g Protein: 1.1 g Total fat: 5.8 g Saturated fat: 0.8 g Healthy fats: 5 g
Carbohydrates: 8 g Sugars: 3.1 g Added sugars: 0 g Sodium: 71 mg Potassium: 153 mg Magnesium: 10 mg Calcium: 21 mg

Dr. C spent weeks and weeks bringing different variations of this black lentil soup to the office for his colleague, Ashley, to try. Eventually, with Ashley's help, he discovered the perfect recipe. Rich in flavor and deep spices, this creamy soup is worth the effort to make. Puree all the vegetables before adding the lentils to let the lentils stand on their own in a flavorful and creamy broth. One of the other tricks to this dish is rose harissa. This spicy paste—a favorite among U.K. chefs—Dr. C's favorite brand is Belazu—is added at the very end and really kicks up the flavor. This recipe makes enough for a crowd, or use leftovers to plan lunches for the week.

¼ cup extra-virgin olive oil

2 large carrots (about 8 ounces), peeled, cut into ⅓-inch dice

1 large red bell pepper (about 8 ounces), cut into ⅓-inch dice

1 large leek, white and light green parts only, cut into ⅓-inch dice

½ red onion, cut into ⅓-inch dice

1 piece fresh ginger (about 2-inch), peeled, finely chopped

2 garlic cloves, minced

1 teaspoon ground coriander

1 teaspoon ground cumin

1 teaspoon smoked paprika

¼ cup tomato paste

Kosher salt, to taste

5 cups water, plus more as needed, divided

2 cups (about 14 ounces) dried black lentils soaked in water for 1 to 4 hours and drained

1 cinnamon stick

3 bay leaves

rose harissa, for serving

1. In a heavy large pot over medium-high, heat olive oil. Add the carrots, bell pepper, leek, and onion. Sauté until softened, lightly browned, and caramelized, 13 to 15 minutes. Add the ginger and garlic, and sauté 2 to 3 minutes. Add the coriander, cumin, and paprika, and stir to combine for 1 minute. Mix in the tomato paste and cook for about 5 minutes, stirring frequently to caramelize. Add 1 heaping cup water to deglaze the pan.

2. Using a large ladle, carefully transfer the contents of the pot to a Vitamix or other high-speed blender. Let cool slightly, about 10 minutes, then puree until smooth. Season to taste with salt. You may need to work in batches.

3. Return the puree to the pot. Add 4 cups water, lentils, cinnamon stick, and bay leaves. Bring to simmer. Reduce to medium-low heat; cover and cook until the lentils are soft, about 45 minutes to 2 hours, depending on the lentils. Stir occasionally and add more water by cupfuls as necessary to thin the soup (soup will get very thick as lentils soften). Season to taste with salt and pepper.

4. Ladle soup into individual bowls. Add about 1 teaspoon rose harissa to each bowl and serve.

What to *Know* When

If you have leftovers, you will need to thin the soup again, as it thickens overnight in the fridge.

MIXED RADICCHIO SALAD WITH WARM ANCHOVY DRESSING

PREP: 10 minutes, plus soaking time   **COOK:** 3 minutes   **MAKES:** 8 servings   **SERVING SIZE:** 1⅓ cups

Calories: 113 kcal   Total fiber: 0.3 g   Soluble fiber: 0.1 g   Protein: 3.6 g   Total fat: 10.8 g   Saturated fat: 1.4 g   Healthy fats: 9.2 g
Carbohydrates: 0.8 g   Sugars: 0.1 g   Added sugars: 0 g   Sodium: 61 mg   Potassium: 70 mg   Magnesium: 11 mg   Calcium: 51 mg

Radicchio is one of those bitter greens you either love or hate. We happen to love it and have a trick to help you love it too. By soaking the leaves in icy cold water, you can get some of the bitterness out. Salads like this one are a great When Way dinner choice, because you want to eat breakfast with family, lunch with friends, and give all your dinner except salads to your enemies.

1 large head radicchio (about 12 ounces), torn into large pieces

¼ cup extra-virgin olive oil

Juice from 1 lemon (optional)

2 large garlic cloves, minced

8 anchovy fillets packed in olive oil

¼ cup walnuts, toasted, coarsely chopped

1. Place the radicchio in a salad spinner bowl. Fill the bowl with cold water and 1 cup ice cubes. Let soak for at least 30 minutes or up to 1 hour. Drain the water and spin the radicchio dry. Transfer to a large bowl.

2. In a small saucepan over medium-low heat, warm the olive oil, garlic, and anchovies, whisking until the anchovies break up into very small pieces and melt into the oil. Add lemon juice, if using, and whisk together. Pour the dressing over the radicchio in the bowl and toss to coat. Sprinkle the walnuts over and serve.

TIP: Depending on your taste buds, a little lemon juice in the dressing will amp the flavor without adding more salt, or be too bitter. You decide.

PERFECT HEIRLOOM TOMATO SALAD

PREP: 15 minutes   **COOK:** None   **MAKES:** 4 servings   **SERVING SIZE:** 2 or 3 (½-inch) slices

Calories: 41 kcal Total fiber: 2.8 g Soluble fiber: 0 g Protein: 2 g Total fat: 0.5 g Saturated fat: 0.1 g Healthy fats: 0.3 g
Carbohydrates: 8.9 g Sugars: 6 g Added sugars: 0 g Sodium: 156 mg Potassium: 538 mg Magnesium: 26 mg Calcium: 23 mg

This is a no-recipe recipe. That's because a perfect heirloom tomato needs almost nothing to make it shine. Still, we've included some ingredients that help add layers of flavor to this fresh dish. First, choose the perfect heirloom tomatoes, which should feel heavy and soft, but not mushy. And because perfect tomatoes are quite delicate, be careful how you transport them from the farmers market (or store).

2 pounds heirloom tomatoes of various colors

Fine sea salt, to taste

Sliced avocado (optional)

Fresh basil (optional)

2 tablespoons extra-virgin olive oil

Freshly ground black pepper, to taste

1. Core the tomatoes. Cut horizontally into ½-inch-thick slices. Season tomatoes lightly on both sides with sea salt.

2. Arrange the tomatoes on a board or platter. If desired, garnish the salad with sliced avocado and/or fresh basil leaves. Drizzle with the oil and grind fresh pepper over top.

WARM ROASTED POTATO & VEGETABLE SALAD

PREP: 2 hours **COOK:** 2 hours **MAKES:** 4 servings **SERVING SIZE:** 2 cups

Calories: 290 kcal Total fiber: 9 g Soluble fiber: 1 g Protein: 7.2 g Total fat: 11.7 g Saturated fat: 1.5 g Healthy fats: 9.6 g
Carbohydrates: 40 g Sugars: 9.1 g Added sugars: 0 g Sodium: 661 mg Potassium: 1260 mg Magnesium: 86 mg Calcium: 152 mg

This filling salad is great for bone health, with plenty of calcium, potassium, and vitamin K_2. We love it because not only does it taste great, but it also follows our When Way principle of making it the night before and eating the next day. The flavors marry perfectly for a delicious leftover lunch.

1½ pounds mixed baby potatoes (gold, red, and purple, about 1-inch-diameter), rinsed, dried

14 teaspoons extra-virgin olive oil, divided

6 garlic cloves, finely chopped, divided

2 teaspoons fresh rosemary, chopped

¾ teaspoon freshly ground black pepper, divided

½ teaspoon kosher salt, plus ⅛ teaspoon, divided

1½ cups (7 to 8 ounces) grape tomatoes

1½ cups carrots, cut into 2- by ¼-inch strips

2 cups beets, ⅛- to ¼-inch-thick slices

1½ cups (7 to 8 ounces) green beans, 1-inch pieces

1½ cups red bell pepper, cut into 1-inch strips

1½ cups red onion (2- to 3-inch), thin strips

5 cups (5 ounces) beet greens or arugula, stemmed, thin strips

½ cup (about 3 ounces) pitted kalamata olives, halved lengthwise

½ cup fresh Italian parsley, coarsely chopped

¼ cup fresh basil, thin strips

1 tablespoon drained capers

4 teaspoons 4-leaf balsamic vinegar

1. Preheat oven to 350°F. Spray a large rimmed baking sheet with nonstick coating. Cut each potato into ¾- to 1-inch pieces. Place them in a large bowl. Add 3 teaspoons oil, 2 teaspoons garlic, and the rosemary; season with ⅛ teaspoon each pepper and salt. Toss to coat evenly. Scatter the potatoes on a prepared sheet. Roast without stirring until the potatoes are tender, 40 to 45 minutes. Transfer to a bowl; set aside.

2. If more baking pans are available, spray another baking pan. Combine the tomatoes, carrots, 1 teaspoon oil, and ⅛ teaspoon each pepper and salt in a medium bowl. Toss to coat. Scatter the vegetables on the sheet. Roast without stirring until the carrots are tender and the tomatoes are softened and wrinkled, 25 to 30 minutes. Transfer to a bowl; set aside.

3. Respray the baking sheet (or spray another pan). Combine the sliced beets, 3 teaspoons oil, and ⅛ teaspoon each pepper and salt in a medium bowl. Toss to coat. Scatter the beets on the prepared sheet. Roast without stirring until the beets are tender, 25 to 30 minutes.

4. Meanwhile, blanch the green beans in a saucepan of boiling water until just tender, 5 to 6 minutes. Drain and set aside.

5. Heat 5 teaspoons oil in a large skillet on medium-high. Add bell pepper and onion. Sauté until the onion starts to brown and the pepper is tender, 8 to 10 minutes. Push the vegetables to one side. Add the remaining 2 teaspoons oil and 4 teaspoons garlic to the other side. Sauté until the garlic is fragrant, 30 to 60 seconds. Add the greens; toss until wilted and tender, 1 to 1½ minutes.

6. Add all the roasted vegetables, green beans, olives, parsley, basil, and capers. Season with the remaining pepper and salt. Reduce to medium-low heat. Continue to toss until everything is heated through, 2 to 3 minutes longer.

7. Drizzle 1 teaspoon vinegar over each serving.

Cauliflower Salad
Véronique
(page 203)

Tempeh Salad
Véronique
(page 202)

TEMPEH SALAD VÉRONIQUE

PREP: 30 minutes   **COOK:** 3 minutes   **MAKES:** 8 servings   **SERVING SIZE:** ½ cup

Calories: 150 kcal Total fiber: 1.5 g Soluble fiber: 0.1 g Protein: 8.4 g Total fat: 8.7 g Saturated fat: 1.2 g Healthy fats: 4.8 g
Carbohydrates: 11.8 g Sugars: 5.6 g Added sugars: 0 g Sodium: 268 mg Potassium: 225 mg Magnesium: 33 mg Calcium: 92 mg

Véronique classically indicates a garnish of seedless white or green grapes, and is typically made with chicken. This recipe follows our When Way plant-forward principles by swapping tempeh for poultry, and adding grapes for moisture to reduce the amount of fat. Tempeh is fermented soy that can have a pungent flavor to someone who is not familiar with eating it. This recipe poaches the tempeh in vegetable broth to make the tempeh milder and more pleasing.

2 cups vegetable broth

1 package (8-ounce) tempeh,
  cut crosswise into ¼-inch slices

½ cup Cashew-naise (page 63)

2 tablespoons Dijon mustard

½ teaspoon kosher salt

¼ teaspoon freshly ground black
  pepper

1½ cups red seedless grapes, halved

⅓ cup (about 1⅔ ounces) pecans or
  walnuts, coarsely chopped

½ cup (about 2 medium stalks) celery,
  finely chopped

⅓ cup red or green onion,
  finely chopped

½ cup firm tofu, well drained,
  patted dry, cut into ½-inch dice

2 tablespoons fresh lemon juice

2 tablespoons fresh parsley, chopped

1. In a small saucepan over medium-high heat, bring the vegetable broth to a simmer. Add the tempeh; reduce to medium-low heat and simmer 3 minutes. Using a slotted spoon, transfer the tempeh to a plate and cool for 5 minutes. Cut tempeh into ¼-inch dice. Discard the broth.

2. In a large bowl, combine the Cashew-naise, mustard, salt, and pepper; whisk to blend. Add tempeh and all the remaining ingredients and toss lightly to blend. Serve immediately or cover and refrigerate up to 6 hours.

CAULIFLOWER SALAD VÉRONIQUE

PREP: 15 minutes   **COOK:** None   **MAKES:** 8–10 servings   **SERVING SIZE:** ½ cup

Calories: 148 kcal Total fiber: 2.5 g Soluble fiber: 0.4 g Protein: 3.6 g Total fat: 9.2 g Saturated fat: 1.1 g Healthy fats: 8 g
Carbohydrates: 11.8 g Sugars: 6 g Added sugars: 0 g Sodium: 280 mg Potassium: 161 mg Magnesium: 18 mg Calcium: 23 mg

This recipe is an excellent option for a Véronique-style salad besides chicken or tempeh. The main ingredient, cauliflower, is surprisingly delicious for breakfast on toast, and definitely as a sandwich with arugula and tomato for lunch. It tastes even better the next day as the moisture and sweetness from the grapes are released. The nuts add both crunch and good-for-you fats.

¼ cup Cashew-naise (page 63)

2 tablespoons (or more) tahini

2 tablespoons Dijon mustard

2 tablespoons fresh lemon juice

½ teaspoon kosher salt

¼ teaspoon freshly ground black
pepper

⅛ teaspoon ground turmeric

1½ cups (5 ounces) cauliflower,
cut into 1-inch florets

½ cup (2½ ounces) carrot,
cut into ½-inch pieces

½ cup (2½ ounces) pecans or walnuts,
halved, lightly toasted

¼ cup (1 ounce) raw unsalted pepitas

½ cup (2½ ounces) celery,
very finely diced

2 tablespoons red onion,
very finely chopped

2 tablespoons fresh Italian parsley,
finely chopped

1½ cups red seedless grapes, each
quartered, then quarters halved

1. In a small bowl, blend the Cashew-naise, tahini, mustard, lemon juice, salt, pepper, and turmeric. Mix in 1 or 2 tablespoons more tahini if desired. Set the dressing aside.

2. Using on/off turns on a food processor, chop the cauliflower until the size of barley grains; transfer to a large bowl. Process the carrots the same way until most pieces are slightly smaller than the cauliflower; add to the same bowl. Process the pecans until the size of barley grains; add to the bowl. Process the pepitas in the processor until most pieces are the size of sesame seeds (smaller than the vegetables or pecans); add to the bowl. Toss to blend.

3. Mix in the celery, onion, and parsley, then the dressing. Gently fold in the grapes.

ROOT-TO-STEM KOHLRABI SALAD

PREP: 30–35 minutes   **COOK:** 22 minutes   **MAKES:** 4–6 servings   **SERVING SIZE:** About 1 cup

Calories: 394 kcal Total fiber: 3.1 g Soluble fiber: 1.9 g Protein: 2.5 g Total fat: 40.4 g Saturated fat: 5.4 g Healthy fats: 34.6 g
Carbohydrates: 7.7 g Sugars: 2.7 g Added sugars: 0 g Sodium: 254 mg Potassium: 306 mg Magnesium: 28 mg Calcium: 28 mg

This is another recipe that is all about eating the whole *vegetable*—roots to stems. It's the best way to get all the great phytonutrients in veggies that love your body. If you haven't had kohlrabi before, you are in for a treat. This unusual-looking vegetable tastes like a cross between broccoli and radish, and is great both raw and cooked. Here, we do both, melding the sweetness of the cooked bulb with crisp and refreshing stems. The leaves are used to make a light and tasty pesto.

Kohlrabi

Kosher salt

1 bunch medium-size kohlrabi (about 1½ pounds), with fresh-looking greens attached

Water for blanching kohlrabi leaves and cooking stems

2 tablespoons extra-virgin olive oil, plus ½ cup, divided

Pesto

8 walnuts, toasted

1 garlic clove

½ teaspoon salt

2 tablespoons fresh lemon juice

Freshly ground black pepper

1. Bring a large pot of water to boil over high heat and season with salt to make it salty like the sea.

2. Cut the kohlrabi bulb away from the stems, and cut the bottom of the stems from the leaves, separating the bulbs, stems, and leaves.

3. Fill a large bowl with cold water; set aside. Add the leaves to the pot of boiling water and blanch for 30 seconds. Using tongs or a spider, transfer the leaves to the bowl of cold water. When cool, spin the leaves dry in a salad spinner. Coarsely chop and reserve.

4. Add the stems to the boiling water and cook until soft but not mushy, about 15 minutes. Using tongs or a spider, transfer to a clean work surface to cool. When cool enough to handle, cut stems into 1-inch pieces.

5. Using a vegetable peeler, remove the tough outer skin of the bulbs. Cut half the bulbs into ½-inch dice and the other half into thin rounds using a knife or mandoline.

6. In a small skillet, heat 2 tablespoons olive oil over medium heat. Add the diced kohlrabi and the cooked stems. Sauté until slightly softened and golden brown in spots, about 7 minutes. Season to taste with salt and pepper. Remove from the heat and let cool.

7. *For the pesto:* In a food processor bowl, combine the walnuts, garlic, and ½ teaspoon salt. Process until a thick paste forms. Add the chopped kohlrabi leaves and lemon juice, and process until the mixture is finely chopped. Gradually add ½ cup olive oil and process the pesto (mixture may not be completely smooth).

8. *For the salad:* In a serving bowl, combine the raw sliced kohlrabi and the cooked diced kohlrabi and stems. Season with salt and pepper to taste, then add half the pesto (about ½ cup; reserve the rest for Farro With Leftover Pesto, page 107). Toss and serve.

FENNEL, CELERY & RADICCHIO SALAD

PREP: 25 minutes   **COOK:** 4 minutes   **MAKES:** 4 servings   **SERVING SIZE:** 1 cup

Calories: 105 kcal Total fiber: 2 g Soluble fiber: 0 g Protein: 0.7 g Total fat: 9.5 g Saturated fat: 1.3 g Healthy fats: 8.1 g
Carbohydrates: 5 g Sugars: 1 g Added sugars: 0 g Sodium: 144 mg Potassium: 257 mg Magnesium: 10 mg Calcium: 37 mg

The way you cut a vegetable makes a big difference in the taste of a dish. A thick piece of fennel tastes very different than a thin one. That's why we recommend investing in a mandoline or V-slicer. These simple devices let you cut ultra-thin vegetables very easily. Just make sure to follow the directions and always use the safety equipment that comes with your tools. Make sure your medical insurance is up to date, too (we really do mean be careful with these tools).

Dressing

4 tablespoons extra-virgin olive oil, divided

1 small shallot (about 3 tablespoons), minced

1 teaspoon capers (preferably packed in salt and rinsed), chopped

¼ cup fresh lemon juice

Kosher salt

Freshly ground black pepper

Salad

1 head radicchio (about 8 cups; 10 ounces), torn into large bite-size pieces

Ice water

1 medium fennel bulb, halved, very thinly sliced

3 tender celery stalks, very thinly sliced

¾ teaspoon kosher salt

½ teaspoon freshly ground black pepper

10 large fresh basil leaves (about ½ cup packed), torn

1. In a small skillet, heat 1 tablespoon olive oil over medium heat. Add the shallot and capers, and sauté until shallot is soft, 3 to 4 minutes. Remove from the heat and let cool. In a small bowl, combine the lemon juice and the shallot mixture; whisk to blend. Whisk in the remaining 3 tablespoons olive oil. Season the dressing to taste with salt and pepper.

2. Place the torn radicchio in a large bowl of ice water. Let soak for 10 to 15 minutes to reduce the bitterness of the radicchio.

3. Meanwhile, put the fennel and celery in a large bowl and season with the salt and pepper; toss to blend.

4. Drain the radicchio, then spin-dry in a salad spinner. Add the radicchio to the bowl with the fennel and celery, and toss. Pour enough dressing over the salad to coat and toss. Garnish with the torn basil and serve.

What to *Know* When

If you don't mind the slight bitterness of the radicchio, you can skip the step of soaking it in ice water.

CHICKPEA, CHESTNUT & KALE SOUP

PREP: 45 minutes, plus soaking/brining time   **COOK:** 36–41 minutes
MAKES: 10 servings   **SERVING SIZE:** 1½ cups

Calories: 202 kcal Total fiber: 11.4 g Soluble fiber: 0.2 g Protein: 4.7 g Total fat: 7.4 g Saturated fat: 1.3 g Healthy fats: 5.2 g
Carbohydrates: 31.7 g Sugars: 5.3 g Added sugars: 0 g Sodium: 293 mg Potassium: 374 mg Magnesium: 28 mg Calcium: 171 mg

---

Dr. C was inspired to make this soup after tasting a chickpea and chestnut soup at a small restaurant called Ristorante Tre Re (Three Kings) in the old city of Viterbo near Rome. This soup is equally delicious, hearty, and creamy—but without the cream! The trick to making it extra creamy is to puree beans in some of the soup before adding the kale.

Beans

2 cups (about 12 ounces) dried or 4 cans cooked chickpeas

If using dried beans you will also need:

1 medium onion, halved

3 dried bay leaves

2 fresh rosemary sprigs

1 teaspoon baking soda

1 teaspoon kosher salt

Soup

¼ cup extra-virgin olive oil

1 large onion, chopped

1 large fennel bulb (2¼ cups; about 12 ounces), chopped

2 large carrots (1¼ cups; about 8 ounces), peeled, chopped

2 large (1 cup) celery stalks, chopped

¾ teaspoon kosher salt

½ teaspoon freshly ground black pepper

12 to 15 ounces peeled roasted chestnuts from a jar, broken up with your hands

1½ tablespoons fresh rosemary, finely chopped

½ teaspoon crushed red pepper flakes (optional)

½ cup tomato paste

10 to 12 cups water

1 bunch kale (about 8 cups; 10 ounces), chopped

1. **For the beans:** If using dried beans, soak and brine the chickpeas overnight in a large pot of 8 cups cold water mixed with 1½ table-spoons salt. (Adding salt helps break down the pectin, which ensures more even cooking.) The chickpeas will more than double in size.

2. Drain the chickpeas in a colander, then rinse with cold water until the water runs clear. Put the beans, onion, bay leaves, rosemary sprigs, baking soda, and salt in a large pot or Dutch oven, and add enough cold water to cover the beans (about 8 cups). Bring to a simmer. Reduce to medium heat and simmer until tender, about 25 minutes. Remove the onion, bay leaves, and rosemary sprigs, then drain the beans in a colander.

3. **For the soup:** Add the olive oil to a Dutch oven or other large heavy-bottomed pot over medium-high heat. Add the onion, fennel, carrots, optional pepper flakes, and celery; season with salt and pepper, and sauté until golden brown, 15 to 16 minutes.

4. Add the chestnuts to the pot and sauté for 3 minutes. Add the rosemary and stir for 1 minute. Move the vegetables to one side of the pot and add the tomato paste. Spread the paste out so it touches the pot surface as much as possible. Cook for 1 minute until it starts to leave a residue on the bottom of the pot, then mix in with the vegetables. Cook 2 to 3 minutes, or until the tomato paste develops a slightly darker color. Add 10 cups water. Using a wooden spoon, scrape the bottom of the pan to release the browned bits. Bring the soup to a simmer for 5 minutes.

5. Combine 2 cups soup with 2 cups cooked chickpeas in a blender or food processor and puree until smooth. Add the puree back to the soup pot. Add the remaining chickpeas to the soup and simmer 5 minutes. If you want a creamier texture, cook the soup longer or puree more of the soup to thicken. Add the kale to the soup and simmer until it softens, about 5 to 7 minutes. Season with salt to taste.

SNAP PEA & STRAWBERRY SALAD

PREP: 20 minutes   **COOK:** 2 minutes   **MAKES:** 4 servings   **SERVING SIZE:** 1 cup

Calories: 163 kcal Total fiber: 2.2 g Soluble fiber: 0.2 g Protein: 1.7 g Total fat: 14.1 g Saturated fat: 2 g Healthy fats: 12 g
Carbohydrates: 7.2 g Sugars: 3.8 g Added sugars: 0 g Sodium: 99 mg Potassium: 67 mg Magnesium: 15 mg

The combination of snap peas and strawberries may sound strange, but it's often said what grows together goes together, and both of these ingredients come in season in the spring. This marriage works because the sweet and tart flavors of the strawberries act like vinaigrette for the snap peas.

1 cup small strawberries, hulled, quartered

1 tablespoon fresh mint leaves, thinly sliced

⅛ teaspoon kosher salt, plus a bit more

8 ounces sugar snap peas

2 teaspoons extra-virgin olive oil

⅛ teaspoon freshly ground black pepper

1. Combine the strawberries, mint, and a pinch of salt in a medium bowl. Crush a few strawberry pieces to extract some juice. Set aside.

2. Bring a large saucepan of water to a boil. Add enough salt to make salty like the sea.

3. Meanwhile, clean the snap peas by pulling the pointy ends toward the inside curve, removing the strings.

4. Add the snap peas to the boiling water and cook 2 minutes. Using a slotted spoon or spider, transfer the snap peas to a colander. Run cold water over the snap peas to cool, then let dry.

5. Thinly slice the snap peas on the diagonal. Place them in a small bowl and season with ⅛ teaspoon each salt and pepper. Add them to the bowl with the strawberries and toss gently to blend. Serve.

What to _Know_ When

It's best if you can use fresh strawberries from the farmers market. In particular, keep your eyes peeled for the Tristar variety, which are smaller and have a great sweet flavor.

CHAPTER SEVEN

FISH & POULTRY

BBQ ARCTIC CHAR

PREP: 20 minutes   COOK: 5 minutes sauce; 10 minutes fish   MAKES: 18 sauce servings; 2 fish servings
SERVING SIZE: ¼ cup sauce; 6-ounce fish fillet

Calories: 281 kcal Total fiber: 0.7 g Soluble fiber: 0.04 g Protein: 33.9 g Total fat: 8.9 g Saturated fat: 1.5 g Healthy fats: 7 g
Carbohydrates: 13.1 g Sugars: 3.6 g Added sugars: 0 g Sodium: 1,384 mg Potassium: 773 mg Magnesium: 41 mg Calcium: 40 mg

Arctic char is from the same family as salmon, which means this fish is equally loaded with healthy omega-3 and omega-7 fats. Turns out, these fish may also be mood boosters; some studies suggest omega-3 fatty acids also help to reduce symptoms of depression. That may be because the fat in fish helps improve the function of neurotransmitters. Pair this delicious, good-for-you fillet with our no-sugar-added barbecue sauce.

Sauce

¼ cup toasted sesame oil

3 large garlic cloves, minced

3¼ cups ketchup (2 grams sugar per serving)

½ cup low-sodium gluten-free tamari

½ cup white grape juice

¼ cup fresh lemon juice

¼ cup Raisin Reduction (page 69)

1 tablespoon freshly ground black pepper

Arctic Char

1 boneless arctic char fillet (12 ounces), about ½ inch thick (have the fishmonger remove the skin if you don't want to do it yourself)

¼ teaspoon smoked paprika

¼ teaspoon kosher salt

¼ teaspoon coarsely ground black pepper

1. In a medium saucepan, combine oil and garlic. Stir over medium-low heat until garlic is aromatic, about 1 minute. Add all remaining sauce ingredients and whisk until well blended. Increase to medium and simmer until heated through, 4 to 5 minutes. Remove from the heat and set aside to cool.

2. Reserve 8 tablespoons of the barbecue sauce for the arctic char. (Label, date, and freeze the remaining sauce for up to 6 months.)

3. Preheat the oven to 350°F. Remove the skin from the arctic char, if necessary, and cut the fish crosswise into four equal-size pieces, each about 3 ounces. Season evenly with smoked paprika, salt, pepper.

4. Place the fish pieces on a small baking sheet, spaced apart. Spoon 2 tablespoons barbecue sauce evenly over each piece. Bake just until the fish pieces are opaque in the center, 9 to 10 minutes. For smaller pieces of char, you will most likely need a shorter baking time to reach opaque perfection.

ROASTED CHICKEN WITH ORANGE & URFA PEPPER

PREP: 25 minutes, plus overnight   **COOK:** 50–55 minutes   **MAKES:** 4 servings
SERVING SIZE: ¼ chicken

Calories: 950 kcal Total fiber: 2 g Soluble fiber: 1.1 g Protein: 68 g Total fat: 66.6 g Saturated fat: 18.5 g Healthy fats: 43 g
Carbohydrates: 9.7 g Sugars: 7.2 g Added sugars: 0 g Sodium: 851 mg Potassium: 926 mg Magnesium: 86 mg Calcium: 77 mg

Urfa pepper is a dried pepper from Turkey that has a sweet and smoky heat. Once you try it, you'll want to add it to everything. One of the best parts of this recipe is the scents it creates. Stop and smell the dish at multiple stages of cooking—good olfactory senses are associated with decreased dementia risk.

2 large oranges

1 teaspoon fine sea salt

1 teaspoon Urfa pepper

1 whole chicken (3½ pounds)

1 tablespoon extra-virgin olive oil

½ cup dry white wine or broth

1. Finely grate the zest (about 3 teaspoons) from the oranges into a small bowl. Wrap the oranges; refrigerate and reserve. Mix the salt and Urfa pepper with the orange zest to blend to make a dry brine.

2. Place the chicken breast side down. Using kitchen shears, cut out and discard the backbone. Break the joints so the legs lay flat. Pat the chicken dry with paper towels. Turn the chicken breast side up and, using your fingers, carefully loosen the skin over the breast, thighs, and legs. Evenly distribute three-quarters of the dry brine under the skin. Rub the remaining dry brine all over the outside of the chicken. Tuck the wingtips underneath the breast, so that the breast skin is completely exposed. Refrigerate, uncovered, for at least 4 hours or overnight.

3. Preheat the oven to 425°F. Place a large cast-iron skillet in the oven to heat for 15 minutes.

4. Pour 1 tablespoon olive oil over the chicken and rub all over the skin to coat. Place the chicken in the skillet. Cut one of the reserved oranges in half and add to the skillet. Roast the chicken for 30 minutes.

5. Add the wine or broth to the skillet. Continue to roast the chicken until the skin is brown and crisp, and a thermometer inserted into the thickest part of the thigh registers 160°F to 165°F, usually about 15 to 20 minutes longer. Transfer the chicken to a plate; let rest for 10 minutes.

6. Meanwhile, using tongs, rub the orange halves, flesh side down, in the bottom of the skillet, to remove any browned bits and to combine the orange juice with the accumulated sauce.

7. Cut the chicken into quarters. Serve with the sauce.

ORANGE SESAME MEATBALLS

PREP: **40 minutes**   COOK: **35–45 minutes**   MAKES: **4–5 servings**   SERVING SIZE: **2 meatballs**

Calories: **278 kcal** Total fiber: **1 g** Soluble fiber: **0.02 g** Protein: **18.9 g** Total fat: **17 g** Saturated fat: **3.8 g** Healthy fats: **10 g**
Carbohydrates: **12.1 g** Sugars: **2.9 g** Added sugars: **0 g** Sodium: **466 mg** Potassium: **567 mg** Magnesium: **26 mg** Calcium: **78 mg**

This version of our Ultimate Chicken Meatballs (page 247) has Mediterranean flavors with citrus from fresh oranges and crunch from toasty sesame seeds. For a complete lunch, pair this protein bomb with our Cucumber, Orange & Mint Salad (page 193) and our Minted Tahini Sauce (page 40).

3 cups whole grain sourdough bread, crust removed, cut into ¼-inch cubes

1 cup buttermilk

2 tablespoons extra-virgin olive oil

⅓ cup red onion, finely chopped

3 large garlic cloves, minced

2 teaspoons orange zest (from 1 large orange), finely grated

¾ teaspoon fine sea salt or kosher salt

½ teaspoon dried crushed red pepper flakes

¼ teaspoon freshly ground black pepper

1 pound ground chicken

2 tablespoons sesame seeds

1. Preheat the oven to 400°F. Line a baking sheet with parchment paper. In a medium bowl, combine the bread cubes and buttermilk, and let soak 10 minutes.

2. Meanwhile, heat the olive oil in a small skillet on medium. Add the onion and garlic, and sauté until softened, about 5 minutes. Set aside and let cool.

3. Using a fork or your hands, mash the bread, making sure any large chunks are broken up to form a uniform mixture. Set a strainer over another bowl and transfer the bread mixture to the strainer, pressing lightly on the mixture to squeeze out any excess liquid. You should have about 1 cup soaked bread; place the soaked bread in a large clean bowl.

4. Add the reserved onion mixture, orange zest, salt, red pepper flakes, and black pepper to the bowl with the bread mixture. Add the ground chicken and mix gently with a fork or your hands until just incorporated and uniform. Using slightly wet hands, form the mixture into 8 to 9 large balls, each about 2 generous inches in diameter. Place the meatballs on a parchment-lined baking sheet, spaced apart. Sprinkle the sesame seeds generously over the top of each meatball. Refrigerate for 30 minutes.

5. Bake the meatballs in the oven until cooked through and the tops are light golden brown, 30 to 40 minutes.

DR. R'S FAMOUS SALMON BURGER

PREP: 1 minute   **COOK:** 4–6 minutes   **MAKES:** 1 serving   **SERVING SIZE:** 1 salmon burger

Calories: 130 kcal Total fiber: 0 g Soluble fiber: 0 g Protein: 14 g Total fat: 7 g Saturated fat: 1 g Healthy fats: 6 g
Carbohydrates: 1 g Sugars: 0 g Added sugars: 0 g Sodium: 80 mg Potassium: 280 mg Magnesium: 32 mg Calcium: 58 mg

Because you've read our first book—*hint, hint*—you know that Dr. R loves salmon burgers. He eats a few of them for breakfast and is even known to travel with them. Dr. R gets his frozen wild salmon burgers (made from overage of the Alaskan salmon run) at Costco, which saves him time and ensures he's getting his daily dose of omega-3s. So this is his recipe for a burger-in-a-hurry.

Extra-virgin olive oil

Garlic salt

1 frozen salmon burger (Dr. R prefers Costco Alaskan Trident-C®)

1. In a grill pan, add a touch of extra-virgin olive oil and garlic salt to taste. Heat the pan over high flame. Add the salmon burger and season liberally with more garlic salt. Cover pan and cook until blackened, about 2 to 3 minutes. Flip, cook uncovered for another 2 to 3 minutes. Plate the burgers and eat with olives and broccoli or your choice of grilled vegetables.

HARISSA-BAKED WILD KING SALMON FILLETS

PREP: 15 minutes   **COOK: 12 minutes**   **MAKES: 2 servings**   **SERVING SIZE: Two 3-ounce fillets**

Calories: 425 kcal Total fiber: 2.7 g Soluble fiber: 0.3 g Protein: 35.4 g Total fat: 28.3 g Saturated fat: 4.1 g Healthy fats: 15.8 g
Carbohydrates: 5.8 g Sugars: 0.5 g Added sugars: 0 g Sodium: 606 mg Potassium: 670 mg Magnesium: 45 mg Calcium: 106 mg

In this recipe, Chef Jim uses healthy king salmon to showcase the North African flavors of harissa. His Harissa Spice Blend (page 71) is on the mild side because everyone has a different tolerance for spice, but don't be afraid to increase the chili pepper in this dish—the salmon's richness and fat content soothe the heat and create a harmonious balance.

1 tablespoon fresh Italian parsley, finely chopped, plus more for garnish

1 tablespoon extra-virgin olive oil

3 garlic cloves, finely chopped

1 tablespoon Harissa Spice Blend (page 71)

1½ teaspoons (packed) lemon peel, finely grated

1 teaspoon fresh lemon juice

¼ teaspoon kosher salt

⅛ teaspoon freshly ground black pepper

4 skinless wild salmon fillets (3 ounces each), preferably king salmon

1. Preheat the oven to 350°F. In a small bowl, combine 1 tablespoon parsley with olive oil, garlic, Harissa Spice Blend, lemon peel and juice, salt, and pepper. Stir until well blended. Spread a quarter of the harissa mixture (about 2 teaspoons) evenly over the top of each salmon fillet.

2. Spray a 12-by-8-inch rimmed baking sheet with nonstick coating. Place the fillets about an inch apart on the prepared sheet. Roast the salmon until the fillets feel almost firm to the touch and are just cooked through, about 12 minutes.

3. Garnish the fillets with some chopped parsley before serving.

ROASTED TROUT WITH CRAUTI

PREP: 15–25 minutes   **COOK:** 25 minutes   **MAKES:** 6 servings
SERVING SIZE: 8–10 ounces of trout with crauti

Calories: 332 kcal Total fiber: 2.7 g Soluble fiber: 0 g Protein: 32.3 g Total fat: 18.5 g Saturated fat: 3.5 g Healthy fats: 13.1 g
Carbohydrates: 6.7 g Sugars: 2 g Added sugars: 0 g Sodium: 690 mg Potassium: 728 mg Magnesium: 59 mg Calcium: 39 mg

---

Sauerkraut—or *crauti*, as it's called in northern Italy—adds a great sour flavor to this fish dish. This fermented cabbage is a both a prebiotic (feeds the good gut bacteria) and a probiotic (carries good bacteria). In this recipe, we load the sauerkraut into a whole steelhead trout (great for those omega-3s!), but you can substitute another fish or serve the kraut on top of a fillet if a whole fish is unavailable. If using a whole fish, ask your fishmonger to butterfly it and remove the bones for you. This recipe is for a crowd, but it is also great for a smaller group; just use less fish.

2 cups (12 ounces) refrigerated sauerkraut, drained

5 tablespoons extra-virgin olive oil, divided

2 carrots (6 ounces), peeled, cut into 2-inch pieces, then ¼-inch matchsticks

¾ cup shallots, finely chopped

3 garlic cloves, finely chopped

1½ to 2 tablespoons tarragon, chopped

1 teaspoon kosher salt, divided

1 teaspoon freshly ground black pepper, divided

6 boned and butterflied steelhead trout with heads (8 to 9 ounces each) or six steelhead trout fillets (7 to 7½ ounces each), with skin

1. Place the sauerkraut in a large sieve. Rinse well with cold water. Place over a bowl; let drain.

2. Heat 2 tablespoons oil in a large skillet on medium-low. Add the carrots, shallots, and garlic. Sauté until the vegetables are tender and beginning to brown, stirring often, about 18 minutes. Mix the sauerkraut with tarragon, ¼ teaspoon salt, and ¼ teaspoon pepper. Let the crauti cool if using to stuff the trout. Keep crauti warm if using to top the fillets.

3. Preheat the oven to 425°F. Line a large rimmed baking sheet with parchment paper. If using whole trout, open the fish like a book. Season the insides each with ⅛ teaspoon each salt and pepper. Spoon ½ cup crauti along one side of each fish. Fold the opposite side over the stuffing to enclose. Wrap kitchen twine around the fish, or skewer it closed with small pins like turkey lacers. Brush the fish all over with the remaining 3 tablespoons oil. Arrange the fish on the baking sheet, spaced evenly apart. Roast the fish until cooked through, 10 to 12 minutes.

4. If using trout fillets, brush the fish with the remaining 3 tablespoons oil. Season with ⅛ teaspoon each salt and pepper. Arrange the fillets on the baking sheet. Roast until just cooked through, about 10 minutes. Transfer the fillets to plates; top each fillet with ½ cup warm crauti.

TIP: Whole fish are great cooked on the grill. To make it easy to flip, use a fish basket and don't snap it shut..

TROUT PICCATA

PREP: 25 minutes   **COOK: 5 minutes**   **MAKES: 2 servings**   **SERVING SIZE: 6 ounces**

Calories: 509 kcal Total fiber: 4.4 g Soluble fiber: 0.6 g Protein: 44.4 g Total fat: 23.5 g Saturated fat: 4.5 g Healthy fats: 16.4 g
Carbohydrates: 29.1 g Sugars: 1.9 g Added sugars: 0 g Sodium: 597 mg Potassium: 977 mg Magnesium: 120 mg Calcium: 81 mg

Ocean trout is the other family of fish besides salmon that hasn't learned to eat corn or soy meal. That means these trout are loaded with beneficial fish oils as they really only eat the algae or plankton.

Sauce

2 teaspoons cornstarch

2 teaspoons cold water

1¼ cups vegetable broth

Trout

2 boneless trout fillet halves
    (6 ounces each), skin removed

¼ teaspoon kosher salt

¼ teaspoon freshly ground
    black pepper

½ cup 100% whole wheat flour or
    gluten-free flour

2 tablespoons extra-virgin olive oil,
    plus 1 teaspoon, divided

3 garlic cloves, minced

2 tablespoons fresh lemon juice

2 tablespoons fresh Italian parsley,
    finely chopped

1 tablespoon capers, drained

1. In a small bowl, whisk the cornstarch and cold water until the cornstarch dissolves. In a small saucepan, bring the vegetable broth to a boil over high heat. Add the cornstarch mixture and whisk until the sauce begins to slightly thicken, 1 to 2 minutes. Remove the saucepan from the heat, cover, and reserve.

2. Cut each trout fillet on a bias into 3 equal-size pieces, for a total of 6 pieces. Season evenly with salt and pepper. Put the flour in a shallow bowl. Dredge the trout pieces on both sides with the flour.

3. In a 12-inch nonstick skillet over medium-high, heat 2 tablespoons olive oil. Add the trout pieces and sauté until golden brown, turning once, 1 to 2 minutes per side. Move trout pieces to one side of the skillet. Add the garlic and the remaining 1 teaspoon olive oil; stir until the garlic is aromatic and just light golden, about 15 to 30 seconds. Add the lemon juice and the reserved sauce. Sprinkle the parsley and capers over the trout pieces. Shake the skillet, allowing all the ingredients to mix. Quickly transfer the trout fillets to a platter to prevent them from overcooking.

4. Reduce the heat to medium-low and simmer the sauce until reduced and thickened to your desired consistency, about 30 seconds. Pour the sauce over the trout and serve.

WOOD-GRILLED WILD SOCKEYE SALMON

PREP: 25–30 minutes, plus 4 hours marinating   **COOK:** 2–3 minutes   **MAKES:** 4 servings
SERVING SIZE: 2 pieces

Calories: 320 kcal Total fiber: 0.5 g Soluble fiber: 0.1 g Protein: 23 g Total fat: 24 g Saturated fat: 3.6 g Healthy fats: 15.5 g
Carbohydrates: 3 g Sugars: 0.5 g Added sugars: 0 g Sodium: 298 mg Potassium: 460 mg Magnesium: 32 mg Calcium: 63 mg

Grilling gives salmon great flavor. Dr. R goes crazy over this at lunch when Chef Jim shares leftovers. This recipe is the *best* way to use an outdoor grill while significantly reducing the risks of carcinogens associated with grilled foods. Because the salmon is thinly sliced on a bias, it remains on the grill less than 3 minutes.

½ cup leek (white part only), finely chopped

3 tablespoons extra-virgin olive oil

4 garlic cloves, minced

1 tablespoon fresh Italian parsley, chopped

1¼ teaspoons lemon zest, finely grated

1 teaspoon fresh ginger, peeled, minced

½ teaspoon kosher salt

¼ teaspoon freshly ground black pepper

¼ teaspoon smoked paprika

8 skinless wild sockeye salmon fillets (2 ounces each)

Lump wood charcoal

2 pieces hickory wood (2 ounces each), soaked in water for at least 30 minutes

1. Combine the leek, olive oil, garlic, parsley, lemon zest, ginger, salt, pepper, and paprika in a large bowl; mix well. Add the salmon fillets and toss to coat well. Cover and refrigerate for at least 1 hour and up to 4 hours.

2. Remove and clean the grill cooking rack from an outdoor grill fitted with a lid. Keep the rack outside the grill to remain cold. Prepare the grill, using lump wood charcoal mounded on one side of the grill. Ignite and heat to 275°F when covered with the lid. Open the grill lid, add the soaked hickory on top of the coals. Arrange the salmon fillets on the cold grill rack, insert the grill rack with salmon into the cooker, cover, and grill for about 1 to 2 minutes at the most. Turn the salmon over, grill about 30 to 40 seconds, or until the salmon is just lightly opaque inside. Remove the salmon from the grill and arrange on a platter and serve.

What to *Know* When

If using a gas outdoor grill, follow the same techniques: Have a cooler side if possible to moderate heat, and use a cold rack that can be placed on top of the grill rack to prevent sear marks. To grill indoors, follow the same salmon preparation, place a wire rack on top of a baking sheet, and roast in the oven at 350°F until done.

SPRING CHICKEN RAGOUT

PREP: 1 hour   **COOK: 1 hour**   **MAKES: 6 servings**   **SERVING SIZE: 2 cups**

Calories: 332 kcal Total fiber: 6.4 g Soluble fiber: 0.6 g Protein: 23.2 g Total fat: 17 g Saturated fat: 3.4 g Healthy fats: 12.5 g
Carbohydrates: 17 g Sugars: 4 g Added sugars: 0 g Sodium: 211 mg Potassium: 833 mg Magnesium: 96 mg Calcium: 273 mg

We had a tough time deciding what to call this recipe, a *ragu* or a *ragout*. Ragu is a traditional sauce from northern Italy made with ground meat and served with pasta; ragout is a French braise of meat, poultry, or vegetables that can be served with a grain or on its own. In the end, because of this dish's versatility, we chose the French ragout. This chicken and veggie combo is great as a warm salad or mixed with yogurt and spread on a piece of toast. The key ingredient is saffron, which adds a luxurious flavor and screams spring.

¼ cup extra-virgin olive oil

2 stalks (about 1¼ cups) celery, cut into ⅓-inch dice

1 small yellow onion or 1 large spring onion with green (about 1¼ cups), finely chopped

1 large leek (about 1¼ cups), finely chopped

1 large carrot (about ¾ cup), peeled, cut into ⅓-inch dice

1 cup hot water

½ teaspoon saffron threads, crumbled

2 pounds bone-in chicken thighs (about 8), skin removed

1 cup dry white wine

4 large fresh thyme sprigs

¼ cup fresh lemon juice, preferably Meyer lemon

1 teaspoon lemon zest, preferably Meyer lemon, finely grated, plus more (optional garnish)

Kosher salt

Freshly ground black pepper

1 bunch asparagus (about 16 ounces), tough ends trimmed, stalks cut into 1-inch pieces

1 bunch (3½ cups) lacinato kale, ribs and stalks removed, leaves cut crosswise into thin strips

½ cup fresh peas, shelled

10 large fresh basil leaves

Dried crushed red pepper flakes or Espelette pepper (optional)

1. Pour the olive oil into a heavy large pot or Dutch oven over medium heat. Add the celery, onion, leek, and carrot, and sauté until slightly softened, 10 to 12 minutes.

2. Meanwhile, combine 1 cup hot water and saffron. Let stand while the vegetables are cooking.

3. Add the chicken, water with saffron, wine, thyme, and lemon juice and zest to the pot. Season with 1 teaspoon each salt and pepper. Bring to a simmer. Reduce to medium-low heat, cover, and simmer for 20 minutes. Turn the chicken over and simmer until the chicken is cooked through, 15 to 20 minutes more.

4. Meanwhile, blanch the asparagus, kale, and peas in another large pot of boiling salted water until crisp-tender, 3 to 5 minutes. Drain well and reserve.

5. Transfer the chicken from the pot to a work surface and let stand until cool enough to handle. Using two forks, shred the chicken, discard the bones, and return meat to the pot. Continue to cook until the liquid is reduced to a sauce consistency.

6. Add the blanched vegetables to the sauce just before serving. Taste and season with more salt and pepper as needed. Garnish with basil, dried crushed red pepper flakes or Espelette pepper, and additional lemon zest, if desired. Serve with long whole grain pasta like linguine, fettuccine, or pappardelle, or as a warm salad, or with romaine or radicchio lettuce cups.

What to *Eat* When

Asparagus, EVOO, and onions are good choices to help manage type 2 diabetes—all help reduce inflammation and insulin resistance.

Roasted Chicken
With Lemon & Thyme
(page 232)

ROASTED CHICKEN WITH LEMON & THYME

PREP: 25 minutes, plus overnight marinating   **COOK:** 50–55 minutes
MAKES: 4 servings   **SERVING SIZE:** ¼ chicken

Calories: 554.16 kcal Total fiber: 0.8 g Soluble fiber: 0 g Protein: 42.9 g Total fat: 38.2 g Saturated fat: 10.4 g Healthy fats: 24.8 g
Carbohydrates: 2.2 g Sugars: 0.3 g Added sugars: 0 g Sodium: 933 mg Potassium: 443 mg Magnesium: 48 mg Calcium: 52 mg

---

Chicken provides great protein power without the amino acids in red meat that cause the bacteria in your gut to turn pro-inflammatory. And lean meats at lunch are a great choice for fighting fatigue. Of course, chicken is the main event here, so try to get the best chicken you can—try the farmers market, where heirloom varieties are often available.

1 large lemon

1 tablespoon fresh thyme, finely chopped

1 teaspoon fine sea salt

¾ teaspoon freshly ground pepper

1 whole chicken (4 pounds)

Extra-virgin olive oil

½ cup dry white wine

1. Finely zest the peel of the lemon into a small bowl (about 1½ teaspoons). Wrap the lemon; refrigerate and reserve for roasting the chicken. Add the thyme, salt, and pepper to the lemon zest, and mix the dry brine to blend.

2. Place the chicken, breast side down, on a work surface. Using kitchen shears, cut out the backbone of the chicken and discard. Break the joints so that the legs lay flat. Pat the chicken dry with paper towels. Turn the chicken breast side up on the work surface. Using your fingers, carefully loosen the skin over the breast, thighs, and legs. Using your fingers, evenly spread and distribute three-quarters of the dry brine mixture under the skin over the breast, thighs, and legs, being careful not to tear the skin. Rub the remaining dry brine all over the outside of the chicken. Place the chicken on a platter. Tuck the wingtips underneath the breast, so that the breast skin is completely exposed. Refrigerate, uncovered, for at least 4 hours or overnight.

3. Preheat the oven to 425°F. Place a large cast-iron skillet in the oven to heat for 15 minutes.

4. Pour 1 tablespoon olive oil over the chicken and rub all over the skin to coat. Remove the skillet from the oven and place the chicken in it. Cut the reserved lemon in half and add to the skillet. Return the skillet to the oven and roast the chicken for 30 minutes. Add the wine to the skillet. Continue to roast the chicken until the skin is brown and crisp and an instant-read thermometer inserted into the thickest part of the thigh registers 160°F to 165°F, 15 to 20 minutes longer. Remove the skillet from the oven and transfer the chicken to a plate; let rest for 10 minutes.

5. Meanwhile, using tongs, rub the lemon halves, flesh side down, in the bottom of the skillet, to remove any browned bits and to combine the lemon juice with the accumulated sauce in the skillet.

6. Cut the chicken into pieces. Serve with the sauce.

ROASTED CHICKEN WITH LIME & MIXED PEPPERCORNS

PREP: 25–30 minutes, plus marinating overnight   **COOK:** 50–55 minutes
MAKES: 4 servings   **SERVING SIZE:** ¼ chicken

Calories: 951 kcal Total fiber: 1 g Soluble fiber: 0 g Protein: 95.1 g Total fat: 56.6 g Saturated fat: 15 g Healthy fats: 36 g
Carbohydrates: 4 g Sugars: 0.3 g Added sugars: 0 g Sodium: 871 mg Potassium: 896 mg Magnesium: 82 mg Calcium: 50 mg

With this roasted chicken, we utilize pink, green, and black peppercorns. For an extra-special flavor, add Szechuan peppercorns or Japanese sansho pepper. These have a heat level often described as numbing, so just use a little. Remember: The chicken needs to be coated with the dry brine and refrigerated at least four hours or overnight before you cook it.

2 limes

1 teaspoon fine sea salt

1 teaspoon ground mixed peppercorns

1 whole chicken (3½ pounds)

1 tablespoon extra-virgin olive oil

½ cup dry white wine or broth

1. Finely zest the peel of the limes into a small bowl. Wrap the limes; refrigerate and reserve for roasting the chicken. Add the salt and ground peppercorns to the lime zest, and mix the dry brine to blend.

2. Place the chicken, breast side down, on a work surface. Using kitchen shears, cut out the backbone of the chicken and discard. Break the joints so that the legs lay flat. Pat the chicken dry with paper towels. Turn the chicken breast side up on the work surface. Using your fingers, carefully loosen the skin over the breast, thighs, and legs. Using your fingers, evenly spread and distribute three-quarters of the dry brine mixture under the skin over the breast, thighs, and legs, being careful not to tear the skin. Rub the remaining dry brine all over the outside of the chicken. Place the chicken on a platter. Tuck the wingtips underneath the breast, so that the breast skin is completely exposed. Refrigerate, uncovered, for at least 4 hours or overnight.

3. Preheat the oven to 425°F. Place a large cast-iron skillet in the oven to heat for 15 minutes.

4. Pour the olive oil over the chicken and rub all over the skin to coat. Remove the skillet from the oven and place the chicken in it. Cut one of the reserved limes in half and add to the skillet. Return the skillet to the oven and roast the chicken for 30 minutes.

5. Add the wine to the skillet. Continue to roast the chicken until the skin is brown and crisp and an instant-read thermometer inserted into the thickest part of the thigh registers 160°F to 165°F, 15 to 25 minutes longer. Remove the skillet from the oven. Transfer the chicken to a plate; let rest for 10 minutes.

6. Meanwhile, using tongs, rub the lime halves, flesh side down, in the bottom of the skillet, to scrape up any browned bits and to combine the lime juice with the accumulated sauce in the skillet. Season the sauce with ¼ teaspoon salt and ⅛ teaspoon pepper.

7. Cut the chicken into pieces. Serve with the sauce.

WILD SOCKEYE SALMON EN PAPILLOTE

PREP: 30 minutes   COOK: 20 minutes   MAKES: 2 servings   SERVING SIZE: 6 ounces salmon

Calories: 545 kcal Total fiber: 3 g Soluble fiber: 0 g Protein: 36.6 g Total fat: 34.3 g Saturated fat: 5.1 g Healthy fats: 21.8 g
Carbohydrates: 14 g Sugars: 4 g Added sugars: 0 g Sodium: 474 mg Potassium: 930 mg Magnesium: 59 mg Calcium: 103 mg

En papillote is French for cooking in paper—a classic technique. Most recipes use high heat and incorporate raw vegetables to steam along with fish, but we sauté the shallots and garlic first to remove and prevent the raw sulfur from being infused in the cooking vapors; sautéing the shiitake and tomato brings out their umami flavors, which are intensified by the Riesling wine and chili paste. Baking the papillote at a lower temperature provides a few more minutes for all these flavors to join together with the salmon's natural juices.

2 tablespoons extra-virgin olive

¼ cup shallot (from about 1 large shallot), finely chopped

2 garlic cloves, minced

1½ cups (about 3 to 4 ounces) fresh shiitake mushrooms, stemmed and sliced

½ cup orange cherry tomatoes, halved lengthwise

¼ teaspoon kosher salt, divided

¼ teaspoon freshly ground black pepper, divided

½ cup Riesling wine

1 teaspoon sambal oelek chili paste

4 fillets wild sockeye salmon (3 ounces each), skin and bones removed

½ teaspoon smoked paprika

2 tablespoons fresh arugula, chopped

4 lemon slices

1. Preheat the oven to 350°F. In a medium skillet over medium heat, combine the olive oil and shallots; sauté until translucent, 3 to 4 minutes. Add the garlic and sauté until aromatic, 1 to 2 minutes. Add the mushrooms and tomatoes; season with half the salt and half the pepper, and sauté until the mushrooms are tender and begin to lightly brown, about 5 to 6 minutes. Add the wine and the chili paste, and sauté until the liquid is reduced by half, stirring frequently, 1 to 2 minutes. Remove the skillet from the heat and allow the mixture to cool for 5 minutes.

2. Meanwhile, fold 2 sheets of parchment paper (16 by 12 inches each) in half. Open the fold, place 2 salmon fillets in the center of the bottom part of each paper. Season the 4 salmon fillets evenly with the remaining salt, pepper, and smoked paprika, then sprinkle with the chopped arugula. Top the salmon with the mushroom and tomato mixture, dividing evenly. Place 1 lemon slice on each salmon fillet, and fold the paper over to cover. Make small overlapping folds at the edge of the folded paper until the content of each packet is fully enclosed, sealing the last fold with a paper clip to ensure a tight seal. It should resemble a half circle when completely folded.

3. Bake the packets just until the fish is opaque in the center, about 12 minutes. Transfer the packets to a serving plate and carefully slit the center open with scissors, making a crosscut to peel back the paper and being careful as hot steam will escape. This dish can be served in the paper or removed by sliding the contents of the packet onto a serving plate.

—What to *Know* When—

Zest the lemon before slicing it to capture more citrus flavor, then add the zest to the fish when seasoning. Remove as much of the outer white pith from the lemon as possible to remove the bitterness.

SALMON RILLETTES

PREP: 30 minutes   **COOK:** 8-10 minutes   **MAKES:** 4-6 servings   **SERVING SIZE:** ⅓-½ cup

Calories: 166 kcal Total fiber: 0.2 g Soluble fiber: 0 g Protein: 18.7 g Total fat: 9.3 g Saturated fat: 1.6 g Healthy fats: 4.7 g
Carbohydrates: 1.8 g Sugars: 0.9 g Added sugars: 0 g Sodium: 114 mg Potassium: 376 mg Magnesium: 23 mg Calcium: 51 mg

This salmon pâte is great on 100% whole grain toast or as a party dip. If you can find it, we like to use wild king salmon (typically freshest from late June to early August and frozen the rest of the year). Wild king salmon is the fattiest and most flavorful of the wild salmons, which means extrahealthy omega-3s for you. This recipe calls for a couple versions of salmon—smoked and king. This synergy makes for a lot of vitamin D, healthy DHA omega-3s, and great amino acids and polyphenols in one bite.

½ teaspoon caraway seeds

1 king salmon fillet (4 ounces) with skin

⅛ teaspoon kosher salt

Pinch of freshly ground black pepper, plus additional to season rillettes

¼ cup red onion, finely chopped

2 garlic cloves, finely chopped

4 ounces smoked wild salmon, finely chopped

6 tablespoons plain Greek yogurt

2 tablespoons cornichons, finely chopped

1 tablespoon fresh lemon juice

1 tablespoon whole grain mustard

1. In a small skillet, stir the caraway seeds over medium heat until fragrant and lightly toasted, 2 to 3 minutes. Cool slightly, then coarsely grind in a spice grinder or coffee grinder. Set aside.

2. If you have a steamer, pour 1 inch water into the bottom of a pot. Bring the water to a simmer. Place the king salmon on the steamer insert. Season the fish with salt and pepper, then top with the chopped onion and garlic. Place the steamer insert in the pot. Cover the pot and steam the salmon until just opaque in the center, about 6 minutes. Remove from the pot and let cool. Reserve the onion and garlic on the salmon.

3. If you don't have a steamer, add about an inch water to your largest diameter pot with a lid. Place the salmon on a small plate that will fit in the pot with room around the sides. Season the salmon with salt and pepper, and place the chopped onion and garlic on top of the fish. Bring the water to a simmer and place the plate with the salmon inside the pot; cover the pot with the lid. The water should not cover the salmon. Steam the salmon just until opaque, about 6 minutes. Remove the salmon from the pot and let cool. Reserve the onion and garlic on the salmon.

4. Put the reserved onion and garlic from the salmon in a medium bowl. Remove the salmon skin and any bones and discard. Add the steamed salmon to the bowl, then add the smoked salmon, yogurt, cornichons, lemon juice, mustard, and the reserved ground caraway seeds. Using a fork, mix all the ingredients together to a uniform paste. Season with additional pepper to taste. Cover and refrigerate for at least an hour before serving. Salmon rillettes will keep for about 3 days in the fridge.

BRAISED
MUSTARD CHICKEN

PREP: 30 minutes   **COOK: 50 minutes**   **MAKES: 8 servings**   **SERVING SIZE: 6 ounces chicken**

Calories: 615 kcal Total fiber: 2.1 g Soluble fiber: 0.2 g Protein: 50.1 g Total fat: 36 g Saturated fat: 9.1 g Healthy fats: 24.3 g
Carbohydrates: 13.7 g Sugars: 6.6 g Added sugars: 0 g Sodium: 345 mg Potassium: 794 mg Magnesium: 57 mg Calcium: 105 mg

This chicken has a rich and creamy sauce—without the cream, thanks to whole grain mustard and plain Greek yogurt. Fair warning: This sauce can separate, so give it a good whisk or stir before serving. If you want to make use of the remainder of the fennel, pair this chicken with our Fennel, Celery & Radicchio Salad (page 207) for a complete lunch.

3½ pounds skinless bone-in chicken legs/thighs (separated)

Kosher salt

Freshly ground black pepper

¼ cup extra-virgin olive oil

1 large red onion (about 12 ounces), halved lengthwise, thinly sliced crosswise

3 garlic cloves, crushed

½ cup fennel fronds (from 1 large bulb), chopped, plus additional for garnish

1 tablespoon fresh thyme, chopped

1 cup dry white wine

¾ cup water

⅓ cup whole grain mustard

1 cup plain Greek yogurt (2%)

1. Season chicken with 1½ teaspoons salt and ¾ teaspoon pepper.

2. Heat the olive oil in a large heavy pot on medium until hot. Working in two batches, add the chicken pieces to the pot and cook until lightly browned on both sides, about 8 to 10 minutes a batch. Transfer the chicken to a platter.

3. Add the sliced onion to the pot and sauté until softened and beginning to brown, about 10 minutes. Add the fennel fronds, garlic, and thyme. Sauté for 2 to 3 minutes more. Add the wine and bring to boil. Add ¾ cup water and the mustard. Stir to blend well, then whisk in the yogurt.

4. Return the chicken to the pot and bring to a simmer. Reduce to medium-low heat; cover and simmer until the chicken is cooked through, turning the chicken pieces halfway through cooking, about 40 minutes total. Season with additional salt and pepper, if desired, and serve in sauce.

Salmon Burgers
With Harissa Yogurt
(page 242)

JP's Wild King
Salmon Patties
(page 243)

SALMON BURGERS WITH HARISSA YOGURT

PREP: 30 minutes to 1 day   **COOK: 8 minutes**   **MAKES: 6 servings**   **SERVING SIZE: 1 burger**

Calories: 454 kcal Total fiber: 3.8 g Soluble fiber: 0.2 g Total fat: 25.5 g Saturated fat: 3.5 g Healthy fats: 19.9 g
Carbohydrates: 12.3 g Sugars: 6.8 g Added sugars: 0 g Sodium: 674 mg Potassium: 1,087 mg Magnesium: 57 mg Calcium: 150 mg

Bears may be onto something because salmon might just be the most perfect food in the world. It is one of the two types of fish that is not fed corn or soy meal so it consistently has great fish oils—DHA. Data imply that eating salmon is much healthier than taking DHA supplements due to its protein and other nutrients, like vitamin D, which a small study found may be key for boosting testosterone. Plus, it will help keep the blood vessels clear.

1½ pounds skinless, boneless wild salmon fillets (preferably king salmon), gray portions trimmed from underside

2 tablespoons extra-virgin olive oil

1 cup red bell pepper, cut into ⅓- to ½-inch dice

1 cup onion, cut into ⅓- to ½-inch dice

½ cup carrot, cut into ⅓- to ½-inch dice

3 garlic cloves, minced

1 tablespoon capers, drained

1½ teaspoons (packed) lemon peel, finely grated

1½ teaspoons kosher salt, divided

½ teaspoon freshly ground black pepper

1½ cups whole milk plain Greek yogurt

1½ tablespoons (or more) rose harissa

2 tablespoons avocado oil

1. Divide the fish into 2 equal parts. Cut 1 half into 1-inch chunks. Place in a bowl and refrigerate. Cut the remaining half into ¼-inch dice. Place in another bowl and refrigerate.

2. In a medium skillet on medium, heat olive oil. Add the bell pepper, onion, and carrot, and sauté for 5 minutes. Reduce to medium-low heat and cook until the vegetables are tender and starting to brown, stirring often, about 5 minutes longer. Add the capers, lemon peel, and 1 teaspoon salt; stir a minute. Remove from the heat. Cool to room temperature, about 30 minutes.

3. Scrape the vegetable mixture and any juices from the skillet into a food processor bowl. Blend with 3 intervals of 10 on/off turns until the vegetables are finely chopped and sticking together. Sprinkle the larger chunks of chilled salmon evenly around the bowl. Blend with 2 intervals of 15 on/off turns until the mixture looks like a paste, scraping down the bowl after each interval.

4. Transfer the salmon mixture to a large bowl. Add the pepper and remaining salt, then the small diced chilled salmon. Fold together until well blended.

5. Line a baking sheet with parchment paper. Drop 6 equal mounds of the salmon mixture, about ⅔ cup each, on the parchment paper. Using wet hands, shape each mound into a ball, then flatten to a 4-inch-diameter patty. Cover the burgers with plastic wrap and refrigerate at least 30 minutes and up to 1 day.

6. Meanwhile, preheat the oven to 350°F and make the harissa yogurt. Blend the yogurt and 1½ tablespoons harissa in a medium bowl, adding more harissa if desired. Cover and refrigerate.

7. Cook in batches. In a hot heavy skillet over medium heat, add 1 tablespoon avocado oil and salmon burgers. Cook for 3 minutes on 1 side. Then using a spatula, flip and transfer pan to oven. Cook for another approximately 5 minutes. Transfer to plates. Serve topped with the harissa yogurt plain or on a whole wheat bun.

JP'S WILD KING SALMON PATTIES

PREP: **35 minutes**   COOK: **3 minutes**   MAKES: **12 servings**   SERVING SIZE: **1 patty**

Calories: 202 kcal Total fiber: 3 g Soluble fiber: 0.2 g Protein: 17.3 g Total fat: 12 g Saturated fat: 1.8 g Healthy fats: 6.6 g
Carbohydrates: 7.3 g Sugars: 1 g Added sugars: 0 g Sodium: 294 mg Potassium: 423 mg Magnesium: 32 mg Calcium: 63 mg

This is Chef Jim's version of a salmon burger, which means it comes with some pro techniques! His biggest pointer: Ice is a fish's best friend. Always keep your salmon very cold on ice packs in the refrigerator. When working with it, remember to refrigerate it after handling—never leave salmon out on the counter while doing other prep. All this cooling helps keep the fish from warming and deteriorating. Chef Jim's recipe makes 12 patties so you can serve some for breakfast, then freeze the rest for another day—rather than run to Costco like Dr. R.

2 pounds skinless, boneless wild salmon fillets (preferably king salmon), gray portions trimmed from underside

3 teaspoons white chia seeds

7½ teaspoons water

2 tablespoon extra-virgin olive oil, plus more for cooking the patties

8 ounces crimini mushrooms, halved and thinly sliced

1½ teaspoons kosher salt, divided

1 teaspoon freshly ground black pepper, divided

½ cup leeks (white part only), finely chopped

½ cup fresh whole grain breadcrumbs

4 tablespoons unsweetened hemp milk

1 cup canned artichoke hearts, drained, chopped

2 tablespoons fresh Italian parsley, chopped

1½ teaspoons garlic powder

½ teaspoon Harissa Spice Blend (page 71)

½ teaspoon fresh thyme, minced

¼ teaspoon smoked paprika

1. Divide the salmon into 2 equal portions. Cut half into medium (½- to ¾-inch) cubes. Place in a bowl; cover and refrigerate. Cut the second half into ¼-inch cubes. Place in a bowl; cover and refrigerate.

2. Place chia seeds in a small cup. Add the water and stir to blend. Let stand until a thick gel forms, at least 10 minutes. (This will become an egg substitute.)

3. Spray a large skillet with nonstick coating. Add the oil and place over medium heat. Add the mushrooms, ¼ teaspoon each of salt and pepper. Sauté until the mushrooms are golden, about 8 minutes. Add the leeks and cook until tender, about 5 minutes. Scrape mixture onto a plate; refrigerate uncovered to cool.

4. In a small bowl, combine the breadcrumbs, hemp milk, and chia mixture.

5. Place the larger ½-inch cubes of salmon in a food processor and process until a coarse and chunky consistency. Add cold mushroom mixture, remaining salt, breadcrumb mixture, artichokes, parsley, garlic powder, harissa, thyme, and paprika. Process 10 to 15 seconds until mixed together, stopping in between to scrape sides of processor.

6. Scrape the paste into a large bowl. Fold in the small fish cubes. Line a small baking sheet with parchment paper. Drop 6 equal mounds, about ½ cup each, onto the paper. Using wet hands, form each mound into a ball, then flatten into a 3-inch-diameter patty. Cover and refrigerate at least 30 minutes

7. Spray a large skillet or two with nonstick coating. Add 1 teaspoon oil to the skillet(s) for each patty. Place over medium heat. Add patties and cook 1½ minutes a side until just cooked through.

EGG-WHITE FRITTATA

PREP: 25 minutes   **COOK:** 18–21 minutes   **MAKES:** 4 servings   **SERVING SIZE:** ¼ frittata

Calories: 199 kcal Total fiber: 2.8 g Soluble fiber: 0.02 g Protein: 9.7 g Total fat: 11.6 g Saturated fat: 1.5 g Healthy fats: 9.1 g
Carbohydrates: 13.6 g Sugars: 3.6 g Added sugars: 0 g Sodium: 296 mg Potassium: 284 mg Magnesium: 20 mg Calcium: 28 mg

A frittata uses eggs to hug vegetables. Use this recipe as a starting point, but swap in whatever vegetables you happen to have on hand. Our version is egg whites only, because yolks are an only-on-occasion When Way food, like red meat. Serve the frittata on top of a 100% whole sprouted grain tortilla to add fiber and protein.

8 egg whites from 8 large eggs

¼ cup fresh chives, thinly sliced

1 tablespoon fresh basil, thinly sliced

3 tablespoons extra-virgin olive oil

1 cup (about 2½ ounces) fresh shiitake mushrooms, stemmed, halved, sliced

¾ cup sweet onion, finely chopped

¾ cup red bell pepper, finely chopped

1 teaspoon fresh ginger, peeled, minced

¼ teaspoon kosher salt

½ teaspoon freshly ground black pepper

½ teaspoon turmeric

2 cups (loosely packed) spinach leaves, thinly sliced

1 100% whole grain tortilla (10-inch)

1. In a large bowl, combine the egg whites, chives, and basil. Whisk to blend well and to lightly aerate the eggs.

2. Add olive oil to a 10-inch nonstick skillet over medium heat. When hot, add the mushrooms and sauté until light brown, 4 to 5 minutes. Add the onion, bell pepper, and ginger, and season with the salt and pepper. Stir until coated with oil, then add the turmeric and cook, stirring frequently until the vegetables are tender, 8 to 10 minutes.

3. Add the spinach and stir until wilted, about 1 minute. Add the beaten egg mixture evenly around the vegetables in the skillet and, using a silicone spatula, begin to gently fold the cooked eggs inward from the rim of the skillet. Tilting the pan in the direction of the fold allows the loose uncooked eggs to fill that area and cook. Continue with this procedure around the skillet and the eggs will cook quickly and begin to create a frittata.

4. Finish cooking the top of the eggs by putting the skillet under a preheated broiler. Or cover the skillet with a plate of the same size as the frittata and, while firmly holding the plate over the frittata, invert the skillet upside down, allowing the frittata to safely settle onto the plate. Slide the frittata back into the skillet, uncooked side down, to finish cooking the eggs for 1 to 2 minutes.

5. Toast the tortilla over medium heat in a dry skillet until lightly browned on both sides, about 2 minutes a side. Place the tortilla on a large platter, set the frittata on top, and serve.

ULTIMATE CHICKEN MEATBALLS

PREP: 35–40 minutes   **COOK:** 1 hour, 10 minutes   **MAKES:** 4 servings   **SERVING SIZE:** 2 large meatballs

Calories: 226 kcal Total fiber: 2.7 g Soluble fiber: 0 g Protein: 12.3 g Total fat: 12.1 g Saturated fat: 2.6 g Healthy fats: 8.3 g
Carbohydrates: 17.1 g Sugars: 6.2 g Added sugars: 0 g Sodium: 411 mg Potassium: 570 mg Magnesium: 19 mg Calcium: 85 mg

Everyone has a favorite meatball recipe—be it your own, your mom's, or your grandmother's. Unfortunately, when you are swapping in chicken for beef, it's not an even trade (beef is fattier, which adds extra moisture and flavor). To make a healthy meatball more enticing, we spent a lot of time on this recipe. Here are our best pointers: Stick to packages labeled "ground chicken," not "ground chicken breast"—ground chicken breast is too lean, which leads to tougher meatballs. Use buttermilk to moisten the bread (it makes what is called a panade), which will add flavor and moisture into the meatballs.

Meatballs

3 cups whole grain sourdough bread, crust removed, cut into ¼-inch cubes

1 cup buttermilk

⅓ cup red onion, finely chopped

3 garlic cloves, minced

3 tablespoons fresh basil or Italian parsley, chopped

2 teaspoons fresh rosemary, minced

½ teaspoon crushed red pepper flakes

¾ teaspoon fine sea salt or kosher salt

¼ teaspoon freshly ground black pepper

1 pound ground chicken

Quick Tomato Sauce

¼ cup extra-virgin olive oil

1 large red onion (about 10 ounces), finely chopped

4 large garlic cloves, minced

2 cans (28 ounces each) crushed tomatoes, preferably San Marzano

⅓ cup fresh basil or 1½ tablespoons dried basil, chopped

1 teaspoon fine sea salt or kosher salt

¼ teaspoon crushed red pepper flakes

¼ teaspoon freshly ground black pepper

1. In a medium bowl combine the bread cubes and buttermilk, and let soak for 10 minutes. Using a fork or your hands, mash the bread, making sure any large chunks are broken up to form a uniform mixture. Set a strainer over another bowl and transfer the bread mixture to the strainer, pressing lightly on the mixture to squeeze out any excess liquid. You should have about 1 cup of soaked bread; place the soaked bread in a large clean bowl.

2. Add the onion, garlic, basil, rosemary, pepper flakes, salt, and pepper to the bowl with the bread mixture, then add the ground chicken and mix gently with your hands or a fork until just incorporated and uniform. Using slightly wet hands, form the mixture into 8 to 9 large balls, each about 2 generous inches in diameter. Place the meatballs on a platter or small baking sheet and refrigerate for 30 minutes.

3. Meanwhile, make the sauce. In a large, deep skillet over medium heat, add the olive oil, then the onion, and sauté until beginning to soften and brown lightly, about 5 minutes. Add the garlic and stir 2 to 3 minutes. Stir in the crushed tomatoes and bring to simmer. Add the basil, salt, crushed pepper flakes, and black pepper. Reduce to medium-low heat and simmer for 30 minutes to blend flavors, stirring frequently (sauce will thicken).

4. Using a large spoon, transfer the meatballs to the sauce in the skillet. Cover the skillet and simmer the meatballs over medium-low heat for 20 minutes, stirring occasionally. Turn the meatballs over; cover the skillet again and simmer until the meatballs are cooked through, about 10 minutes longer.

SEA BASS WITH HERB & RHUBARB SALAD

PREP: 15 minutes   **COOK:** 6 minutes   **MAKES:** 2 servings   **SERVING SIZE:** 1 sea bass fillet and ½ salad

Calories: 358 kcal Total fiber: 1 g Soluble fiber: 0.2 g Protein: 24.7 g Total fat: 27.3 g Saturated fat: 4.1 g Healthy fats: 22.8 g
Carbohydrates: 2.4 g Sugars: 0.8 g Added sugars: 0 g Sodium: 576 mg Potassium: 507 mg Magnesium: 68 mg Calcium: 73 mg

Rhubarb looks a lot like celery but has a much different taste. It's tart and citrusy and most often used in dessert. We like to add it to salad for a great tart crunch, like in this herb-forward one served with seared sea bass (the leafy greens are great for arteries). This recipe is excellent for brawn and brains: Sea bass offers muscle-building proteins and omega-3 DHA fish oil—the key fish oil for your brain. Pair the sea bass with our Creamed Corn (page 173) for a well-rounded meal.

Salad

1 slender and tender rhubarb stalk
    (3 to 3½ ounces)

2 cups arugula

5 small fresh mint sprigs

5 small fresh basil sprigs

2 tablespoons extra-virgin olive oil

¼ teaspoon kosher salt

⅛ teaspoon freshly ground
    black pepper

Sea Bass

2 sea bass fillets (6 ounces each),
    with skin

⅛ teaspoon kosher salt

⅛ teaspoon freshly ground
    black pepper

1½ tablespoons extra-virgin olive oil

1. **For the salad:** Use a vegetable peeler to remove the tough outer layer of the rhubarb stalk. Thinly cut the rhubarb stalk crosswise into ⅛-inch slices.

2. In a medium bowl, combine the rhubarb slices, arugula, and herbs. In a separate bowl, whisk the olive oil, salt, and pepper. Set the salad and dressing aside while preparing the fish.

3. **For the fish:** Pat the fish fillets dry with paper towels. Season each fillet with salt and pepper. In a hot, large nonstick skillet over medium heat, add the olive oil. Add the fish to the skillet, skin side down, and cook just until opaque in the center, about 3 minutes a side. (Fish thicker than about 1 inch may take a minute longer to cook.) Transfer to a plate.

4. Toss the salad with the olive oil dressing. Top the fish with the salad and serve.

CHAPTER EIGHT

DRINKS & DESSERTS

WHOLE GRAIN & DARK CHOCOLATE WTEW BARS

PREP: 30 minutes **COOL:** 2 hours **MAKES:** 24 servings **SERVING SIZE:** 1 bar

Calories: 289 kcal Total fiber: 3.4 g Soluble fiber: 0.05 g Protein: 4.3 g Total fat: 9.2 g Saturated fat: 5 g Healthy fats: 2.8 g
Carbohydrates: 34 g Sugars: 14 g Added sugars: 0 g Sodium: 17 mg Potassium: 130 mg Magnesium: 3 mg Calcium: 27 mg

This recipe is a crowd favorite. It requires no baking, stays fresh for five days, and freezes well for three months. It has no added sugars, but it's plenty sweet from the apricots and raisins. Have this to satisfy a sweet tooth or as a treat for breakfast.

½ cup (about 2 ounces) walnuts, toasted

½ cup (about 2 ounces) unsalted pecans, toasted

1 cup (about 5½ ounces) Turkish dried apricots

¾ cup (about 2¾ ounces) golden raisins

3 cups (about 3 ounces) 100% whole grain puffed wheat

2 tablespoons vanilla extract

½ teaspoon ground cinnamon

1¼ cup unsweetened hemp milk or almond milk

16 ounces bittersweet chocolate (70%), finely chopped

1. Combine the walnuts and pecans in a food processor. Using on/off turns, pulse until finely ground. Add the apricots and raisins, and pulse until the mixture becomes sticky and starts to form a ball. Add the puffed wheat; pulse until finely ground and a loose mixture. Add the vanilla and cinnamon, and process until the mixture is very sticky and begins to clump together.

2. Transfer the mixture to an 8-by-8-inch glass or metal baking dish. Spread the mixture evenly over the bottom of the dish. Using a flexible spatula, press firmly on the mixture to achieve even thickness. Or you can cover the mixture with plastic wrap and press into the bottom of the dish with a heavy flat-bottomed object to evenly spread and compact the mixture, then remove the plastic wrap.

3. In a heavy medium saucepan, bring the milk to a simmer over medium heat. Remove the saucepan from the heat. Immediately add the chopped chocolate to the milk and whisk until the chocolate is melted and smooth. Pour the melted chocolate over the top of the pressed walnut mixture, then spread the chocolate evenly to cover completely (chocolate layer will be as thick as the walnut mixture). Cover and refrigerate until the chocolate is set, at least 2 hours. Using a sharp knife, cut into 24 bars.

What to *Know* When

You can make these bars up to two days before serving. Just let them stand at room temperature for an hour before eating.

VEGAN POTICA: FROM MY FAMILY TO YOURS

PREP: 1 hour, 10 minutes, plus overnight   **BAKE:** 30–35 minutes   **MAKES:** Six 6-inch loaves
SERVING SIZE: One ½-inch-thick slice

Calories: 236 kcal Total fiber: 3 g Soluble fiber: 0.2 g Protein: 5.4 g Total fat: 19 g Saturated fat: 1.8 g Healthy fats: 16 g
Carbohydrates: 14.5 g Sugars: 3.8 g Added sugars: 0 g Sodium: 31.4 mg Potassium: 80 mg Magnesium: 14 mg Calcium: 41 mg

This is Chef Jim's most cherished reinvented family recipe. It tastes like it won't love your body back, but trust us, it does. One slice is less than 250 calories and is loaded with omega-rich walnuts. This is a time-intensive dessert meant to be prepared for a special celebration. Start preparing the walnut mixture and the dough a day ahead so they can chill overnight. Trust us, the work is time well spent for a tasty treat—without any guilt!

Walnut Mixture

3 pounds (about 14 cups) walnuts, divided

2¼ cups (12 ounces total weight) lightly packed yellow raisins

1¼ cups unsweetened and unflavored almond milk, plus 2 tablespoons

½ cup Raisin Reduction (page 69)

½ cup canola oil

3 tablespoons vanilla extract

2 tablespoons orange zest (from 2 very large oranges), finely grated

1 tablespoon lemon zest (from 2 very large lemons), finely grated

Dough

2½ cups warm water (105°F to 110°F), divided

2 packages (¼-ounce each) dry active yeast (not instant yeast)

3 teaspoons sugar, divided

½ cup canola oil

1 teaspoon kosher salt

6 cups 100% whole wheat flour, divided

Canola oil spray

1. **For the walnut mixture:** In a food processor, combine 1 pound walnuts and half the raisins. Process until the nuts are finely ground and the mixture is beginning to clump together and stick to the sides of the bowl. Transfer the mixture to a very large bowl. Repeat the process with another 1 pound walnuts and the remaining raisins. Add to the very large bowl. Finely grind the remaining walnuts in the processor and add to the same bowl.

2. In a medium bowl, combine almond milk with Raisin Reduction, canola oil, vanilla, orange zest, and lemon zest; whisk to blend well. Add the milk mixture to the walnut mixture; stir to mix. Cover and refrigerate overnight.

3. **For the dough:** In a small bowl, combine ½ cup warm water, yeast, and 1 teaspoon sugar. Set aside until bubbly, doubled in size, and yeast is dissolved.

4. In another small bowl, mix 2 cups warm water, 2 teaspoons sugar, canola oil, and salt.

5. In a large electric mixer bowl fitted with a dough hook, place 4 cups flour. Add canola oil mixture, then yeast mixture, and mix on low, starting slowly and increasing speed as needed until well blended. Slowly add the remaining 2 cups flour and mix until the dough is pliable and leaves the sides of the bowl. If more water is needed, use warm water from the faucet by teaspoonfuls. Dough should be moist on the outside but not wet. Cover the dough and refrigerate overnight.

6. When ready to use, remove the dough from the refrigerator and separate into two equal portions (25 to 27 ounces each). Return one portion of the dough to the refrigerator. Using a long rolling pin, roll out the dough on a large lightly floured wooden board into a 21-by-18-inch rectangle, adding more flour under the dough on the board as needed to keep it from sticking but not so much to make it dry.

Continued on next page

7. Halve the walnut mixture into two equal portions (about 38 ounces each). Return a portion of the walnut mixture to the refrigerator. Drop the other part of the walnut mixture on the dough by tablespoonfuls scattering it all over the surface and covering it completely. Using a rubber spatula, spread the nuts all over the dough as evenly as possible until the entire dough is covered.

8. Starting at the short side of the dough rectangle, roll the dough as tightly as you can—like making a jelly roll—enclosing the filling completely. If the dough sticks to the board, lightly scrape it off into the direction you're rolling with a stiff rubber scraper.

9. Line three 9-by-5-inch loaf pans with wax paper, leaving some paper hanging over the edge. Lightly spray the paper with a vegetable oil–based spray.

10. Using a sharp knife, cut the dough roll crosswise into 3 equal pieces, each about 6 inches long. Place a dough piece in each prepared pan. Lightly brush canola oil over the top of each piece. Cover each with a clean kitchen towel and let the rolls rise in a warm draft-free area until puffed and increased in volume, about 1½ hours (they will not double in size). Repeat steps 6 through 10 with the other half of the dough and nut mixture. Position the rack in the center of the oven and preheat to 350°F. Bake the potica rolls until lightly tan to brown on top, 30 minutes. (It is better to underbake than overbake.) Let cool in pans for ½ hour. Using the wax paper as an aid, lift out the potica rolls and cool completely on a rack. Cut crosswise into ½-inch-thick slices and serve. You can freeze potica loaves for up to 6 months.

———

CASHEW WHIP

PREP: 15 minutes, plus overnight soaking   **COOK:** None   **MAKES:** 16 servings   **SERVING SIZE:** 2 tablespoons

Calories: 58 kcal Total fiber: 0.4 g Soluble fiber: 0 g Protein: 1.8 g Total fat: 4.4 g Saturated fat: 0.8 g Healthy fats: 2.5 g
Carbohydrates: 3.4 g Sugars: 0.8 g Added sugars: 0.3 g Sodium: 20 mg Potassium: 57 mg Magnesium: 24 mg Calcium: 7 mg

Traditional buttercream frosting is loaded with lots of butter, sugar, and heavy whipping cream; likewise, whipped cream is made from heavy cream, vanilla, and sugar. Neither is good for you. Instead, this Cashew Whip can satisfy a person's indulgent desires to top cupcakes and pies—*and* loves your body back with healthy cashews and healthier fats and polyphenols. Use this as an excellent topper for our Heavenly Good & Fudgy Cupcakes (page 263), Papa's Pumpkin Pie-less (page 273), or mixed with fresh berries.

2 cups firmly packed (about 9.6 ounces) raw cashews

4 cups water

½ cup unsweetened and unflavored almond milk

¼ cup cashew butter

4 teaspoons Raisin Reduction (page 69)

2 teaspoons pure maple syrup

2 teaspoons vanilla extract

¼ teaspoon kosher salt

1. Place the cashews in a medium-size bowl. Add water; cover and refrigerate overnight.

2. Drain the cashews thoroughly before using (excess water will dilute the whip). Put the cashews in a high-speed blender. Add all the remaining ingredients and blend until the mixture is as smooth as possible, occasionally scraping down the sides of the blender jar as needed.

3. Using a silicone spatula, transfer the Cashew Whip to an airtight container. Cover and refrigerate at least an hour before using. (You can store the whip for 3 days in the fridge.)

PECAN CRESCENTS

PREP: 25–30 minutes   **BAKE:** 13 minutes   **MAKES:** 28 servings   **SERVING SIZE:** 1 cookie

Calories: 111 kcal Total fiber: 1.3 g Soluble fiber: 0 g Protein: 1.8 g Total fat: 8.8 g Saturated fat: 0.8 g Healthy fats: 0.8 g
Carbohydrates: 6.4 g Sugars: 0.5 g Added sugars: 0 g Sodium: 20 mg Potassium: 25 mg Magnesium: 0 mg Calcium: 8 mg

Most pecan desserts contain too much sugar, which we all know may be delightful for your taste buds, but bad for your health. These are not too sweet, and not too dry or moist. But they do pair perfectly with morning coffee.

2 cups (8 ounces) pecan pieces

2 cups (9 ounces) whole wheat pastry flour

¼ teaspoon kosher salt

½ cup Raisin Reduction (page 69)

½ cup unsweetened and unflavored almond milk

⅓ cup canola oil

1 tablespoon vanilla extract

1. Preheat the oven to 350°F. Line a large rimmed baking sheet with parchment paper.

2. Scatter the pecans on another 12-by-8-inch baking sheet. Toast the nuts until fragrant and lightly colored, 7 to 8 minutes. Cool the nuts completely.

3. Grind the nuts in a food processor for 13 seconds until a coarse meal (there will be some small bits and pieces), occasionally scraping around the bottom edge.

4. Transfer the nut meal to a medium bowl. Add the flour and salt, and whisk to blend. In a separate large bowl, combine the Raisin Reduction, almond milk, oil, and vanilla. Whisk to blend. Using a flexible spatula, stir in the dry ingredients. Continue to stir and fold until a moist dough. Let the dough rest 5 minutes.

5. Scoop up a rounded tablespoon of dough. Roll the dough into a ball, then roll it on a work surface into a 3½- by ½-inch log. Shape the dough into a crescent and place it on the parchment-lined baking sheet. Repeat to make 28 crescents, spaced about 1 inch apart on the sheet (the dough does not spread).

6. Bake the crescents for 13 minutes. Set the crescents aside on the baking sheet 15 minutes. Transfer to a rack and cool completely.

What to *Eat* When

These cookies are great for brain health, especially when paired with coffee. The whole grains, nuts, and coffee all help keep your brain younger—and each of the ingredients contains nutrients that help prevent type 2 diabetes.

WHEN WAY GOLDEN MILK

PREP: 10 minutes   **COOK: 30 minutes**   **MAKES: 6 servings**   **SERVING SIZE: ½ cup**

Calories: 120 kcal Total fiber: 2.5 g Soluble fiber: 0.1 g Protein: 3.1 g Total fat: 5 g Saturated fat: 0.4 g Healthy fats: 2.5 g
Carbohydrates: 15.3 g Sugars: 10 g Added sugars: 0 g Sodium: 112 mg Potassium: 3 mg Magnesium: 47 mg Calcium: 2 mg

Instead of having hot chocolate or even worse—eggnog—on cold winter days, try our When Way Golden Milk (for an extra treat, we'll even let you top it with our Cashew Whip from page 256). This milk gets its golden color from turmeric, a great anti-inflammatory spice that's also associated with lower risk of dementia.

2 cups unsweetened and unflavored almond milk

2 cups unsweetened hemp milk

8 large dried Turkish apricots (2 ounces)

1 teaspoon fresh ginger, peeled, minced

1 teaspoon vanilla extract

½ teaspoon ground cinnamon

½ teaspoon ground turmeric

¼ teaspoon white chia seeds

Pinch of freshly ground black pepper

2 tablespoons pure almond butter (made with only dry roasted almonds)

Pinch of kosher salt (optional)

1. Place everything but the last two ingredients in a large saucepan. Bring to a low boil, whisking often. Adjust the heat to maintain the same active bubbling and cook until the volume is reduced to 3 cups, stirring and scraping down the sides of the pan occasionally, 24 to 25 minutes. Remove the pan from the heat. Let cool to lukewarm, about 30 minutes.

2. Transfer the mixture to a blender. Add the almond butter and blend at the highest speed until the milk is very smooth and slightly thickened, at least 1 minute. If desired, add the salt and blend another 10 seconds. Divide the golden milk among 6 glasses.

What to *Know* When

It is important to allow golden milk to cool a little bit before blending to prevent steam and pressure buildup in the blender. Blend with the top slightly vented to allow steam and pressure to escape. Be careful to keep hands away from the vented area.

NO-BAKE COCOA
& APRICOT NUT BARS

PREP: 20 minutes   **COOL: 1 hour**   **MAKES: 16 servings**   **SERVING SIZE: 1 bar**

Calories: 137 kcal Total fiber: 3.7 g Soluble fiber: 0.3 g Protein: 3.3 g Total fat: 9.6 g Saturated fat: 0.8 g Healthy fats: 8 g
Carbohydrates: 12.3 g Sugars: 6.9 g Added sugars: 0 g Sodium: 12 mg Potassium: 266 mg Magnesium: 29 mg Calcium: 34 mg

These bars are a great breakfast-on-the-go, dessert, or pick-me-up snack (you know, for when you're extra hangry). The apricots help keep your gut healthy and your digestive system moving. Bear in mind, these bars aren't meant to be super sweet, but rather a hint of sweetness loaded with crunch to satisfy cravings. These bars can be frozen for up to two months, so you can always have them on hand.

1 cup (about 3½ ounces) walnuts, toasted

8 ounces (about 1⅔ cups) dried unsweetened Turkish apricots

½ cup unsweetened cocoa powder

⅓ cup unsweetened almond butter

⅓ cup pecans, toasted, roughly chopped

1. Place the walnuts in a food processor and pulse using on/off turns for about 15 seconds until finely chopped but not smooth. Add the apricots and process for about 25 to 30 seconds until finely ground and just before the mixture begins to form a ball. Add cocoa powder and almond butter and process until all the ingredients are well blended and the mixture begins to clump together, about 20 to 30 seconds.

2. Transfer the mixture to an 8-by 8-inch glass baking dish. Spread and pat down the mixture with a rubber spatula to an even thickness. Sprinkle the chopped pecans over the top and press down again with a rubber spatula to set pecans. Refrigerate for an hour.

3. Cut into 16 bars and serve.

What to *Swap* When

For an energized breakfast version and caffeine kick, add 1 teaspoon instant espresso powder when you add the cocoa powder! Dr. R likes his bars with macadamia nuts on top, which add healthy omega-7 fats.

CHOCOLATE ESPRESSO MOUSSE

PREP: 20–30 minutes, plus overnight soaking   **COOL:** 8 hours or more   MAKES: **10 servings**   SERVING SIZE: **¼ cup**

Calories: 166 kcal Total fiber: 2.6 g Soluble fiber: 0 g Protein: 3.8 g Total fat: 10.7 g Saturated fat: 4.1 g Healthy fats: 3.6 g
Carbohydrates: 13.5 g Sugars: 6.3 g Added sugars: 0 g Sodium: 8 mg Potassium: 51 mg Magnesium: 7 mg Calcium: 32 mg

A small amount of chocolate is actually good for you because of its great flavonoids, which help the endothelial cells of your blood vessels thrive and also help ameliorate pain. Chef Jim's version of chocolate mousse is a no-fail recipe full of creamy, dense chocolate flavor—a chocoholic's delight.

4 cups water

1 cup (about 5 ounces) raw cashews

1 bar (4 ounces) bittersweet chocolate (70% cocoa), broken into small pieces

⅔ cup unsweetened hemp milk

3 tablespoons Raisin Reduction (page 69)

1 tablespoon vanilla extract

1 tablespoon instant espresso coffee powder (optional)

1 medium fully ripe banana, broken into pieces

6 tablespoons unsweetened cocoa powder

Pinch of kosher salt

1. Combine the water and cashews in a medium bowl. Cover and refrigerate overnight. Drain the cashews well just before using.

2. Place the chocolate pieces in a small microwave-safe bowl. Microwave in a couple 15-second intervals until the chocolate begins to melt (do not overheat; chocolate may seize or stiffen). Stir gently until the chocolate stops melting. Microwave again in a couple 15-second intervals. Let chocolate pieces soften 1 minute. Stir until smooth. Or, melt the chocolate in a double-boiler over a pan of barely simmering water.

3. Combine the cashews, hemp milk, Raisin Reduction, vanilla, and espresso powder (if using) in a high-speed blender. Blend until creamy smooth, then add the banana and blend until smooth. Scrape down the sides of the jar. Add the cocoa and salt, and blend until well mixed. Add the melted chocolate, blending until fully mixed and smooth.

4. Transfer the mousse to individual dishes or to a medium bowl. Cover and refrigerate until set, at least 8 hours or overnight.

What to *Swap* When

This recipe can be made with decaffeinated coffee powder to reduce the overall caffeine or eliminate instant coffee entirely if you are trying to avoid caffeine.

HEAVENLY GOOD & FUDGY CUPCAKES

PREP: 30 minutes   COOK: 35–40 minutes   BAKE: 20–21 minutes

MAKES: 12 cupcakes   SERVING SIZE: 1 cupcake

Calories: 260 kcal Total fiber: 5 g Soluble fiber: 0.2 g Protein: 3.3 g Total fat: 14.2 g Saturated fat: 3.8 g Healthy fats: 9.6 g
Carbohydrates: 33.3 g Sugars: 7.7 g Added sugars: 0 g Sodium: 160 mg Potassium: 353 mg Magnesium: 35 mg Calcium: 67 mg

Chocolate cravings are no joke. We all get them. But indulging in a rich piece of chocolate cake only satisfies our taste buds for a minute—then we're left with guilt, and a gut full of food that doesn't love you back. That's why we've made this recipe: a healthy, yet indulgent celebratory dessert. These cupcakes are *plenty* sweet and moist, and even have a red velvet color from their main ingredient—beets! For even more indulgence, top them with our recipe for Cashew Whip (page 256).

2 cups (packed) raw beets, peeled, cut into ½-inch pieces

½ cup extra-virgin olive oil

¾ cup Raisin Reduction (page 69)

½ cup unsweetened hemp milk

1 tablespoon vanilla extract

1½ cups whole wheat pastry flour

½ cup unsweetened 100% cocoa powder

2 teaspoons baking powder

¼ teaspoon kosher salt

1 cup bittersweet chocolate (70%) chunks or chips

1. Place beets in a medium saucepan; cover with 2 inches cold water. Boil over medium-high heat until the beets are very soft, about 35 to 40 minutes. Drain. Cool to room temperature.

2. Preheat the oven to 350°F. Line 12 standard muffin cups with paper liners. Puree the beets in a food processor until smooth (if necessary add 1 to 2 teaspoons water to make the puree as smooth as possible). Measure out 1 cup beet puree into a medium bowl. Add the olive oil, Raisin Reduction, hemp milk, and vanilla; whisk to blend.

3. In another medium bowl, whisk the flour, cocoa, baking powder, and salt to blend. Add the dry ingredients to the beet mixture in 3 batches, stirring with a silicone spatula after each addition just until incorporated. Fold in the chocolate chunks. Spoon the batter into muffin cups, dividing equally and filling the cups about three-quarters full.

4. Bake the cupcakes until they have risen, are dry on top, and a toothpick inserted into the center comes out with some moist crumbs attached, 20 to 21 minutes. Let cool in the muffin cups for 5 minutes, then transfer the cupcakes to a rack and cool completely.

What to *Know* When

The beet puree, which can take about a half hour to make, can be prepared a day or two before and refrigerated to save time when making cupcakes. Or you can use precooked beets that are well drained.

MANGO ALMOND CELEBRATION CAKE

PREP: 30–35 minutes   **BAKE:** 38–40 minutes   **MAKES:** 12 servings   **SERVING SIZE:** 1 slice

Calories: 197 kcal Total fiber: 3.2 g Soluble fiber: 0.3 g Protein: 7.7 g Total fat: 12.7 g Saturated fat: 0.9 g Healthy fats: 11.7 g
Carbohydrates: 15 g Sugars: 7.7 g Added sugars: 0 g Sodium: 201 mg Potassium: 108 mg Magnesium: 6 mg Calcium: 99 mg

Even one slice of cake—no matter how harmless you feel it is—reintroduces bad sugars and fats into our diets and reignites those sweet tooth cravings. Try this cake instead, which will help keep your taste buds satisfied, with ingredients that love you back.

Cake

Canola oil or extra-virgin olive oil

2½ cups (about 10 ounces) slivered almonds, toasted

3 teaspoons baking powder

¼ teaspoon kosher salt

¾ cup Raisin Reduction (page 69)

1 tablespoon vanilla extract

2 teaspoons orange zest (orange part only), finely grated

1 teaspoon lemon zest (yellow part only), finely grated

5 large egg whites

Mango Topping

2 tablespoons sugar-free apricot jelly or preserves

2 ripe mangoes (about 2 cups), peeled, pitted, cut into ⅓-inch dice

1. Position the rack in the center and preheat the oven to 350°F. Lightly coat a 9-inch springform pan with canola oil or extra-virgin olive oil.

2. Put the almonds in a food processor and finely grind, about 30 seconds.

3. In a large bowl, mix the ground almonds, baking powder, and salt. In a small bowl, mix the Raisin Reduction, vanilla, orange zest, and lemon zest. Add the Raisin Reduction mixture to the bowl with the dry ingredients and stir to blend well.

4. In another large bowl, use an electric mixer to beat the egg whites until soft peaks form. Gently fold a third of the beaten egg whites into the nut mixture. Fold in the remaining egg whites in a couple more additions, until just incorporated but careful not to deflate the batter. Do not overmix.

5. Transfer the batter to the prepared springform pan. Bake until the center looks light golden and the edges are deep golden brown and start to shrink away from the sides of the pan, 38 to 40 minutes. Transfer to a rack and let cool in the pan for 5 minutes. Using a small sharp knife, cut around the outer edges of the cake and remove the outside pan ring. Let cool 5 minutes more.

6. Spread the apricot preserves over top of the warm cake, then let cool completely. Remove the cake from the pan bottom with two spatulas, and place on a serving platter. Top the cake with the diced mango.

What to *Swap* When

Swap the apricot preserves for a variety of sugar-free jellies, and top with fresh fruit like peaches or blueberries.

VANILLA SHAKE

PREP: 5 minutes   **COOK:** None   **MAKES:** 2 servings   **SERVING SIZE:** ¾ cup

Calories: 213 kcal Total fiber: 5.6 g Soluble fiber: 0.5 g Protein: 5.4 g Total fat: 11.1 g Saturated fat: 1.1 g Healthy fats: 2.4 g
Carbohydrates: 21.8 g Sugars: 11.5 g Added sugars: 0 g Sodium: 88 mg Potassium: 81 mg Magnesium: 7 mg Calcium: 106 mg

You know all those overripe bananas you hate to throw away? This recipe will take care of them. Loved by adults and children alike, this smoothie makes a great breakfast or dinner when old frozen bananas are all you have on hand and time is limited. It's also a delicious dessert when those sweet tooth cravings hit. Remember: Don't chug this shake. Like with all smoothies, the sugar content—even when all natural—can increase your blood sugar too much if consumed too quickly.

1 ripe banana, peeled, frozen

¾ cup cold unsweetened and unflavored almond milk

1 tablespoon pure unsweetened almond butter

1 tablespoon pure unsweetened cashew butter (no added oils)

1 tablespoon vanilla extract

2 teaspoons flax seeds, ground

1. Break the frozen banana into quarters for easier blending, then place in a blender along with all the remaining ingredients. Blend until smooth. Serve immediately.

What to *Swap* When

For a richer, creamier shake, replace ¼ cup almond milk with ¼ cup unsweetened hemp or soy milk.

WHEN WAY
CHOCOLATE MOUSSE

PREP: 10–15 minutes   **COOL:** 1 hour   **MAKES:** 4 servings   **SERVING SIZE:** ⅓ cup

Calories: 370 kcal Total fiber: 6.2 g Soluble fiber: 0 g Protein: 4.4 g Total fat: 24.2 g Saturated fat: 13.9 g Healthy fats: 8 g
Carbohydrates: 30 g Sugars: 17.1 g Added sugars: 0 g Sodium: 19 mg Potassium: 405 mg Magnesium: 131 mg Calcium: 47 mg

There are lots of ways to make chocolate mousse, but most of them involve cream and egg yolks—no foods on the When Way. Our version of mousse is When Way approved because it swaps cream for water, which helps the chocolate really shine—and is enhanced by salt and Grand Mariner liqueur, which adds a whole other level of flavor. Even without the added fat and eggs, you'll find this dessert decadent and satisfying.

8 ounces dark (70 %) chocolate, such as Valrhona or Lindt, chopped

⅔ cup water

2 tablespoons liqueur, such as Grand Marnier or Chambord

Pinch of salt

Grated dark chocolate or cocoa powder, for serving

1. Place the chocolate in a metal mixing bowl or metal bowl of a stand mixer.

2. In a small saucepan bring ⅔ cup water to boil. Pour the water over the chocolate in the bowl, then add the liqueur and the salt. Whisk by hand or with attachment to combine until smooth. Continue to whisk until the chocolate mixture begins to cool and thicken just slightly but is still pourable, 2 to 3 minutes.

3. Divide the chocolate mixture evenly among 4 small ramekins or glasses. Chill until cold, about 1 hour. Serve cold or at room temperature as desired.

WTEW BERRY CRISP

PREP: **30 minutes**   BAKE: **25 minutes**   MAKES: **12 servings**   SERVING SIZE: **1 cup**

Calories: **190 kcal** Total fiber: **5.5 g** Soluble fiber: **0.4 g** Protein: **5.1 g** Total fat: **8.5 g** Saturated fat: **0.9 g** Healthy fats: **6.3 g**
Carbohydrates: **25 g** Sugars: **7.1 g** Added sugars: **0 g** Sodium: **238 mg** Potassium: **205 mg** Magnesium: **35 mg** Calcium: **49 mg**

This recipe is the perfect example of how dessert can be breakfast and vice versa. It's loaded with health benefits from fresh raspberries, blueberries, and strawberries, which are packed with polyphenols that are great for brain health. It makes for a great start-your-day meal, with oats and walnuts mixed in. Plus, it's easy to make ahead of time and keep in the fridge (for up to three days).

4 cups (about 20 ounces) fresh blueberries, rinsed

1½ cups (8 to 9 ounces) fresh strawberries, rinsed, hulled, quartered

1 cup (4 to 5 ounces) fresh raspberries, rinsed

3 tablespoons Raisin Reduction (page 69), divided

1 tablespoon chia seeds

1 teaspoon orange zest (from 1 orange), finely grated

6 tablespoons unsweetened and unflavored almond milk

2 cups quick-cooking oats

1 cup walnuts, toasted, chopped

¼ cup gluten-free or whole wheat flour

2 tablespoons flax seeds, ground

1 teaspoon baking powder

1 teaspoon baking soda

½ teaspoon kosher salt

1. Position the rack in the center of the oven and preheat to 400°F. In a large mixing bowl, combine all the berries, 2 tablespoons Raisin Reduction, chia seeds, and orange zest; toss gently to blend. Transfer to a 13-by-9-inch glass baking dish and spread evenly.

2. In the same bowl, whisk the almond milk and the remaining Raisin Reduction to blend.

3. In another large mixing bowl, combine the oats and all the remaining dry ingredients and whisk to thoroughly mix. Add the almond milk mixture to the oat mixture and stir to mix well for a crumb topping. Sprinkle the oat mixture evenly on top of the berry mixture. Bake until the topping is golden brown and the berries begin to juice, about 25 minutes. Remove from the oven and let stand for 15 minutes before serving.

PAPA'S PUMPKIN PIE-LESS

PREP: 25 minutes, plus overnight soaking   **BAKE:** 1 hour   **COOL:** 2 hours or more   **MAKES:** 11 servings
SERVING SIZE: ½ cup

Calories: 375 kcal Total fiber: 8.7 g Soluble fiber: 0.02 g Protein: 11.9 g Total fat: 24.4 g Saturated fat: 3.2 g Healthy fats: 19.2 g
Carbohydrates: 33.7 g Sugars: 15 g Added sugars: 4 g Sodium: 30 mg Potassium: 376 mg Magnesium: 164 mg Calcium: 116 mg

It is easy to get derailed trying to make food that loves you back during the holiday season. When Chef Jim's family recipes contain excessive added sugars, sodium, and saturated fats, he creates new versions that are healthy, taste great, and can become new family traditions. This version of crustless pumpkin pie—or as his grandkid's call it "Papa's Pumpkin Pie"—offers all the pumpkin and spice flavors you crave, without the added fat and sugar. We think this is a keeper your family will love adding to the holiday menu. (Keep in mind, this dish still packs a lot of naturally occurring sugar, so only serve it on special occasions.)

1 cup raw cashews

4 cups water

1 sweet potato (14 to 16 ounces)

1 large ripe banana, broken into chunks

½ cup pure unsweetened almond butter

6 tablespoons Raisin Reduction (page 69)

¼ cup unsweetened almond milk

2 teaspoons vanilla extract

1 can (15-ounce) pure pumpkin

5 teaspoons pure maple syrup

1½ teaspoons ground cinnamon

¾ teaspoon ground ginger

¾ teaspoon ground nutmeg

1. Place the cashews in a medium bowl; pour water over. Cover and refrigerate overnight. Drain well just before using.

2. Preheat the oven to 350°F. Bake the sweet potato until very tender, about 1 hour. Cool slightly, then peel. Scoop out the flesh and measure 1 cup; set aside.

3. Mix the drained cashews, banana, almond butter, Raisin Reduction, almond milk, and vanilla in a high-speed blender until smooth. Transfer to a medium bowl and set aside.

4. In a food processor, puree the reserved 1 cup sweet potato until smooth. Add the cashew mixture, pumpkin, maple syrup, and all spices, and process until as smooth as possible, occasionally scraping down the sides of the bowl.

5. Transfer the mixture to a clean medium bowl and refrigerate at least 2 hours before serving.

—**What to *Know* When**—
Save time and bake the sweet potato a day ahead. Refrigerate overnight while the cashews are soaking.

Grape
Escape
(page 276)

Vitality
Smoothie
(page 277)

GRAPE ESCAPE

PREP: 8–10 minutes   **COOK: None**   **MAKES: 4 servings**   **SERVING SIZE: ½ cup**

Calories: 75 kcal Total fiber: 2.1 g Soluble fiber: 0.5 g Protein: 0.8 g Total fat: 0.2 g Saturated fat: 0.1 g Healthy fats: 0.1 g
Carbohydrates: 19.8 g Sugars: 15.4 g Added sugars: 0 g Sodium: 2 mg Potassium: 227 mg Magnesium: 9 mg Calcium: 24 mg

This smoothie is great for cooling off on a hot summer day. The flavors are intense, thanks to using frozen grapes instead of ice. The grapes make it healthier too—their polyphenols are reported to give you a testosterone boost for muscle building in both men and women, so pour a glass before you hit the gym.

1 cup seedless green grapes, frozen

1 cup cold seedless green grapes

1 large orange, all peel and white pith removed, segmented

1 lime, all peel and white pith removed, segmented

1. Place all the ingredients in a blender. Cover and puree until smooth and frothy, about 2 minutes.

What to *Know* When

Be sure to remove all the pith from the lime and lemon to prevent their bitterness from affecting the smoothie's sweet flavor.

VITALITY SMOOTHIE

PREP: 15 minutes   COOK: None   MAKES: 4 servings   SERVING SIZE: 1 cup

Calories: 121 kcal Total fiber: 5 g Soluble fiber: 1 g Protein: 2.1 g Total fat: 0.8 g Saturated fat: 0.1 g Healthy fats: 0.4 g
Carbohydrates: 30 g Sugars: 18.6 g Added sugars: 0 g Sodium: 23 mg Potassium: 430 mg Magnesium: 31 mg Calcium: 70 mg

This is one of the most delicious green smoothies you will ever have, and we bet you'll happily drink it every day. It has the perfect balance of greens and flavorful, sweet, ripe fruits. *And it's actually good for you!* Green smoothie drinks are a wonderful option for any time of day when you need a quick meal on the go. In this drink, plenty of phytochemicals allow your circulation to function optimally—great for your heart, skin, and reproductive apparatus.

1 cup green seedless grapes

1 orange, all peel and white pith removed, coarsely chopped

1 cup (packed; about 1½ ounces) spinach leaves

1 ripe Bartlett pear, unpeeled, core and stem removed, coarsely chopped

1 cup (packed; about 1¼ ounces) kale leaves, stems removed, coarsely chopped

1 ripe banana, peeled and sliced

½ cup fresh Italian parsley leaves

1 teaspoon chia seeds

1½ cups ice cubes

1. Alternate the ingredients in a high-speed blender: First add the grapes and orange, pulse, then alternate adding the greens and the remaining ingredients. Cover the blender and blend until very smooth. (The grapes and orange will easily liquefy, as will the other fruits, helping to pull in the greens for easier blending.)

CHOCOLATE CHUNK & NUT CHEWIES

PREP: 25 minutes   **BAKE:** 12–13 minutes   **MAKES:** 28 cookies   **SERVING SIZE:** One cookie

Calories: 113 kcal Total fiber: 2 g Soluble fiber: 0.2 g Protein: 2.2 g Total fat: 8.1 g Saturated fat: 2 g Healthy fats: 4.8 g
Carbohydrates: 8.7 g Sugars: 4 g Added sugars: 0 g Sodium: 97 mg Potassium: 58 mg Magnesium: 11 mg Calcium: 11 mg

If you have a desire for a chocolate chip cookie but want one that loves you back, then you'll enjoy these delicious chocolate chewies. Made with healthy walnuts, pecans, raisins, dark chocolate, and no added sugar (trust us, you won't even miss it), this is one cookie that is good for you. We'll bet a When Way book that they'll more than satisfy.

1½ cups 100% whole grain old-fashioned oats

1 cup (about 4.2 ounces) pecans, toasted

1 cup (about 3.6 ounces) walnuts, toasted

½ cup golden raisins

1 teaspoon baking soda

¾ teaspoon kosher salt

½ teaspoon ground cinnamon

3 tablespoons Raisin Reduction (page 69)

2 tablespoons water

1 tablespoon vanilla extract

1 cup (5 ounces) dark chocolate (70% cacao), cut into about ⅓-inch pieces

1. Preheat oven to 350°F.

2. In a food processor, pulse the oats until coarsely ground, about 25 seconds. Add the pecans and walnuts, and process until the mixture is finely ground, about 20 seconds. Add the raisins and process until the mixture begins to stick together, about 20 seconds. Add the baking soda, salt, and cinnamon; pulse using on/off turns just until well blended. Add the Raisin Reduction, water, and vanilla; pulse until well blended. The dough will be sticky.

3. Transfer the dough to mixing bowl. Using a rubber spatula, gently fold in the chocolate chunks until well incorporated. Scoop out the dough by heaping tablespoonfuls (about 1½ tablespoons for each) and form balls using your hands. Place the cookies on large nonstick baking sheets, spacing at least 1½ inches apart. Lightly press down on each cookie by hand to flatten slightly.

4. Bake for 12 minutes. Cool on the baking sheets for 15 minutes, then transfer to a rack to cool completely.

What to *Know* When

These cookies freeze very well, and defrost quickly because they're so small. Pack them with a bagged lunch right from the freezer and they'll be ready to eat by noon.

BLUEBERRY RHUBARB PIE

PREP: 60 minutes **BAKE:** 55 minutes **MAKES:** 8 servings **SERVING SIZE:** 1 slice

Calories: 272 kcal Total fiber: 4.6 g Soluble fiber: 0.4 g Protein: 3.9 g Total fat: 14.7 g Saturated fat: 1.1 g Healthy fats: 13 g
Carbohydrates: 33.5 g Sugars: 8.2 g Added sugars: 0 g Sodium: 183 mg Potassium: 219 mg Magnesium: 9 mg Calcium: 47 mg

What's not to love about a pie that combines fresh blueberries and rhubarb? This spring-forward dessert has a 100% whole grain crust for extra fiber. It freezes exceptionally well for up to six months, so we recommend making a few pies at once and storing them to whip out for the next family celebration.

Pie Crust

2 cups whole wheat pastry flour

½ teaspoon salt

½ cup canola oil

½ cup cold water

1 tablespoon white vinegar

Filling

4 cups blueberries, rinsed

2 cups rhubarb, diced

Pinch of salt

2 tablespoons minute tapioca

1 tablespoon cornstarch

1½ cups Raisin Reduction (page 69)

1. Preheat the oven to 350°F. In mixing bowl, whisk together the flour and salt. Add the canola oil, water, and white vinegar; mix well, until a dough forms.

2. Place the dough on a wooden cutting board and knead 10 to 15 times. Wrap it in plastic and set aside.

3. In a separate large mixing bowl, combine blueberries, rhubarb, salt, tapioca, and cornstarch. Set aside.

4. Divide the dough into two even portions. Roll out half the dough into an 11-inch circle. Transfer to a 9-inch pie pan (fold the dough in half to make for an easier transfer). Cover the bottom and sides of the pan in dough.

5. Stir the Raisin Reduction into the blueberry and rhubarb mixture. Combine well, then pour into the pie pan on top of the dough.

6. Roll out the second portion of dough into an 11-inch circle and place on top of the pie. Crimp the dough around the pan with a scalloped edge. Use the tip of a knife to cut air holes in the top of the crust—mark the holes where you would cut 8 slices.

7. Place the pie pan on a baking sheet and bake in the oven for 55 minutes or until juice begins to bubble out of the air holes. Cool, then refrigerate and serve.

—**What to *Know* When**—

It is very important to knead the dough before rolling. If you've frozen this pie for future use, move the pie from the freezer and place the frozen pie on a baking sheet. Bake in a 350°F oven for an hour and 15 to 25 minutes. Pie is ready when juices are bubbling out of the holes.

ACKNOWLEDGMENTS

All of the authors would like to thank the incredible team at National Geographic for all of their work, commitment, and passion for turning our concepts and recipes into a spectacularly delicious reality. Without their dedication, you wouldn't be holding what we truly believe will be your go-to place for recipes and inspiration. Specifically, our deepest appreciation goes to: senior project editor Allyson Johnson, art director Sanaa Akkach, photo editor Adrian Coakley, and senior production editor Judith Klein. Our sincerest thanks also goes out to photographer Scott Suchman, food stylist Lisa Cherkasky, prop stylist Kristi Hunter, and our wonderful recipe editors Lena Birnbaum and Selma Morrow.

From Dr. R

All I write is secondary to my motivation to help people live longer healthy lives (and have a younger RealAge). All of this has happened only because of a super editor, thought leader, and agent Candice Fuhrman. Thank you for so much, Candice. And, of course, all of this would not be doable without the support of my family members—especially the encouragement and review from my spectacularly wonderful saint of a wife; thank you, Dr. Nancy. Jen, the family chemist, and Jeff, the family pediatric endocrinologist, have contributed much support too. My wife's 100-plus-year-old mother, Marion, showed me that aging can be a very vibrant time—and made great soups. Her influence is squeezed into this book, as is that of my sister Marsha and brother-in-law Richard Lowry, who were critical readers. This family was joined at times by the "enlarged family" of the Katzes, Unobskeys, and Campodonicos. I also need to thank Mehmet and Lisa Oz and their family, including master chef

Daphne, John Mauldin, Zack Wasserman, and others, for encouraging and critiquing the concepts.

We've had a lot of help testing these recipes to ensure they are tongue pleasers and make life much more fun. Co-authors Dr. C. and Chef Jim keep teaching me techniques and pushing me to try new recipes. They build on the foundation created by many others who taught me about healthy lifestyles and food: the many co-workers, clinicians, scientists, and experts at the Cleveland Clinic and in the Wellness Institute. Mladen Golubic, M.D., Ph.D., has pushed scientific rigor. John La Puma, M.D., is a super doc and super chef who taught me how to enjoy food more and how to cook (and how to engage medical co-workers to do the same). He deserves much of my applause. Helping him teach me were Donna Szymanski and Dan Zakri.

I am so appreciative of the entire Nat Geo team as listed above who worked on this project. A special thank you goes to Allyson Johnson, who as a superb editor oversaw the whole project and challenged us to make this the best cookbook possible. Her attentive eye and thoughtful leadership made this book possible. Many thanks go to National Geographic Editor in Chief Susan Goldberg for her deep support of this book and its message.

I am fortunate to work with many caregivers who have broken traditional molds and are making the Cleveland Clinic the best place to work and the best place to receive care—especially if you want wellness as a culture and long-term outcome. Former CEO Toby Cosgrove has said, and new CEO Dr. Tom Mihaljevic even more adamantly stated, that while the clinic will continue to be known as one of the best in illness care, wellness is part and parcel of what we do and must continue to do for every employee and every person we touch. Especially important was chief nutritionist Kristin Kirkpatrick. I want to thank all of them for tasty suggestions and scientific contributions and constructive criticisms, and for allowing me the time and encouraging me to complete this work. They have kept the food great for you without sacrificing taste. I am grateful to have worked with such a talented and creative group as Dr. Martin Harris; Dr. Bridget Duffy; Dr. Mike O'Donnell; Dennis Kenny; many nutritionists and exercise physiologists; Dr. Rich Lang; Dr. Raul Seballos; Dr. Steven Feinleib; Dr. Barbara Messinger-Rapport; Dr. Roxanne Sukol; and Dr. Rich Cartabuke. I also need to thank Mira Ilic; Karen Tabor; Karen Jones; Dr. Jim Young; and the Canyon Ranch experts, including Dr. Rich Carmona, who span the gamut from inner-city schoolteachers (thank you, Rosalind Strickland and the Reverend Otis Moss) to executive coaches.

The list of scientific contributors is long too, but I extend a special thanks to Keith Roach and the late Anita Shreve, along with the many gerontologists and internists who read sections of the book for accuracy; others on the RealAge team validated and verified the content and contributed their expertise to the book.

My administrative associates Beth Grubb and especially Jackie Frey made this work possible. It's no accident that U.S. News & World Report has ranked the Cleveland Clinic number one in cardiac care 35 years in a row. My prior associate, Anne-Marie Prince, deserves special thanks, as does Diane Reverand—she started this process by telling me not to worry about offending medical colleagues. As long as the science was solid, they would understand that we were trying to motivate you to understand that you can control your genes.

And, of course, Ted Spiker made writing much more accurate and enjoyable—you will see what I mean. I cannot say enough about how fantastic Ted is.

I hope and believe this book will help you to love healthy food, make great choices, and live younger and longer. Having fewer people need the illness treatment part of our medical system for many, many years will be the best reward any physician could want.

From Dr. C

When I started medical school, my plan was to be a neurosurgeon, but after two years of residency, I feared that I had made the wrong choice. Although I thought neurosurgery would combine all of my interests, I discovered that while I liked it, I didn't love it, and it took me too far away from one of my passions—cooking. It was during my vacation that second year that I made a trip to The Awaiting Table cooking school in Puglia, Italy. There I was immersed in the real culture of the region and the origins of the Mediterranean diet. The recipes were great, but even more inspiring were the words of our teacher, Silvestro Silvestori, who on the last day of the school thanked us for coming and helping him to live the life he had always wanted. I want to thank Silvestro for that message, which helped me leave my residency and take the unconventional career path I've been on since.

That path led me to discover the field of preventive medicine, a specialty that I always wanted to practice but never knew existed. I appreciate Dr. Miriam Alexander, who took a chance on an unusual candidate and accepted me into the Johns Hopkins Bloomberg School of Public Health Preventive Medicine Residency. There Miriam created a program that prepared me well for my profession and allowed me to explore interests in both food and media. I also had the privilege of meeting another important mentor and friend at the school of public health, Dr. Bob Lawrence. Bob, a true visionary leader, helped me follow my passion for food and agriculture and also taught me the value of the Socratic method. Finally, I want to thank one more professor, Dr. Tom Burke. Tom encouraged me to do a rotation at *The Dr. Oz Show,* an experience that made a profound impact on my career. His class in risk assessment also gave me the skills I needed to make an impression during that rotation and to later get a job at *Consumer Reports.*

I never planned to write a book, let alone two, and I want to thank Dr. Mike Roizen for asking me to join him on this exploration of the science of our circadian rhythm. Mike is one of the smartest, most passionate, generous, and just about nicest guys I know, and it has been such great fun to become co-authors and great friends. I also want to give a big shout-out to Jim Perko, a great partner and chef, who challenged me to think differently about the way I cook. I also have to thank Ted Spiker, another great partner and smart and clever writer, who knew just how to help us tell our story and keep us organized. And of course, special thanks to the whole crew at Nat Geo, especially Allyson Johnson for being such a great editor, and Ann Day and Daneen Goodwin for making sure people know our books exist. Our recipe editor, Lena Birnbaum, taught me a lot about writing recipes, which is much harder than I originally thought.

Of course, I have to acknowledge Mehmet Oz, who I have had the privilege of working with for many years now. Mehmet is a great teacher and advocate, and also introduced me to Mike R. Thanks to all of the folks at *The Dr. Oz Show:* Amy, Stacy, Kathy, Christine, Tina, Cheryl, Jacqueline, Jessica, Lisa, Maybe Hilary, Ann, Marty, and everyone else who taught me so much about how to talk to real people. And finally, a very special thanks to Ashley Archer. Ashley shares an office wall with me and is a brilliant chef and producer—she never complains (too much) about talking through or brainstorming new recipes with me.

I couldn't write a cookbook without thanking Walter Luque, an amazing pastry chef who helped me find my passion for food and cooking and showed me how to appreciate both elevated cuisine and the basics. Thanks to my other favorite chefs, Sue Torres, Björn Böttcher, and Franco Taruschio, who let me cook with them and learn in their kitchens. A big thanks to my good friend and former roommate Corey Young, who helped support my cooking habit in medical school and always did the dishes. And of course, I am grateful to all of my closest friends and family, who have learned to accept that I'm either going to be cooking or taking them on a culinary adventure.

Finally, thanks to my parents, Diane and Daniel Crupain, who not only gave me life but all the love and support I need, no matter what. It was my mom who first inspired my love for cooking and never discouraged me from trying something new, complicated, or messy, and my dad who inspired my love of food and health, and to both of them I will be forever grateful.

From Chef Jim

It has been a lifetime of learning that's formed my ideas, skills, and judgment to create the recipes I have contributed in this book. Mastering culinary literacy, skills, and especially culinary medicine techniques is what I hope you will gain from my contributions. This brings me joy, and for this I am so grateful to the many people who helped and inspired me. Dr. Michael Roizen, it is because of *you* that I am the chef I am today! You have imprinted me with your passion, wisdom, and knowledge. Your zest for life and learning and your quest to innovate is infectious. I am forever grateful and honored to know you, learn from you, and be a partner in this book. Thank you!

I am thankful to all the patients I've cooked for, lectured to, and instructed for the past 34 years in hospitals. What I learned from you was invaluable, and I'm a better chef for it. Seeing your struggles, hardships, and transformations from changing life-long eating habits has been no less than awe inspiring.

Thank you, Dr. Michael Crupain, for challenging me with other points of view. I've learned a great deal from them, and I am privileged to be a co-author with you. Thank you, Ted Spiker, for your genius literary talents and contributions. Thank you to the whole team at National Geographic who provided so much support, ideas, and guidance from start to finish.

To my closest physician friend, Dr. Mladen Golubić, I cherish the countless educational conversations over the past 18 years. Your honesty, sincerity, humbleness, and passion for *true* patient care has been my driving force in developing and teaching Culinary Medicine. I'm forever grateful to Jules W. Bouthillet, Lakewood Hospital's CEO, and John Tomlinson, Director of Dietary Management, for hiring me as Lakewood Hospital's executive chef which launched my career in healthcare. Thank you to all the dietitians I've worked with in the last 34 years, especially Bonny Ayers (the first), Romina Yee, and Kristin Kirkpatrick. We were chefs and dietitians working together, pre-culinary medicine! I must also thank Gary Rossen for letting me introduce culinary medicine principles to his patrons at Rozis.

Thanks also to Gabby Shipta, sous-chef extraordinaire for helping to keep our professional Culinary Medicine Teaching Kitchen and my work life running smoothly.

I thank my father, Robert Perko, Sr., and mother, Eleanor Perko, for teaching me the values that have guided me through life. I will always be thankful to them for instilling in me by their example the passion, effort, and desire to always put deliciousness in food. Thank you to my brother, Robert Perko, Jr. You do more than support me, from driving to the Culinary Institute of America in New York all the way from Cleveland to presenting culinary medicine with me to your fellow firefighters.

Most important, and above all, to my wife, Debbie—my soulmate, best friend, haven, love of my life, and best ever sous-chef: Thank you for helping me with this book. Your incredibly instinctive culinary gifts contributed immensely to the recipes, especially many of the desserts. Our potica is the best and healthiest I've ever eaten! I wouldn't have been able to do this book without you. You've helped me chop, cook, clean, and prepare recipe mise en place for many months with passion, care, and attention to every detail from measuring to making notes to taking photos. You're my best critic, taster, and motivator. Your laughter, smiles, and humor make our lives fun, and doing this book with you will forever be one of the special joys in my life. Thank you for marrying me!

To our daughter, Katie, thank you for the endless proofing of recipes for literary and grammatical errors. You're always looking out for us to be the best we can be. To our son, Jim Jr., thanks for your professional legal advisement. Like Katie, you always look out for Mom and Dad. To our son-in-law, Michael, and daughter-in-law, Acacia, thank you for your patience, support, love, and encouragement. Finally, thank you to my special recipe tasters, our grandsons Austin, Connor, Gideon, and Gabriel, who give quick, unbiased, and honest critiques. Your priceless hugs and kisses keep Papa young and motivated to stay as healthy as I can be.

I hope our recipes will help you to cook more and love the foods that love you back!

MEET THE CHEFS

Our Authors Show You Why Cooking Is Part Science, Part Art, Very Personal, and a Whole Lot of Fun

Michael Roizen, M.D., First Chief Wellness Officer of the Cleveland Clinic, @DrMikeRoizen

Dr. Roizen initiated and developed the RealAge concept to motivate behavior change. He has served as Cleveland Clinic's first chief wellness officer from 2007 to 2019 and is the founding chair of its Wellness Institute. The clinic's wellness programs have helped the clinic avoid spending more than $848 million in health care costs for its 101,000 employees and dependents over 10 years, compared with national averages, and have reduced unscheduled sick leave by 28 percent. The wellness programs have also helped more than 43.6 percent of participants achieve "6+2 normals®"—six measures of good health and two measures of good lifestyle behaviors that can lead to a reduction in chronic diseases.

Dr. Roizen is certified in internal medicine and anesthesiology. He is a Phi Beta Kappa graduate of Williams College, AOA from University of California, San Francisco School of Medicine. He now serves as Cleveland Clinic's chief wellness officer emeritus and is a professor at the Lerner College of Medicine of the Cleveland Clinic at Case Western Reserve University.

He has written more than 190 peer-reviewed scientific publications, four *New York Times* #1 best sellers, and nine overall best sellers, including *RealAge, AgeProof,* and his latest book, *What to Eat When.* He served 16 years on U.S. Food and Drug Administration advisory committees, helped start 13 companies, co-invented a drug approved by the U.S.

FDA, and has a weekly podcast. Together with Dr. Mehmet Oz, Roizen writes a daily column syndicated to more than 100 newspapers that translates current scientific reports into actionable steps for lay audiences. He is a recipient of an Emmy, an Elle, and the Paul Rogers Best Medical Communicator Award from the National Library of Medicine.

Dr. Roizen is devoted to helping people live younger. He consults with patients in Cleveland Clinic's Executive Health Program and is an avid believer in smartphone technology tied with human coaching as well as incentives for motivating health through behavioral change to reduce the need for illness care and give people more healthy years, thereby reducing health care costs.

Michael Crupain, M.D., M.P.H., Chief Medical Officer of Sharecare

Dr. Crupain is the chief medical officer of Sharecare, the leading digital health company that helps people—no matter where they are in their health journey—build a longer, better life by enabling health transformation at the individual, organizational, and community level. Board-certified in preventive medicine, he is dedicated to making the world a healthier place. Dr. Crupain is a multiple Emmy Award–winning producer and the medical unit chief of staff at *The Dr. Oz Show,* where he directs the research team.

Before joining *The Dr. Oz Show,* Dr. Crupain was the director of food safety testing at *Consumer Reports,* where he ran large studies on contaminants in everyday foods to educate consumers and drive policy change. He worked on a wide variety of issues that became magazine cover stories and that led to U.S. Food and Drug Administration actions. These topics included pesticides in produce, antibiotic-resistant bacteria in meat and poultry, and mercury in fish.

Dr. Crupain completed his undergraduate degree at Duke University and received his medical degree from New York Medical College. He went on to complete a residency in preventive medicine and obtained a master's in public health degree at the Johns Hopkins Bloomberg School of Public Health, where he is also a member of the faculty. Dr. Crupain is a fellow of the American College of Preventive Medicine.

Dr. Crupain's other passion is food, and he cooks every day.

Chef Jim Perko, Sr., Executive Chef for the Cleveland Clinic's Center for Integrative and Lifestyle Medicine

Chef Jim Perko has collaborated with physicians to develop the first evidence-based, technique-driven culinary medicine initiatives for the Cleveland Clinic. He developed curricula and recipes for four patient programs, including Culinary Medicine for Chronic Disease. He is the creator and provider of the first Cleveland Clinic Culinary Medicine Patient Consult, created to help patients execute prescribed nutritional plans and to find true enjoyment in them. He provides culinary medicine education for physicians, resident physicians, nurses, patients, caregivers, and community initiatives.

Perko is a graduate of the Culinary Institute of America in Hyde Park, New York, and one of four apprentices to the 1976 U.S. Culinary Olympic Team. He was also a member of the 1977/78 U.S. Antarctic expedition, where he cooked for scientists and support staff at the South Pole. After seven years as a chef in hotels, Jim started his health care career in 1985 as executive chef of Lakewood Hospital in Lakewood, Ohio. In 1988, he founded the national award-winning Food Is Knowledge program—designed for pre-K and kindergartners—that became a signature part of the Cleveland Clinic community outreach wellness programs.

In 1990, Jim competed nationally to become a member of the American Culinary Federation (ACF) 1992 U.S. Culinary Olympic Team, Northeast Region. He and his team finished third out of 52 teams from 30 countries He is one of 114 current ACF-certified culinary judges and the recipient of numerous ACF national and local awards.

Perko's passion is to widely implement culinary medicine that's evidence based in both clinical and culinary disciplines. He also wants to educate about how foods can be powerful medicine without compromising the flavor of your meals or your health.

WHAT IS YOUR FOOD PHILOSOPHY?

Dr. R: It's what Chef Jim taught me: Only eat food that loves you back.

Dr. C: Watching cooking shows really taught me the fundamentals of cooking—that how you prepare something really matters. Ingredients matter. Technique matters.

The book *The Omnivore's Dilemma* changed my life and my food philosophy. It inspired me to think about where food comes from, how we grow and raise it, and that when you buy great ingredients, you don't need to do much to them. Again: Ingredients matter.

Chef Jim: I believe that how we make a family meal matters just as much as the time shared during a family meal. We do not have to give up the principles of good cooking to eat nutritiously. Instead, they become the core factors in determining cooking time, temperature, and method, as well as quality and combinations of ingredients.

With work, patience, thought, and practice, we increase our culinary skills and literacy. Simultaneously, we also begin to recognize that cooking healthy is just as much about the process, as it is about the final product.

WHAT ARE THREE THINGS YOU WOULD EAT EVERY DAY?

Dr. R: Salmon burgers, walnuts, dark chocolate.

Dr. C: In the summer, tomatoes, tomatoes, tomatoes. Year-round? Broccoli. And I love pasta, but I wouldn't eat it every day. Maybe every other day.

Chef Jim: Garlic, broccoli, and blueberries.

WHAT ARE THREE THINGS YOU WILL NEVER EAT AGAIN?

Dr. R: Processed red meat, high-fructose corn syrup, anything with added sugar (except ice cream three times a year at baseball games and a soufflé on my wedding anniversary).

Dr. C: Fish high in mercury like tilefish, shark, king mackerel, and swordfish.

Chef Jim: Meat, dairy, and white pasta.

WHAT'S YOUR FAVORITE COOKING TOOL?

Dr. R: I love my cast-iron skillet and my chef's knife.

Dr. C: I like my Vitamix. A Vitamix really enables you to make perfectly smooth soups and sauces in a way a food processor or blender can't. I also have an awesome Chinese spatula that is really a cross between a spatula and a shovel. It's great to use when sautéing. I love my pots and pans, too: Each brand makes certain types I like, so I have a mix.

Chef Jim: My half-bolster Messermeister Meridian Elite 8-inch chef's knife. The bolster is a thick part of the knife that tapers to where the handle meets the blade. Messermeister nailed the design for eliminating the half of the bolster while still having durable strength, and for me it has the best hand comfort and feel. I have several sizes of spiders,

which are used to remove foods from pots so the cooking liquid can be saved. I like them made from smooth stainless steel because they're easier to clean. And I love my "waiter's style" corkscrew.

HOW DID YOU GET INTO COOKING?

Dr. R: As I went through my career as a doctor and began to figure out how to help people make their RealAges younger, I learned about the medicinal power of food and cooking techniques. In fact, when I became dean of the College of Medicine at SUNY Upstate Medical University, I quickly developed an elective called Culinary Medicine to teach students how to cook healthy. I made 10 recipes a day, 5 days a week, for 50 weeks with a cooking partner, Donna Szymanski, and my nutritional doc/cooking partner Dr. John La Puma. John was fabulous—he taught me how to pause and smell the food, the herbs, and the spices at each stage.

I used to look at cooking as a chore. But in creating and teaching that Culinary Medicine course I really *found* food. I learned that food was more than just ingredients; it is also preparation and technique. Through cooking, you will help your body by making foods that you love and that love you back. By making food choices, you are influencing your gene expression, determining how fast you age or develop chronic diseases. This is key new science.

Dr. C: Cooking with my mom is one of my first memories and it's just always been a passion of mine. I really started to take it seriously during the year I moved home in preparation to apply to medical school, when I worked with a chef on the weekends. Since then, most of my vacations revolve around eating and cooking the local ingredients, and I'm always trying to learn and explore new cuisines.

Chef Jim: My passion for food was ingrained in me as a child from parents who were instinctively good cooks. My professional experience began as a busboy at a high-end Italian restaurant. I was soon promoted to a line cook and worked there full-time after graduating high school, all while saving money to attend the Culinary Institute of America (CIA) in Hyde Park, New York. At the CIA, I became one of four apprentices of the 1976 United States Culinary Olympic team, which exposed me to the international stage of food and cooking.

I became an executive chef at the age of 26. Desiring more family time with my wife and our two children, I left the glamour of hotels after seven years to accept a position at Lakewood Hospital in Ohio. This journey began my introduction to serving patients, which has become my passion.

WHAT IS THE RELATIONSHIP BETWEEN FOOD AND HEALTH?

Dr. R: At the Cleveland Clinic, we found that if we could get people to normal levels of important medical markers (like blood pressure and blood sugar), we could radically change the presence of disease by up to 80 percent (and cut medical costs significantly). We help patients and employees discover foods that taste great and love you back for optimum health.

Dr. C: Food is health. It's not just what you eat, but of course when you eat and also the way you grow the food that matters.

Chef Jim: Culinary Medicine combines the evidence-based science of food, nutrition, and medicine with the joy and art of cooking. You don't have to compromise the taste of your meals for good health! It's easy to make foods taste good with added sugars, sodium, and saturated fats. But it becomes really challenging to eliminate these addictive ingredients and still make meals taste fantastic. This is what culinary medicine is all about. It is about how to sweeten recipes without adding sugar (see Raisin Reduction, page 69), and how to help someone on a restricted diet regain enjoyment in meals again.

WHAT'S A FUN FOOD FACT ABOUT YOU?

Dr. R: Seventy percent of our freezer is salmon burgers, and half of the rest is walnuts or dark chocolate. I drink several cups of black coffee every day.

Dr. C: I have well over 300 cookbooks.

Chef Jim: My wife and I rarely go out to eat. The best food and wine are at home, and Saturday night date nights rank at the top!

WHAT'S YOUR GUILTY PLEASURE?

Dr. R: None. I get pleasure in love-you-back foods. But on the four days I celebrate with my wife, we enjoy soufflés together.

Dr. C: Cheese. Don't tell Dr. R.

Chef Jim: Good red wine with meals.

WHAT DO YOU DO WHEN YOU'RE COOKING?

Dr. R: I usually have a news or comedy show on. And I try to smell the food at multiple times.

Dr. C: I just cook. For me, cooking is a time to be mindful of what I'm doing. It's not only relaxing, but it also helps make me a better cook. I pay attention to the sound of a knife on a cutting board. I listen to the sizzling of a pan or the rolling of boiling water to judge when things are done. I take in the smells.

Chef Jim: I wear two chef hats. One is professional and serious at the Cleveland Clinic. My personal hat is much different. I'm happiest cooking on Saturday date nights with my wife of 41 years while listening to classic rock-and-roll. I'm relaxed, and in a "mental umami" state of mind cooking alongside my wife, sipping on red wine, and being creative. We create the best meals together!

WHAT'S YOUR BEST ADVICE FOR HOW PEOPLE CAN ENJOY COOKING MORE?

Dr. R: Watch a Chef Jim Facebook Live session.

Dr. C: Do it with someone who loves to cook. You'll have fun and pick up a few things along the way.

Chef Jim: Think about all the things you *can* have and *not* what you can't or are advised not to have.

Make your
new normal
become your
new healthy.

THE WHEN WAY:
A 31-DAY PLAN

One Month to Shift Your Eating Habits & Improve Your Health

Patience has become the dinosaur of human qualities. Today, we want—and get—everything instantly. Our coffee. Our news. Our mail. That efficiency has changed the world, yes, but it has also helped create an environment where we cannot even tolerate waiting 30 seconds for a red light to turn green. This systematic impatience has extended to all areas of our lives.

And from where we sit, that message is loud and clear when it comes to your health. Maybe you've spent a year, a decade, or your whole life in a sort of a health malaise—not giving your body, your diet, or your habits a lot of thought or attention. But when something snaps (seeing a number on a scale, getting a cholesterol scare, or living life with general malaise), you're ready. Like right now.

All you want is to flip a switch or swallow a pill—and get your desired health outcome instantly. The body, however, cannot microwave your new desires in a matter of seconds. It needs a little time to let new habits take effect. It needs you to coax it in the right direction.

But here's the good news: Eating better, eating smarter, and eating the When Way doesn't have to take an entire ice age to take effect. In fact, in just one month, you can adjust your habits and eating approach so that your new normal becomes your

new healthy. And you'll reap all the benefits we have outlined—with a healthier weight, healthier organs, lower stress, lower risk of disease, and better energy.

With this 31-day plan, you're going to gradually shift your eating habits to achieve two things: consume better foods, and maximize your chrono-nutrition by syncing your food intake with how your body wants to operate.

DAYS 1 TO 3

Record what you eat and when you eat. Take note of all foods, portion sizes, and the time of day; this will count for meals, snacks, and "nobody's looking" swipes in the cookie jar. Then, make charts like the one on page 292, where you estimate the portion of your calories in relationship to the time of day you're eating them. On day 4, we will use this information to figure out the perfect plan for you.

DAYS 4 TO 8

Your goal for the next few days is to eat more of your daily calories earlier in the day and fewer calories later, without worrying too much about what you're eating. Take a look at the charts you filled out over the last three days. Do they look like any of the following three we listed, in terms of what time of day you eat most of your food?

Like most people, you're probably eating a lot more of your calories at night for dinner or even after. Starting today, we want you to shift to eating your calories earlier. We recommend you do this over the next three or four days to give your body time to adjust to the change. But if you are like Dr. R and that doesn't fit with your personality, go ahead and make the change all at once; your body will catch up with you.

You also have to decide if you want to shift your calories to breakfast, lunch, or somewhere in between. So, let's take a look at your log again. If you find that you're not at all hungry and don't have any time in the morning, then it might be better to switch your calories to late morning or an early afternoon lunch. But if you do have time for breakfast, earlier is always better. You could also split the calories between the two meals.

10% **Breakfast 7 a.m.**	10% **Breakfast 8 a.m.**	10% **Breakfast 7:30 a.m.**
20% **Breakfast**	20% **Breakfast**	20% **Breakfast**
30% **Breakfast**	30% **Lunch**	30% **Breakfast**
40% **Lunch**	40% **Lunch**	40% **Breakfast**
50% **Lunch**	50% **Lunch**	50% **Lunch**
60% **Lunch**	60% **Lunch**	60% **Lunch**
70% **Snack**	70% **Lunch**	70% **Lunch**
80% **Snack**	80% **Snack**	80% **Lunch**
90% **Dinner**	90% **Dinner**	90% **Dinner**
100% **Dinner Finish 7 p.m.**	100% **Dinner Finish 7 p.m.**	100% **Dinner Finish 6:30 p.m.**

Your log can help you decide what would work best for you.

Whatever time you choose, try the following few techniques over the next four days:

- Look at your regular dinner. Let's say it represents about 50 percent of your typical daily calories, based on the estimate you made in your log. Your goal is to bring it closer to 20 percent. Therefore, you essentially need to cut your typical dinner in half. If you're like Dr. C whose dinner used to represent almost all of his calories, you may need to cut dinner by 75 percent.

- Divide your dinner into quarters in your head. Starting today, we want you to take the food in one of those quarters and save it for breakfast or lunch tomorrow—whichever meal you've decided to increase in size. If your goal is to cut your dinner in half, then the next day, plan to do the same. On the third day, take two of those quarters (half the plate) and save it for breakfast or lunch the next day. By the third night, you should be eating a When Way–size dinner. On day four, do the same thing again.

Now, to pull this off, you're going to have to think the When Way and stop stereotyping foods. It's OK to eat the same foods for breakfast, lunch, and dinner.

You may be worried that you're going to be really hungry eating a much smaller dinner—but in all likelihood, you probably won't be. You're still eating the same total amount in a day; you've just shifted the timing of the main calorie consumption. The meals you ate earlier should help make you less hungry at dinner. Both Drs. R and C have successfully shifted most of their eating to breakfast and lunch,

and both saw their hunger patterns change very quickly to fit the new schedule. They both slept better and had more energy!

That said, if you do find yourself hungry anyway, we have a few tricks to try:

1. Add a salad or two. Actually, add as much salad as you want. Salad contains fiber and other micronutrients, but not that many calories (as long as you don't load it up with meat and cheese and tons of creamy or sugary dressing). We are talking about lettuce and other fiber-rich vegetables, extra-virgin olive oil, and maybe balsamic vinegar.

2. Expand your plate with as many vegetables as you want. Again, vegetables are fiber rich, filling, and low in calories—provided they aren't smothered in cheese or dressing.

3. Eat a pear for dessert; it's a fiber-rich fruit with a good amount of sweetness. A pear or berries at the end of dinner can help satisfy cravings for sugar and make you feel full.

4. Save one of your snacks for 20 minutes before dinner. It can take about this long for your body to feel full after you eat, so having a snack before dinner may dull your appetite and help you feel satisfied with a smaller meal.

Want to see how this works in practice? Here's how Dr. C pulled off this switch to make his bigger meal earlier. On most days, Dr. C was an intermittent faster. He may have had a very small breakfast in the morning (a half cup of yogurt), then ate nothing all day until the evening (usually 7 or 8 p.m.), and was typically finished eating around 9. He had the fasting (or time restriction) right, but his biggest meal was at the completely wrong time.

His day looked like this when he put it on the chart:

10% **Breakfast 8 a.m.**
20% **Dinner**
30% **Dinner**
40% **Dinner**
50% **Dinner**
60% **Dinner**
70% **Dinner**
80% **Dinner**
90% **Dinner**
100% **Dinner Finish 9 p.m.**

Dr. C realized he needed to make a big change. He needed to shift his calories from dinner to earlier in the day. On most days it would be hard for him to make breakfast his largest meal, so he decided

Night Snackers

If you're a late-night snacker, we want you to count that snack as part of your dinner. Based on all the biology, it should be pretty clear that snacking late at night is just about the worst thing for you, as this is when insulin resistance is at its max. As a result, regular late-night snacks have no place in the When Way of eating.

he would start by shifting the bulk of his calories to lunch. He wanted his chart to look more like this:

10% **Breakfast start 8 a.m.**
20% **Breakfast**
30% **Lunch**
40% **Lunch**
50% **Lunch**
60% **Lunch**
70% **Lunch**
80% **Lunch**
90% **Dinner**
100% **Dinner Finish 7 p.m.**

To do it, he used the strategy mentioned previously, quartering his dinner. When Dr. C made dinner, he ate just a small amount and saved the rest for his lunch the following day. Now he typically doesn't eat dinner at all and saves the meal he makes at night for the next day.

DAYS 9 TO 14

After shifting your eating schedule, you may feel different. When Dr. C began eating most of his calories earlier, he started to sleep better and wasn't hungry in the evening. The downside: Even though he's now eating the same amount of food as before, he's had to buy new, smaller pants.

You can take these few days to work on making a further adjustment: trying to eat all your meals between sunrise and sunset. If you're eating after dark (it's especially hard not to in the winter), it's time to move your breakfast later or your dinner earlier. Now that you're eating a smaller dinner, you should be able to nudge it a little earlier if you need to (take a few days to get there; you can do it in increments, starting 30 minutes earlier a day).

If you're already eating only when the sun shines, you can skip ahead to an advanced technique like time-restricted feeding. Ideally you should be eating within a window of 12 hours or less. Remember the studies we mentioned earlier: Humans and animals with shorter eating windows tend to be healthier. So, use this time to shorten the window during which you eat even more.

DAY 15

Take today to log how you eat. See how much you've changed since you started. If you haven't quite made the full shift—eating more of your calories earlier and shifting your eating window to between sunrise and sunset—just keep working toward that goal as you start focusing more on the kinds of foods you eat.

DAYS 16 TO 19

Now is the time you're going to start focusing on what you're eating. On Day 16, take this quiz to note how you're doing with the When Way foods.

AVOID FOODS

How often do you eat processed foods?

Never	1/Month	1/Week	2-6/Week	Daily	Multiple Times a Day

How often do you eat simple carbs (sugar, white flour foods)?

Never	1/Month	1/Week	2-6/Week	Daily	Multiple Times a Day

How often do you eat fried foods?

Never	1/Month	1/Week	2-6/Week	Daily	Multiple Times a Day

How often do you eat processed meat, red meat, or pork?

Never	1/Month	1/Week	2-6/Week	Daily	Multiple Times a Day

WHEN WAY FOODS

How many servings of vegetables do you eat a day?

5 or more	4	3	2	1	0

How many servings of whole grains do you eat a day?

4 or more	3	2	1	0

How often do you eat nuts or seeds?

Daily	2–6/Week	1/Week	1/Month	Never

How often do you eat plant protein, fish, or skinless chicken or turkey as your protein source?

Multiple Times a Day	Daily	2–6/Week	1/Week	1/Month	Never

Take a look at how you answered these questions. Ideally all your responses would be on the lighter end of the spectrum. If your answers are toward the darker end of the spectrum, your goal over the next two weeks is to shift what you eat toward the lighter end of the spectrum.

Of course, just stopping isn't easy, so we have devised a series of substitutions (called the Sub Shop) that will make it simpler for you to eat under this new schedule.

For the next three days, we want you to focus on processed foods. On your first day, substitute healthier options for processed snacks. Collect all the processed food snacks you would have eaten and put them in a plastic bag. This will help you see what you've been eating—and you'll feel good at the end of the day when you haven't touched any of it! (Just make sure you throw the bag away at the end of the day. Temptation is real!)

Crunch Time

One of our favorite foods—which you can use as a go-to snack and to help you feel satisfied—is the almighty nut. We especially like walnuts, because eating them is associated with eating more fruits and vegetables, as well as with weight loss. Also, nuts (especially walnuts) are known to lower the risk of heart attacks and strokes, as well as the risk of death. Walnuts in particular are a powerhouse snack that appear to help boost four types of good gut bacteria (*Faecalibacterium*, *Clostridium*, *Dialister*, and *Roseburia*). In practice, that means that nuts, especially walnuts, on breakfast cereal or avocado toast make for excellent choices to help you start the day.

DAYS 20 TO 23

We hope you are well on your way to eliminating processed foods from your diet. (Don't worry if you need more time; just keep working on it.) For the next three days, focus on this When Way principle: Stop stereotyping your foods.

Probably no meal is more stereotyped than breakfast. People often think of breakfast as either bacon and eggs; an egg, ham, and cheese sandwich; sugary cereal with milk; pancakes; waffles; or muffins and pastries. Hmm, none of those really fit into the When Way of eating, so if you are a breakfast person, this could mean some big changes are in store. But if you realize that "traditional breakfast foods" don't actually have to be eaten for breakfast—or ever—and that lunch and dinner foods are just fine in the morning, you'll be well on your way.

DAYS 24 TO 26

For these three days, we want you to focus on getting more whole grains into your diet. Carbs have been much maligned in recent years, but a study published not long ago found that we as a nation are not eating enough whole grains. Eating them actually helps you live younger and longer, and they are delicious to boot! Remember, you want to eat about four servings of whole grains a day.

DAYS 27 TO 28

Use these two days to focus on some of the previous steps you are still trying to achieve. If you haven't quite made the switch from your old lunch to the When Way option, now's your chance to catch up.

For most of you, lunch will probably be your easiest biggest meal. But it's also hard to prepare on the run. A good solution is to plan on eating your leftover dinner for lunch. One of Dr. C's favorites is a vegetable and bean stir-fry. This is yet another way to add more vegetables into your day, and it tastes great cold. You can eat it with some whole grains mixed in or on the side.

Another great trick, especially in the winter, is hot homemade soup. Believe it or not, an old-fashioned thermos can actually keep soup hot for 12 hours. Dr. C just started taking soup to work, and was skeptical that his old-looking thermos would do the trick. On the first day, he tried the soup after it had been in the thermos for six hours and he burned his tongue!

DAYS 29 TO 30

For this two-day period, focus on making your now smallest meal (dinner) something that's filling and satisfying. We like to make dinner a mini-feast of fiber-rich vegetables, soups, and salad. Both of us love broccoli and both believe we cook it the best.

Another great choice for dinner is a small bowl of vegetable soup with a little whole grain like quinoa or whole grain farro added in. As we mentioned before, you can have as much salad as you want.

DAY 31

Look back on all you've accomplished toward eating the When Way. Even if you skipped some steps or want to change your eating regimen and aren't all the way there yet, you've still come a long way. Remember that you don't have to fully make the switch in 30 days; after all, you've probably been eating the same way for a lifetime. You can revisit any of the days in this plan anytime to keep adjusting.

Now is the time to work on consistency with what you eat and when you eat. Even if you take a day off during the weekend, you're still doing great and well on the path to better health.

METRIC CONVERSIONS

The recipes in this book were developed using standard U.S. measures following U.S. government guidelines. The charts below offer equivalents for U.S. and metric measures. All conversions are approximate and have been rounded up or down to the nearest whole number.

ounces	grams
½	14
¾	21
1	28
1 ½	43
2	57
2 ½	71
3	85
3 ½	99
4	113
4 ½	128
5	142
6	170
7	198
8	227
9	255
10	283
12	340
16 (1 pound)	454

U.S.	metric
1 teaspoon	5 milliliters
2 teaspoons	10 milliliters
1 tablespoon	15 milliliters
2 tablespoons	30 milliliters
¼ cup	59 milliliters
⅓ cup	79 milliliters
½ cup	118 milliliters
¾ cup	177 milliliters
1 cup	237 milliliters
1 ¼ cups	296 milliliters
1 ½ cups	355 milliliters
2 cups (1 pint)	473 milliliters
2 ½ cups	591 milliliters
3 cups	710 milliliters
4 cups (1 quart)	0.946 liter
1.06 quarts	1 liter
4 quarts (1 gallon)	3.8 liters

Fahrenheit	Celsius	gas mark
225	105	¼
250	120	½
275	135	1
300	150	2
325	165	3
350	180	4
375	190	5
400	200	6
425	220	7
450	230	8
475	245	9

ILLUSTRATIONS CREDITS

THE WHAT TO EAT WHEN COOKBOOK

Since 1888, the National Geographic Society has funded more than 13,000 research, exploration, and preservation projects around the world. National Geographic Partners distributes a portion of the funds it receives from your purchase to National Geographic Society to support programs including the conservation of animals and their habitats.

National Geographic Partners
1145 17th Street NW
Washington, DC 20036-4688 USA

Get closer to National Geographic explorers and photographers, and connect with our global community. Join us today at nationalgeographic.com/join

For rights or permissions inquiries, please contact National Geographic Books Subsidiary Rights: bookrights@natgeo.com

Library of Congress Cataloging-in-Publication Data
Names: Roizen, Michael F., author. I Crupain, Michael, author. I Perko, Jim, author.
Title: The what to eat when cookbook : 135+ deliciously timed recipes / Michael F. Roizen, M.D., Michael Crupain, M.D., M.P.H., Jim Perko, CEC, AAC, chef.
Description: Washington, D.C. : National Geographic, [2020] I Includes index. I Summary: "A cookbook that puts into effect a strategic eating plan developed by the authors to help promote healthier living, disease prevention, better performance and a longer life"-- Provided by publisher.
Identifiers: LCCN 2019054076 I ISBN 9781426221033 (hardcover) I ISBN 9781426221040 (ebook)
Subjects: LCSH: Cooking (Natural foods) I Longevity--Nutritional aspects--Popular works. I LCGFT: Cookbooks.
Classification: LCC TX741 .R65 2020 I DDC 641.5/63--dc23
LC record available at https://lccn.loc.gov/2019054076

Printed in the United States of America

20/WOR/1